# Contradictions of Capitalist Society and Culture

# Studies in Critical Social Sciences Book Series

Haymarket Books is proud to be working with Brill Academic Publishers (www.brill.nl) to republish the *Studies in Critical Social Sciences* book series in paperback editions. This peer-reviewed book series offers insights into our current reality by exploring the content and consequences of power relationships under capitalism, and by considering the spaces of opposition and resistance to these changes that have been defining our new age. Our full catalog of *SCSS* volumes can be viewed at https://www.haymarketbooks .org/series_collections/4-studies-in-critical-social-sciences.

# CONTRADICTIONS OF CAPITALIST SOCIETY AND CULTURE

## Dialectics of Love and Lying

RAJU J. DAS

Haymarket Books
Chicago, IL

First published in 2023 by Brill Academic Publishers, The Netherlands
© 2023 Koninklijke Brill NV, Leiden, The Netherlands

Published in paperback in 2024 by
Haymarket Books
P.O. Box 180165
Chicago, IL 60618
773-583-7884
www.haymarketbooks.org

ISBN: 979-8-88890-237-0

Distributed to the trade in the US through Consortium Book Sales and
Distribution (www.cbsd.com) and internationally through Ingram Publisher
Services International (www.ingramcontent.com).

This book was published with the generous support of Lannan Foundation,
Wallace Action Fund, and the Marguerite Casey Foundation.

Special discounts are available for bulk purchases by organizations and
institutions. Please call 773-583-7884 or email info@haymarketbooks.org for more
information.

Cover design by Jamie Kerry and Ragina Johnson.

Printed in the United States.

Library of Congress Cataloging-in-Publication data is available.

*This book is dedicated to all the people of the world, in particular those living in North America and India, who are fighting against the politics of lying (post-truth politics) which is also the politics of hatred. It is dedicated to young people, who are fighting against alienation and the suffering caused by capitalism, as they fail to experience genuine love and have to endure a world of hatred. Finally, this book is dedicated to all the people of the world who are fighting for an alternative culture, one which loves truth, and which promises real love. That culture can only arrive with socialism, a genuinely truthful and profoundly loving social order.*

∴

# Contents

# Acknowledgements

This book began on June 15, 2015, in the form of a few lines I wrote to a friend. I was explaining the meaning of 'I love/respect x' in the context of Marx's comment that 'the human essence is no abstraction inherent in each single individual. In its reality it is the ensemble of the social relations'. My point was that love or anything considered inter-personal is a deeply social matter. Later on, I began thinking a little about lying – political lying – in the context of Far Right politics of hatred (anti-love) which is also a politics of what has come to be known as post-truth. Gradually, I began exploring the connection between the two aspects of capitalist culture. So basically, what began as a couple of pages on love and lying has become this book. I imagine this book as a concrete theoretical 'application' of the ideas laid out in my *Marxist class theory for a skeptical world* published in 2017. But I would have definitely not written this book, if it was not for the kind encouragement that I received from Professor David Fasenfest, the editor of Brill's Studies in Critical Social Sciences book series. And, I certainly would not have explored the *connection* between love and lying without his encouragement to write the book. In many ways, this book is a gift of love for him.

# List of Figures and Tables

### Figures

### Tables

# CHAPTER 1

# Introduction

Love and lying are two important aspects of human culture. There is something trans-historical about them. In all societies, people have fallen in love. In all societies, people have deserted truth and resorted to lying. However, things that are more universal take historically specific forms: these forms are dominantly shaped by historically changing social relations of production/exchange and their politics. In modern society, love and lying have assumed forms that are shaped by the dynamics of capitalist class society, i.e., by capitalist economic and political processes.

In the last 10 years or so, there has been a turn towards what is called post-truth, a situation where facts are considered to be less important than feelings or personal beliefs, so much so that blatant lies and mistaken views (or half-truths) are openly peddled if they serve a specific ideological-political purpose. Businesspeople, politicians and laypeople have engaged in post-truth politics. Besides, political lying is based on, and feeds into, not love, but hatred of fellow citizens, especially, those who look different in terms of race, or who practice a different religion or who are not born in the country/region they currently live in. Political hatred, i.e., the opposite of love for fellow citizens, like political lying, has no basis in facts or reason.[1] Lying makes the persons lied to live an imaginary world created by the liars.

In the post-truth world, not only is the relation between facts (= what is true) and truths (= true statements) that relate to the facts broken, but also is the relation between truth and love broken. Lies, and not a commitment to truth about fellow citizens, and hatred, not a commitment to love for fellow citizens, come together in post-truth capitalism.

We often see that two individuals love each other but they do not care if their neighbours or fellow citizens are lynched upon by a fascistic mob because of the lies that the mob believes in. We also see that two individuals love each other but they do not care about the wellbeing of people around them because they ideologically/politically accept the unjust conditions under which people experience economic deprivation. In these cases, the corrupted and mutilated form of inter-personal love between the two individuals is potentially

---

1   'All emotions of hatred are evil, and, therefore, the man who lives according to the guidance of reason will strive as much as possible to keep himself from being agitated by the emotions of hatred' (Spinoza, 1954: 223). Spinoza, of course, deals with hatred at the inter-personal level.

complicit in the broader fascistic and unjust social environment in which millions are living.[2] Indeed, in their book *Commonwealth*, Hardt and Negri (2009: 183) say that in modern society, love is corrupted when: one loves one's family or one's romantic partners but not the needy people outside or one loves one's own ethnic or religious community but hates others. Why? Why is love between two individuals separated from their love for many?

Why do attitudes towards truth and love appear in the form and in the way that they do? Questions of love (or hatred) and truth (or lying) are not to be treated as (supra-class) moral questions, nor are they to be treated merely as dimensions of individual lives. I seek to explore the supra-individual and class-origins of the two important aspects of culture: attitudes towards truth (i.e., post-truth attitude) and attitudes towards love (i.e., attitudes that produce a narrow, mutilated form of love). Common to both are significant underlying aspects of capitalist economy and capitalist politics.

1       Love

Love is a much more complex process than it appears to be. Some say that love is universal, that it exists everywhere. Others say that love in a true sense does not exist. According to some, love has also been ignored in social and political thought. Given the complexity of love, more attention should be paid to it than has been the case. Luckily, there *have been* some writings on the topic of love recently. This is a part of 'an emotional turn' in social and political thought. This is also a part of a new turn within neuroscience and psychology which are increasingly turning to the study of positive emotions such as love.

Whatever else love might be, it is to be seen as a *social* relationship, and as a form of *social* consciousness. And Marxism treats social relations and social consciousness as fundamental categories (Marx, 1859), so love is a proper topic in Marxist (or materialist-dialectical) analysis. There are actually a number of Marxist writers in the classical tradition who wrote about love. They included, apart from Marx and Engels, the famous Alexandra Kollontai. A few contemporary Marxists have written about the topic too. Apart from Marx, Engels, and Kollontai, in this book, I also selectively build on writers who are influenced by Marxism, such as Allain Badiou, Simone de Beauvoir, Antonio Negri and Michael Hardt, Erich Fromm, Richard Gilman-Opalsky and others. I also draw

---

2    This is true to the extent that the human consciousness has a role in reproducing the society we live in.

on non-Marxist writers: they include classical writers (Plato and Spinoza) and modern writers such as those in philosophy, sociology, neuroscience and psychology. While I build on many Marx-influenced writers and non-Marxist writers, I do not necessarily share the dominant worldviews or the politics of these latter writers. To me, love deserves to be seriously examined by Marxists and that there is a need for a more adequate theorization of love than has been the case.

Love, especially, in the sense of romantic or passionate love, is generally considered to be a private matter, a matter between two *individuals*. And love in its romantic form is supposed to be driven by spontaneous feelings, propelled by neuro-biological drives: it is often said that one just falls in love. These two views – love just happens, and love is between two individuals – reinforce each other. I contest these views.

This book examines love both in its general form (love as caring and solidarity) and in its specific form (romantic love). In discussing love in its two forms, I emphasize the social character of love, including its politics. Like everything else, I argue, love must be seen at multiple levels: human society (in its relation to nature and in relation to the materiality of human life itself); specific forms of class society such as capitalism. In terms of the first level (human society), love is a trans-historical process, so it does have a natural/biological aspect (e.g., physical drives), as revealed in the philosophical and neuroscientific literature. But love is more than a 'thing'. It is a deeply social process. There are multiple ways in which love is a social process and a social relation.

Love as a form of consciousness and as a form of a relationship between individuals are impacted by class relations and is in turn made use of in the reproduction of specific forms of class society. In particular, capitalist alienation and other material conditions as well as certain forms of political consciousness and certain forms of oppression (e.g., gender) that are promoted by capitalism, lead to certain kinds of conception and practice of love under capitalism, and love *in* capitalism helps reproduce love *with* capitalism.

Love must be rescued both from the principle of love of *all humans* (i.e., class-neutral love) and from the principle of love between two humans. Instead, it must be based in the principle of love of *class* brothers and sisters, and in the principle of love of the struggle against class enemies, but in a manner that does not ignore passionate/erotic love between (two) people. Because love is social, it is also political: this is in part because it has a role to play in the fight against capitalism and in the process of the construction of socialism, a society permeated by the spirit/content of democracy and comradely love everywhere. Yet, one must refrain from exaggerated claims about the (political) power of love. In terms of the political character of love, it is necessary to address questions such as the following. Is there a difference between two fascistic bigots being in love vs two communists in love? Can a communist, or even radical bourgeois democrat, have an enduring relation of love with a fascistic individual? Is there a difference between two people in love who just care about each other and two people in love whose lives are also devoted to the creation of a socialist society, a goal that they love? What is the connection between class consciousness and love as a form of consciousness? What kind of love might exist under socialism/communism, and how might it be different from love under capitalism? Why is it that in contemporary (late) capitalism, the politics of hatred (= anti-love) is observed widely?

## 2      Lying

It is not just that human beings' universal need for, and the power to, love has been mutilated and restricted to narrow social spaces (of the lives of two individuals-in-love). Human beings' universal ability to make an effort to use reason and evidence in their lives (i.e., their ability to value truth) is also being severely compromised.[3] The latter tendency has been there for quite some time, but it has been manifested in the last 10–15 years or so with the arrival of right-wing politics in the US, India, and elsewhere. There is an increasing rejection of the fact that certain statements about the natural and social world are true and that certain statements are false. Scholars have begun to lament 'the death of truth'. It is being increasingly recognized that a post-truth phenomenon has arrived where lies and deception inform politics and everyday life as a normal state of affairs in capitalist societies. In the post-truth world, feelings are more accurate than facts, and lies are constantly told for the purpose of the political subordination of reality. The post-truth condition is deeply skeptical of objective truth and of experts/scientists.

I discuss the various traits of the post-truth phenomenon, explain its connection to postmodernist idealist philosophy, and its association with Far Right politics. I also explain the post-truth phenomenon in terms of the crisis-ridden bourgeois political economy and bourgeois politics, including the contradictions of imperialism. I argue that the post-truth phenomenon is only partly because of Far Right *politics*, and that its ultimate cause lies in the capitalist system as a whole.

---

3   Human beings are characterized by 'our natural effort to apprehend the real state of affairs', says philosopher, Frankfurt (2006: 76–77). Lying interferes with, and impairs this effort.

In its early stage, capitalism *was* a progressive mode of production. It fought against unreason and (religious) superstition, etc. that were characteristic of pre-capitalist forms of society. However, gradually, capitalism has been also conducive to lying and an anti-science attitude. Why? I discuss several reasons, all of which concern the nature of the capitalist economy and politics. The post-truth condition is expressed in a particularly virulent form in the world's largest democracy, India, where the post-truth politics generates religious conflicts and suppression of democratic rights of common people. Such post-truth politics is also a politics of hatred (anti-love).

This book presents what can be called a dialectical analysis of love and lying.[4] a) In the process of analyzing love, and in part, relying on Spinoza and some modern philosophers, I examine the opposite of love, i.e. hatred or anti-love (at the inter-personal as well as societal levels). b) In analyzing lying (post-truth), I examine its opposite: truth. I argue that in pursuit of their material and emotional interests, human beings must be truth-seekers: their interest is in seeking truth. c) Lying and loving are connected: genuine love – love as caring, warmth, solidarity, etc., which under certain conditions can take the romantic form – cannot be based on lying. One aspect of love that is not fleeting is conscious decision-making which requires reason and truthful analysis of objects of love, including romantic partners. d) Lying and love are connected structurally, in the realm of political economy. Capitalism – and here I refer to capitalists and their state -- systematically resorts to lying to cover up its structural contradictions that cause suffering of the masses, so much so that given widespread suffering, conditions for genuine love are severely undermined. e) Lying and loving are also connected in the realm of capitalist politics. The state that is fundamentally a social machine to suppress, by violent and ideological measures, the actions and thoughts of the popular masses against the exploiting class cannot be an object of genuine love in the everyday life of the masses. Besides, the right-wing politics of post-truth (= lying), as a consequence of the crisis-ridden capitalist system, is also a politics of anti-love, i.e., hatred. This is the hatred against religious, racial or ethnic minorities, immigrants and against democrats and socialists who oppose the right-wing politics. Politics of anti-love (= hatred) – one might even call it the politics of 'post-love' – requires, and is based on, politics of lying (= post-truth). This is

---

4  Strictly speaking, the term dialectics should be used where one talks about the relation between two (or more) 'things' (x and y, or x, y and z, etc.), along with the contradictions between/among them as well as the internal contradictions within each of them, and where the 'things' – including the contradictions just mentioned – are seen as parts or aspects of the totality, and so on (see Das, 2017a, chapter 5).

true in Far Right circles: the Far Right has to intentionally say blatantly unscientific and un-true things about minorities, the majority community, 'the nation', etc., in order to justify their hate – anti-love – politics. f) Underlying both the politics of post-truth and the politics of post- or anti-love, are capitalist class relations. If the notion/practice of love has been mutilated and corrupted, with love being confined to the narrow circles of the lives of two individuals or of family members, insensitive towards the distress of fellow citizens, and if there is increasingly hatred among people and if people resort to lying on a massive scale, then the fundamental reason lies in capitalism: capitalist class relations are not allowing human beings to be truthful and to experience genuine love.[5] Loving and being truthful, as two crucially important aspects of human culture, now exist in their corrupted forms. g) So, the fight against the politics of hatred   (= anti-love or 'post-love') and the fight against the politics of lying ( = anti-truth or post-truth) must be part of the fight for a post-capitalist world, and more specifically, for a socialist world, which must be imagined as, and which must be, a truthful and loving world beyond the rule of capital.

## 3    Outline

The remainder of the book has 7 chapters. Chapters 2-4 deal with love. Chapter 2 deals with the existing literature on love in philosophy, psychology, sociology and neuroscience, including different concepts of love (and anti-love, or hatred). It then critiques this literature.

Chapters 3-4 provide a Marxist theory of love in the sense of a general explanation of love. Chapter 3 discusses love at a trans-historical level. Chapter 4 focusses on the ways in which capitalism shapes romantic love and how love as a form of consciousness is connected to the kinds of social consciousness that capitalism promotes. It also explains the extent to which love between two people can – and cannot – abstract from the wider political context. Indeed, the question of love is always linked to that of anti-love or hatred. When the bourgeois form of love that most people experience is isolated from the wider

---

5   Connected to love and truth is trust. Trust, considered to be an aspect of 'social capital' in the sense of a social resource, is obviously an important part of culture (on this, see Das, Gough and Eisenschitz, 2023). Trust is also a part of culture in a more specific sense: if love is a part of culture, trust as a part of love (as will be discussed later) is also a part of culture. Trust is also connected to truth: one cannot trust a liar. Class relations of capitalism not only promote lying and hatred, which are the opposites of truth and love, respectively. They also undermine relations of trust.

society and its problems, the two people can be intensely in mutual love but they can at the same time be entirely comfortable with their fellow citizens experiencing hatred, and the two people in love may themselves indeed practice hatred against their fellow citizens. Why have love and anti-love come to be connected like this? Chapter 4 finally discusses the potential contribution of love to the struggle for a socialist society and presents the conception of a socialized romantic love – as opposed to a romanticized socialized love – as a part of the imagination of socialism as a loving society. It is indeed necessary to have a conception of love under socialism.

Chapters 5-7 deal with lying. Chapter 5 discusses the various traits of the post-truth phenomenon and explains its association both with the postmodernist idealist philosophy and Far Right post-truth politics. This discussion sets the context for the next chapter (Chapter 6) which provides a Marxist theory of the post-truth phenomenon. As with the mutilation and corruption of love, whereby love between two individuals can coexist with hatred – or lack of love – on their part for others, so with lying: capitalism is at its root of both. Capitalism has certain contradictions, the justification for which requires lying. Capitalist social relations produce lies as a commodity for profit. As well, the media as a means of spreading lies is also capitalist commodity. While capitalism needs lies and produces the means of lying, common people also believe these lies as if lying has become an opium in their lives over which they have limited control. Chapter 7 considers the post-truth condition in India, the world's largest democracy, where the vast majority do not have regular and adequate access to nutritious food, and yet a big appetite has been produced for big lies. The chapter describes India's post-truth phenomenon and explains it in terms of the contradictions of India's class society. It also critiques the right-wing's post-truth strategy.

The concluding chapter (Chapter 8) summarizes the ideas about love and lying discussed in the book and draws political conclusions from the discussions. It concludes by claiming that the fight against the post-truth condition and the fight against the narrow conception/practice of love must be both a part of the fight against capitalism and for socialism.

# CHAPTER 2

# Love and Politics: Some Existing Views

## 1    Introduction

Love is a much more complex process than it appears to be.[1] Helen Fisher, a biological anthropologist and an expert in the science of human attraction and romantic relation, says that 'Being in love is universal to humanity' (Fisher, 2004: 6). Allain Badiou, the French philosopher, also says that there is something universal about love, which is 'why we like to love' and which is why 'love stories appeal to so many' (Badiou, 2012: 39). Others, however, say that love in a true sense does not exist. For example, according to the sociologist, Mary Evans (2002), love is deeply desirable but it is extremely difficult to find. The Marxist psycho-analysist, Erich Fromm (1956: 133), says that love is a 'real need in every human being' but the love that many people need is missing. 'To analyze the nature of love is to discover its general absence today and to criticize the social conditions which are responsible for this absence' (ibid.).

Kováts (2015: 5) states that love is 'an essential part of human existence', and that it 'carries the possibility for truly symmetric, mutual relationships between people'. Yet love relations are often unequal and/or help reproduce inequality in the wider society. So, how we think about love has 'far-reaching consequences', including 'for the gender relations and for the societal practices amongst which we get socialised and rear our children' (Kováts, 2015: 5).

While many scholars say that love is an important topic for scholarly investigation, according to Morrison et al (2012: 507), 'love – and all the emotionality associated with love – has been passed over for topics that are associated with rationality and reason'. Likewise, Negri and his co-author, Hardt, the two autonomists-Marxists, complain that 'Love has been so charged with sentimentality that it seems hardly fit for philosophical and much less political discourse' and that love 'makes many readers uncomfortable' (Hardt and Negri, 2009: 179). They claim that 'love is an essential concept for philosophy and politics, and the failure to interrogate and develop it is one central cause of the weakness of contemporary thought'. (ibid.). They argue that 'It is unwise to leave love to the priests, poets, and psychoanalysts' and that therefore 'It is necessary for us ... to do some conceptual housecleaning, clearing away some

---

1    This chapter and the next two chapters draw on Das (2022a).

of the misconceptions that disqualify love for philosophical and political discourse and redefining the concept in such a way as to demonstrate its utility'. (p. 179). This is what they seek to do.

It is difficult to agree that love as an intellectual topic has been entirely neglected. Indeed, recent scholarly work on love has been a part of what Illouz (2010) calls 'an emotional turn in all of the social sciences and even the humanities'. Recent scholarly work on love is also part of a new turn within neuroscience and psychology which are increasingly turning to the study of positive emotions such as love and compassion rather than remaining solely focussed on afflictive or negative emotions (Davidson, 2012; Goleman, 2003). Davidson (2019), the US-based neuroscientist and psychologist, says that love in the wider sense 'is going to be the next frontier for science and for neuroscience. I'm not afraid to speak about love ... [L]love is a quality which obliterates certain kinds of boundaries. So, I think that it certainly will be associated with pervasive differences in the brain and is really something that needs to be studied'. In this chapter I discuss some of the existing views on love (sections 2–4). I then subject these views to a critique (section 5).

## 2      What Is Love?

Scholars have written about love from many perspectives. These include: concept of love; the question of why/how people fall in love; and the relation between love and politics.

Plato's *Symposium* contains some interesting ideas. Here we learn that: 'The generic concept [of love] embraces every desire for good and for happiness', so the generic name is used for many 'kinds of love' (Plato, 1956: 85). This means that love shares with other things a passionate desire for something that is good and that makes us happy. '[W]e must ask in what way and by what type of action [people] must show their intense desire if it is to deserve the name of love'. Plato himself provides an answer: 'The object [or the function] of love ... is to procreate and bring forth in beauty', because 'procreation is the nearest thing to ... immortality that a mortal being can attain' (p. 87). Love indeed creates two kinds of progeny, physical (children) and spiritual (wisdom, virtue, etc.), both of which we leave behind when we die (p. 86).

Love in its physical sense is a 'lower' (or poorer) form (or stage) of love. A person who 'is to make beauty of outward form the object of his quest' will realize 'that the beauty exhibited in all bodies is one and the same'; that person 'will become a lover of all physical beauty, and will relax the intensity of [their] passion for one particular person' (p. 92). 'The next stage is for him to reckon beauty of soul more valuable than beauty of body; the result will be that, when he encounters a virtuous soul in a body which has little of the bloom of beauty, he will be content to love and cherish it and ... in this way he will be compelled to contemplate beauty as it exists in *activities and institutions'* (p. 92; italics added).

If in Plato's discussion on love in *Symposium*, beauty has an important place, in Spinoza's *Ethics*, love is related to joy: 'Love is nothing but joy accompanied with the idea of an external cause' (Spinoza, 1954: 139; 150). To the extent that it is a property (not the essence) of love that love is 'the will of the lover to unite himself to the beloved object', Spinoza understands this will to be 'the satisfaction that the beloved object produces in the lover by its presence by virtue of which the joy of the lover is strengthened or at any rate supported' (p. 177). 'We see, too, that he who loves a thing necessarily endeavors to keep it before him and to preserve it' (p. 139). 'If we love a thing which is of the same nature as ourselves, we endeavor as much as possible to cause it to love us in return' (p. 159). According to Spinoza, there is a relation between compassion and love – or love's relation to joy: 'Compassion is love in so far as it affects a man so that he is glad [or, he is experiencing joy or happiness] at the prosperity of another person and is sad when any evil happens to him' (Spinoza, 1954: 179; parenthesis added).

We see that Spinoza links love to joy as the essence of love. Frankfurt, a contemporary American philosopher, usefully elaborates on this link. Joy is what makes people pass on to higher perfection. Joy is 'a feeling of enlargement of one's power to live, and to continue to live, in accord with one's most authentic nature' (Frankfurt, 2006: 44). If a person 'identifies someone or something as the object to which he owes his joy and on which his joy *depends*', then 'the person inevitably *loves* that object' (Frankfurt, 2006: 44). So, people invariably fall in love with 'whatever they recognize as being, for them, a source of joy' and they 'invariably love what they believe helps them to continue in existence and to become more fully themselves' (Frankfurt, 2006: 4). 'People do tend to love what they feel helps them to "find themselves", to discover "who they really are.", and to face life successfully without betraying or compromising their fundamental natures' (Frankfurt, 2006: 45). As well, people cannot help loving truth: this is because truth is essential to their life. So, if you despise truth, you must despise your own life (Frankfurt, 2006: 47).

Spinoza's views get clearer and assume more relevance, when we juxtapose these views with his views on anti-love (or, 'post-love'), i.e., hatred. 'The man whom we hate we endeavor to destroy, that is to say, we endeavor to do something which is evil' (Spinoza, 1954: 221; 139; 158). Hatred is related to a whole host of negative (or afflictive) emotions such as contempt, envy, etc. which are opposite of love. 'Contempt consists in thinking too little of another person in consequence of our hatred for him ... [C]ontempt may be defined as hatred in so far as it affects a man so that he thinks too little of the object he hates' (p. 179). 'Envy is hatred in so far as it affects a man so that he is sad at the good fortune of another person and is glad when any evil happens to him' (p. 179). 'Anger is the desire by which we are impelled, through hatred, to injure those whom we hate' (p. 183). 'Everything which we desire because we are affected by hatred is base and unjust' (p. 222). 'Hatred can never be good' (p. 221). 'Vengeance is the desire which, springing from mutual hatred, urges us to injure those who, from a similar emotion, have injured us' (p. 183). 'Envy, mockery, contempt, anger, revenge, and the other emotions which are related to hatred or arise from it are evil ... and, therefore, the man who lives according to the guidance of reason will strive as much as possible to keep himself from being agitated by the emotions of hatred' (p. 222–223).

For some scholars, love is fundamentally a matter of acknowledging and responding to the unique qualities of the people we love (Velleman, 1999), an idea that connects to Plato's second stage in love. There are others who think that caring about the loved person for their own sake and feeling the pain if they are hurt are a part of what being in love is (Soble 1990; White 2001), an idea that connects to Spinoza's point about one's love for an object and one's desire to 'preserve it'. Giles (1994: 341), a Canadian philosopher and psychologist, says that love involves the expectation that if I love someone, 'I want that person to love me back', a point that echoes Spinoza's (and also Marx's) that 'If we love a thing which is of the same nature as ourselves, we endeavor as much as possible to cause it to love us in return' (Spinoza, 1954: 159).

Love involves the multitude of desires such as blue eyes; intellect; wanting children; and so on. They are, however, 'not basic to the structure of the experience of love. They are rather individual preferences about the way in which love is to be realized' (Giles, 1994: 354). Most fundamentally, 'being in love seems to imply the existence of sexual desire' (p. 352). But why? Giles explains this in terms of vulnerability, which 'is best understood as meaning 'psychologically or emotionally in need" (p. 344). He thinks that 'at the very core of the experience of love lies a complex of intense desires': these desires involve 'the desire to be vulnerable before another person in order that one may be nurtured or cared for by that person, and, at the same time, the desire to have the other person vulnerable before oneself in order that one may nurture or care for that person' (ibid.).[2] '[S]exual desire is but one more way of

---

2   There is a relation between the element of vulnerability and the element of care. 'For the desire to be psychologically or emotionally in need before someone already suggests the desire to have someone look after or show concern for one's needs. And the same could be said about the reciprocal desire for the other person to be emotionally in need' (Giles, 1994: 344).

wanting what love wants: a reciprocity of vulnerability and care' (p. 352). Can two people be in love and 'yet not engage in the desires for bodily baring and caressing?' (ibid.). The answer here, it seems, is that because of the intense and all-encompassing nature of the desires that make up love, they will naturally tend to include physical ways of expressing themselves. 'In my desiring complete reciprocal vulnerability and care with the one I love, my desire does not rest content with wanting reciprocal psychological and emotional vulnerability and care, but at the same time wants reciprocal physical vulnerability and care' (ibid.). The latter is the desire 'to be bare before the one I love in order to be caressed, and have the beloved bare before me in order to caress her. To sexually engage with another person is a powerful way of entering into a relation of reciprocal vulnerability and care' (ibid.).

According to the American psychologist, Robert Sternberg (1986: 119), 'Love is a complex whole that appears to derive in part from genetically transmitted instincts and drives but probably in larger part from socially learned role modeling that, through observation, comes to be defined as love'. (p. 120). A relation of love has three different components (p. 119–120) (see Table 2.1). One is intimacy: it encompasses the feelings of closeness, connectedness, and bondedness – the feelings 'that give rise, essentially, to the experience of warmth in a loving relationship' (ibid.). Another is passion encompassing the drives that lead to romance, physical attraction, and sexual consummation. The third component of love is decision/commitment encompassing, in the short term, the decision that one loves another, and in the long term, the commitment to maintain that love: in other words, love includes 'the cognitive elements that are involved in decision making about the existence of and potential long-term commitment to a loving relationship' (ibid.). According to Sternberg's triangular theory of love, the *amount* of love that one experiences is a function of the absolute strength of these components, and *the kind* of love that one experiences depends on their strengths relative to each other.

These different kinds of love can be represented on a spectrum below, in terms of the number of Ys (which varies from 1 to 3) (Y is as it is defined in Table 2.1). The greater the number of Ys, the stronger is love assumed to be.

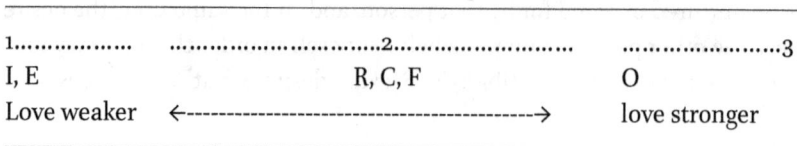

1................        ................2..............                ..............3
I, E                              R, C, F                      O
Love weaker   ←--------------------------------→   love stronger

Note: I, E, R, C, F and O are as explained in Table 2.1 below.

TABLE 2.1    Taxonomy of love

| | Components of love | | | |
|---|---|---|---|---|
| | Intimacy | Passion | Decision/ commitment | # of Ys |
| *Kinds of love* | | | | |
| Infatuated love[a] (I) | N | Y | N | 1 |
| Empty love[b] (E) | N | N | Y | 1 |
| Romantic love (R) | Y | Y | N | 2 |
| Companionate love[c] (C) | Y | N | Y | 2 |
| Fatuous love[d] (F) | N | Y | Y | 2 |
| Consummate love[e] (O) | Y | Y | Y | 3 |

Y = Yes (component present;); N = No (component not present).

Most loving relationships will fit between categories, because the various components of love are expressed along continua. The Table is adapted from Sternberg (1986: 123).

a   This is love at first sight.

b   In societies where people are freely able to choose their partners, empty love 'occurs as a final or near-final stage of a long-term relationship' but in societies, where marriages are arranged, 'empty love may be the first stage of a long-term relationship', where 'the marital partners may start with the commitment to love each other, or to try to love each other, and not much more' (p 124).

c   'This kind of love …is essentially a long-term, committed friendship, the kind that frequently occurs in marriages in which the physical attraction (a major source of passion) has died down' (p. 124).

d   'It is fatuous in the sense that a commitment is made on the basis of passion without the stabilizing element of intimate involvement' as happens when 'a couple meets on Day X, gets engaged two weeks later, and marries the next month' (p. 124).

e   'Consummate, or complete, love results from the full combination of the three components. It is a kind of love toward which many of us strive, especially in romantic relationships' (p. 124).

## 3    Why Do People Fall in Love?

Why/how do people fall in love? There are biological and social-psychological explanations. We have seen Plato's explanation for love: physical and spiritual procreation. Stephanie Cacioppo, a neuroscientist, says that love – including romantic love – is a superpower that makes the brain thrive and that it is a biological necessity just like water or food is (Cacioppo, 2022). According to the biologist, Fisher (2004: 6), 'Being in love … is part of human nature', so, one can say, that is why people fall in love. From an evolutionary biology perspective, love is also said to keep human beings together against external menaces and to facilitate the continuation of the species (Fisher, 2004). Charles Darwin himself is said to have identified unique features of human love compared to other mammals; he credits love as a major factor for creating social support systems that enabled the development and expansion of the human species (Loye, 2000).

The American philosopher of love, Frankfurt (2004: 46), says that 'it is a necessary feature of love that it is not under our direct and immediate voluntary control' and that 'what we love and what we fail to love is not up to us'. This is the case even if the necessity that 'love imposes on the will is rarely absolute' as evidenced by the fact that we do love something more than other things (ibid.).

According to neuroscience, romantic love and sexual attraction/arousal have some common neural basis. Not surprisingly, people refer to sex as *making love*. This also makes evolutionary sense since they are both species-survival mechanisms: we copulate to have offspring and we fall in love to better care for them (Castro, 2014). Love and pleasure ensure the survival of individuals and their species, as love is a joyful and useful activity that encompasses wellness and feelings of well-being (Esch and Stefano, 2005).

Love actually has a geographical location in the brain. The experience of romantic love is associated with three major neurotransmitters. One is dopamine. As the primary pleasure neurotransmitter of the brain's reward circuitry, dopamine plays an important role in both sexual arousal *and* romantic feelings. Then there are oxytocin and vasopressin which are more related to attachment and bonding. When one is in love, one experiences decreased activation in a brain area called frontal cortex, which is the center of executive functioning, judgement, planning, and logic. The prefrontal cortex, the parieto-temporal junction and the temporal poles constitute a network of areas invariably active with 'mentalizing'. The latter is the individual's ability to determine other people's emotions and intentions and to *distinguish* between self and others, with the potential of ascribing different sets of beliefs and desires to others and to oneself. To obtain an imagined "unity-in-love", where the self and the other become one, the process of mentalizing must be rendered *inactive*. This leads to, among other things, what Spinoza would call over-estimation, which is 'an effect or property of love': 'Overestimation consists in thinking too highly of another person in consequence of our love for him' (Spinoza, 1954: 179–80). Here, then, is a neural basis in the brain not only for saying (and feeling) that love is blind, but for the concept of "unity-in-love". 'Love is often irrational because rational judgments are suspended or no longer applied with the same rigour. ... [Even the] judgement in moral matters is suspended as well. ... And morality, too, has been associated with activity of the frontal cortex' (Zeki, 2007). However, even if love is blind, it can still be regulated through a conscious process (Langeslag and Strien, 2016). (See the Appendix for more details).

From a nonbiological angle, love has a social explanation: human beings have a universal need for union. Erich Fromm (1956) says that 'love [is] the overcoming of human separateness, as the fulfillment of the longing for union' (p. 33; see also Solomon, 1988). '[L]ove and marriage' are seen as an important source of 'a refuge from an otherwise unbearable sense of aloneness', and love 'forms an alliance of two against the world' (p. 88). And this loneliness is partly created by capitalism, which is based on competition and individualism from which a refuse is needed, although capitalism constrains the ways in which people can freely express their love (more on this later).

> Love is an active power in man; a power which breaks through the walls which separate man from his fellow men, which unites him with others; love makes him overcome the sense of isolation and separateness, yet it permits him to be himself, to retain his integrity. In love the paradox occurs that two beings become one and yet remain two.
>
> ibid.: 20–21

Of course, the social explanation of love includes a material – biological – aspect: 'above the universal, existential need for union rises a more specific, biological one: the desire for union between the masculine and feminine poles' (Fromm, 1956: 33; see also Solomon, 1988). Love in terms of difference and unity is also a theme in some of Engels' (1891) thinking:

> you, as a bridegroom, have a striking example of the inseparability of identity and difference in yourself and your bride. It is absolutely impossible to decide whether sexual love is pleasure in the identity in difference or in the difference in identity. Take away the difference (in this case of sex) or the identity (the human nature of both) and what have you got left?

Fromm's idea about love as a refuge is contradicted by Marcuse (1955) according to whom love has a repressive social function in modern society. 'Underlying the societal organization of the human existence are basic libidinal wants and needs ... [T]he libidinal impulses and their satisfaction (and deflection) are coordinated with the interests of domination and thereby become a stabilizing force which binds the majority to the ruling minority' (Marcuse, 1955). So, love, along with other emotions such as anxiety, etc., 'serve the economically structured relationships of domination and subordination' (ibid.). Approvingly discussing Freud, Marcuse says that 'love, in our culture, can and must be practiced as "aim-inhibited sexuality," with all the taboos and constraints placed upon it by a monogamic-patriarchal society. Beyond its legitimate manifestations, love is destructive and by no means conducive to productiveness and constructive work. Love, taken seriously, is outlawed: "There is no longer any place in present-day civilized life for a simple natural love between two human beings."' (ibid.).

Like Fromm, Badiou (2012) emphasizes the fact that love is a relation between two people based on difference and unity/alliance.[3] He develops his theory of love through a series of concepts: encounter; difference and identity; and truth procedure. When two people meet, it is initially a chance or contingent encounter based on difference. 'Starting out from something that is simply an encounter, a trifle, you learn that you can experience the world on the basis of difference and not only in terms of identity'. (p 16). '[L]ove involves a separation or disjuncture based on the simple difference between two people and their infinite subjectivities. This disjuncture is, in most cases, sexual difference' (p. 27).

'The declaration of love' the moment of explicit recognition that two people are in love, 'marks the transition from chance to destiny' (p. 43), so 'love really is a unique trust placed in chance' (p. 16). However, 'in retrospect the encounter doesn't seem at all random and contingent, as it appeared initially, but almost a necessity' (p. 42–43). In fact, 'the absolute contingency of the encounter with someone I didn't know finally takes on the appearance of destiny' (p. 43). Thus love 'has universal implications: it is an individual experience of potential universality, and is thus central to philosophy' (p. 17).

The two people being in love means that 'two different interpretive stances are set in opposition ... You have *Two*. Love involves *Two*' (Badiou, 2012: 28). This union view of love claims that when in love, two individuals 'can encounter and experience the world other than through a solitary consciousness' (ibid.: 39; also see Solomon, 1988). Love 'is a quest for truth', in the sense that love produces answers to important questions such as: '[W]hat kind of world does one see when one experiences it from the point of view of two and not one? What is the world like when it is experienced, developed and lived from

---

3   He says that: 'many people still cling to a romantic conception of love that in a way absorbs love in the encounter. Love is simultaneously ignited, consummated and consumed in the meeting, in a magical moment' (p. 30).

the point of view of difference and not identity?' (Badiou, 2012: 22). Love is 'a "truth procedure", that is, an experience whereby a certain kind of truth is constructed. This truth is quite simply the truth about Two: the truth that derives from difference as such' (p. 38).

Badiou says that love, or what he calls 'the Two scene', is the experience of truth construction (p. 38). This is the case even when the two lovers 'don't belong to the same class, group, clan or country' (p. 28). Two people with different identities can fall in love: 'identities in themselves aren't hurdles to the creation of love' (p. 62–63). 'We shouldn't underestimate the power love possesses to slice diagonally through the most powerful oppositions and radical separations' (p. 29). Beginning as a contingent encounter between two people, love necessarily unites them into one subject: they are 'incorporated into ... the [unitary] Subject of love that views the panorama of the world through the prism of [their] difference' (p. 26).

## 4      Consequences and Politics of Love

While Badiou, and others talk about love as a positive emotion, there are those who think love is both good and bad. Richard Davidson, the neuroscientist and psychologist, says: 'There's biased love, and there's unbiased love' (Davidson, 2019). Biased love is toward your in-group. Unbiased love is love towards all beings. 'The cultivation of unbiased love is really challenging. That's where, I think, the next frontier is' (ibid.). In their book *Commonwealth*, Hardt and Negri (2009) who devote numerous pages to the topic of love, discuss the negative and positive aspects of love too. They say that society's 'institutions silently compel individuals to follow established patterns of behavior' in their everyday life (p. 358). An important part of human behaviour, love appears in corrupted forms. This happens when one loves one's family but not the needy people outside or when one loves one's own community but hates others. Thus, love has been corrupted in many ways.

> One corrupt form of love is identitarian love, that is, love of the same, which can be based, for example, on a narrow interpretation of the mandate to love thy neighbor, understanding it as a call to love those most proximate, those most like you. Family love – the pressure to love first and most those within the family to the exclusion or subordination of those outside – is one form of identitarian love.
>
> HARDT AND NEGRI, 2009: 182

There is another form of the corruption of love:

> A second form of corrupt love poses love as a process of unification, of becoming the same. The contemporary dominant notion of romantic love in our cultures, ... requires that the couple merge in unity. The mandatory sequence of this corrupted romantic love – couple marriage-family – imagines people finding their match, like lost puzzle pieces, that now together make (or restore) a whole. Marriage and family close the couple in a unit that subsequently ... corrupts the common.
>
>     p. 183

Love also appears in its uncorrupt form. This is the love that constitutes the common, the multitude or the poor (which we will discuss below).

There is also an explicit attempt in the existing literature to see love in relation to politics. There are at least two approaches to this. One is what I would call 'an indifferent approach': love is indifferent to politics. Another is 'a positive approach': love contributes to emancipatory politics. Let us explore both of these approaches.

For Badiou, the realm of love and that of politics are different: 'love and political passion should never be confused' (p. 70).[4] Badiou says: 'I don't think you can mix up love and politics' (p. 57). Why? '[I]n love it is about two people being able to handle *difference*', but in politics, it 'is about finding out whether a number of people, a mass of people in fact, can create *equality*' (p. 54). Besides, 'there are people in politics one doesn't love' (p. 57). Politics is essentially about 'what are individuals capable of when they meet, organize, think and take decisions' (p. 53),[5] so people inevitably need to identify their 'real enemy' (p. 59), i.e., 'an individual you won't tolerate taking decisions on anything that impacts on yourself' (p. 58). In contrast, 'The issue of enemy is completely foreign to the question of love. In love, ... there are no enemies' (p. 59).

Love is communistic in the sense that it is an antidote to self-interest, which is the opposite of the communist value (Badiou, 2012: 16), yet there is no relation between love and communist politics which is the politics of emancipation in search of 'a world that isn't given over to the avarice of private property, a world of free association and equality' (p. 73). Badiou says: 'The meaning of the word "communism" doesn't immediately relate to love' (p. 73).

---

4  At best, 'only ambiguous connections exist between politics and love, a kind of porous separation or forbidden passage' (p. 103).
5  And 'just as the family exists as the level of love to socialize its impact, at the level of politics the power of the state exists to repress its enthusiasms' (p. 54).

Opposed to Badiou's approach is that of Hardt and Negri (2009). 'To understand love as a philosophical and political concept, it is useful to begin from the perspective of the poor and the innumerable forms of social solidarity and social production that one recognizes everywhere among those who live in poverty' (p. 180). Aspects of love such as solidarity, care for others, building a community, and cooperating in common projects, constitute for the poor, 'an essential survival mechanism'. (ibid.). There are: 'three operations or fields of activity for the power of love'. 'First, and primarily, the power of love is the constitution of the common and ultimately the formation of society'. In the second field of operation of love, 'the power of love [is] ... a force to combat evil', where evil includes the corruption of love (as manifested in the fact that a religious group, bound by ties of a degree of solidarity, hates another religious group). In this field, 'Love now takes the form of indignation, disobedience, and antagonism'. Finally, 'These two first guises of the power of love – its powers of association and rebellion, its constitution of the common and its combat against corruption [of love] – function together in the third: making the multitude' (Hardt and Negri, 2009: 195). The two authors say that 'Love is the power of the poor to exit a life of misery and solitude, and engage the project to make the multitude'. (Hardt and Negri, 2009: 189). When we 'band together' to 'form a social body', that becomes 'more powerful than any of our individual bodies alone', and this is how 'we are constructing a new and common subjectivity'. Love is political.

Similarly, in her book, *A Politics of love*, Williamson (2019: 10) says: 'Where racism, bigotry, and hatred have been harnessed for political purposes, we need to harness love for political purposes'. Politics should include the capacity for love, says Harris (2017): 'the capacity to practise love – to direct a deep sense of warmth towards another – should be ... valued in politics'. This is why 'We should admire and encourage those who are motivated by love in their political practice (rather than being motivated by the 'power and domination' to which hooks refers), and who express love through political action' (ibid.). To Harris, 'the securing of love [should be] ... a fundamental aim of what is done in politics' (ibid.).

## 5    A Critique of Existing Views on Love

Whether it is Plato or Spinoza or more modern writers, scholars tend to consider love to be, more than anything else, a relation which is confined to the lives of two individuals. Fromm (1956) says that 'most people believe that ... it is a proof of the intensity of their love when they do not love anybody except the "loved" person' (p. 26).

In my view, the idea that love is a relation between two people, whether advanced by neuroscientists or philosophers and others, is not entirely wrong. But this view is inadequately social. Love is more than about a relation between two individuals. This is at least in two senses. One is that each of the two individuals comes from specific 'networks' of people and families. When two people are tied to one another, the people who they are related to come to have some sort of ties with them too, weaker or stronger, depending on the social-cultural contexts. Further: the conception of what love is, how to live that relation, what is important to life of which love is a part, etc. are all social, and transcend the boundary of the two-in-one subject of love.

Love is often equated to desire and sex. This is not entirely wrong. But the conscious and decision-making aspect of love is under-estimated. While some neuroscientists say that love is driven by operations of certain neurons and flooding of certain transmitters such as dopamine, other neuro-scientists say that the impulse can be countered and that unbiased love – love that is confined to two individuals or a narrow family circle – can be cultivated (Davidson, 2012). 'Love is not about getting married and having lots of children' (Badiou, 2012: 32). Of course, 'the birth of a child is part of love' but one cannot conclude that that is 'the fulfilment of love' (p. 33). 'The idea that love is exclusively fulfilled or enacted via the creation of a family universe is far from satisfactory' (ibid.). When two people say they are in love, 'this declaration, even if it remains latent, is what produces the effects of desire, and not the desire itself' (p. 36). 'Love proves itself by permeating [physical] desire. The ritual of bodies is then the material expression of the word' (p. 36–37). '[L]ove cannot be ... a mere cloak for sexual desire, a sophisticated, chimerical ploy to ensure the survival of the species' (p. 37). The relation between love and sex must then be seen as socially mediated to a much greater extent than is the case in the literature.

Thinkers have rightly pointed to the societal constraints on people's ability to freely fall in love (this will be discussed later), but there is no indication that there are class constraints on the very notion of love itself. Class society tends to confine love to the love between two individuals based on mutual – sexual – attraction. What makes people fall in love, including through a chance encounter, is often confused with what makes love *enduring*. That there are neurotransmitters behind the act of falling in love cannot *themselves* adequately explain that act or how that act happens, because the neurotransmitters themselves are shaped by how people feel and act, as the neuroscience of plasticity itself says.

Further, the subjects of love, the lovers, are assumed to be non-class subjects, as if lovers' class position and social consciousness do not matter. Lovers are treated merely as individuals who just fall in love. Badiou says that two lovers who 'don't' belong to the same class, group, clan or country' (p. 28) can love each other and form a subject of love. Love has the power to blur boundaries across classes (p. 29). Badiou's concept of love has nothing to do with class.

Frankfurt does have interesting things to say about love. But he also has an individual-centric, particularistic and personalistic conception of love. Frankfurt (2004: 43) contrasts a person who loves another *person* to someone who loves, say, *the poor people* of society. 'Someone who is devoted to helping the sick or the poor for their own sakes may be quite indifferent to the particularity of those whom he seeks to help' (ibid.). What qualifies these people to benefit from 'his charitable concern is not that he loves them. His generosity is not a response to their identities as individuals; it is not aroused by their personal characteristics' (ibid.). Much rather, 'It is induced merely by the fact that he regards them as members of a relevant class [or a stratus or group]. For someone who is eager to help the sick or the poor, any sick or poor person will do' (ibid.). 'The significance to the lover of what he loves is not that his beloved is an instance or an exemplar. Its importance to him is not generic; it is ineluctably *particular*' (Frankfurt, 2004: 44; italics added). 'For a person who simply wants to help the sick or the poor,... it does not matter who in particular the needy persons are', i.e. which poor person he/she helps, and 'he does not really care about any of them as such', i.e. any specific poor person in particular, as all the poor people 'are entirely acceptable substitutes for each another'. In contrast, 'The situation of a lover is very different. There can be no equivalent substitute for [a person's] beloved' (Frankfurt, 2004: 44).

So, the object of love cannot be a class in the above view. I disagree. According to Frankfurt, if I help the poor, it is not because I love them but because I engage in charity. The poor as a group, as a class-fraction, cannot be the object of my love. Love's object is always a particular individual, to Frankfurt. To be an object of love, one has to be *an individual*, and a unique one at that. This is, more or less, an a-social view of love. Love that is theorized by Frankfurt and others is the love that exists, and that can only exist, in a class-less society. The fact is that when society is class divided, love in it cannot be as innocent of class as it appears to be. The idea that love involves first a chance encounter, and then an enduring relation, between *two* individuals, underestimates not only its social character but also its (class-) political character. The (class-) political character of love is either denied (as in Badiou's and Frankfurt's work) or under-conceptualized (as in Hardt and Negri).

Badiou thinks that love is a relation between just two individuals, so even if he rightly under-emphasizes the physical aspect of love, he wrongly underestimates the social, and therefore, the political, character of love. For Badiou, politics involves fighting enemies while love recognizes no enemy. He says that the essence of politics is about identifying and fighting enemies and about 'what are individuals capable of when they meet, organize, think and take decisions' (p. 53). 'Only political difference with the enemy is "irreconcilable" as Marx said', and this fact 'has no equivalent in the process of love' (p. 63). Badiou forgets that alliance building (i.e., connecting to like-minded people) is crucial to politics, and that such act of connecting can connect love to politics. For Badiou, love is communistic (and I agree), but he wrongly thinks that love has no relation to politics, let alone communist politics. Badiou's approach would suggest that a worker can have an enduring love relation with a bourgeois *as a bourgeois*. Badiou would accept that when two people, one with a working class consciousness and one with a socialist consciousness, are in love, they can produce 'a Subject of love'. If so, one might ask: what would be the class character of that Love Subject? Or will they become a class-neutral love subject, or a 'popular front' at a personal level? Will love then neutralize class identity of the worker? Badiou's concept of love is in line with the age-old concept of love for humanity, a concept in which individuals are not bearers of class relations or shaped by specific forms of social/political consciousness. People in love are just seen as trans-historical subjects.

There are others, who, to their credit, recognize the political aspect of love. But they under-conceptualize it. Harris (2017) says that 'Love should ... be a *virtue* in, and an *end-goal* of, politics: this is what I mean by a 'politics of love''. To him, 'The project of strengthening a general politics of love involves building up the power of the rhetoric of love, in the same way that, arguably, the neoliberal economic project has involved building up the power of ideas of individualism, freedom and efficiency'. Views on love like this are an improvement of politics-less love. But what is not clear is: how are these views different from those that help reproduce a slightly better, more compassionate, form of capitalism? This is because the class nature of politics in the politics of love remains under-conceptualized.

Hardt and Negri emphasize the political character of love, but their problem is because of the kind of Marxism that they advocate of which their view of love is a part. This is a Marxism that is, among other things, idealistic in a philosophical sense, and that papers over the dialectical and material *contradictions* of capitalism, which is why there is no explicit statement about the revolutionary anti-capitalist class subject (i.e., the working class) in their theory of love. They think that love is going to contribute to revolutionary politics, but it is not clear how. It is not clear how it is that love as such, apart from a class-conscious and organized proletariat, will make the 'multitude' and combat the evil. Is love-consciousness (feeling of love) more important than class consciousness? Does the recognition of the importance of love allow one to ignore the supreme necessity for conscious action and organizing in the fight for socialism?

Cidam (2013) says that in his recent writings, Negri has supplemented the notion of 'love' for his earlier emphasis on antagonism, to address autonomist Marxism's unresolved question of political organization. In Negri's work, 'emancipatory politics is theorized in terms of 'direct and immediate' forms of action' which is why 'the political organization of the revolutionary subject presents itself as an insurmountable problem' (p. 42). 'Negri's understanding of love as a productive force helps him evade this thorny issue by erasing the process of political contestation and mediation from his accounts' (ibid.).

The spirit of Marasco's (2010) complaint about some of the Marxist thinking about love, including about 'communist lovesickness', which is the idea that gives excessive emphasis on the power of love in the fight for communism, might apply to Hardt and Negri's approach. While many scholars (such as Hardt and Negri) talk about love's reconciliatory 'promise of a communitarian ethic for our age' (p. 644), Marasco argues that the renewal of intellectual interest in love 'has much to do with political exhaustion and despair' within the anti-capitalist movement, in the aftermath of the collapse of what was called socialism (p. 646; 648). Can an account of love counter this sense of despair?

### Appendix: Neuroscience and Love

Aided by the advent of brain imaging techniques allowing them to ask questions about the neural correlates of subjective mental states, neuroscientists probe the neural basis of love (Zeki, 2007; Cacioppo, 2022). Usually, romantic love is triggered by a visual input, so one falls in love with individuals who are physically attractive.[6] This is not to say that other factors, such as the voice, intellect, charm or social and financial status do not come into play. Among the brain areas engaged when people are in love, three are in the cerebral cortex itself and several others are located in subcortical stations. All constitute parts of 'the emotional brain' (Zeki, 2007). One can have lust and

---

6   '[T]he intimate experiential connection between love and beauty is probably nothing more than an expression of the intimate anatomical connection between the centres that are involved in these two experiences' (Zeki, 2007).

engage in sex without love, so one can actually tell the difference between love and sex because different brain areas are involved. Like sex, love is a rewarding and pleasurable experience our brains are wired to seek and enjoy. Behind this are the neural mechanisms.

Love can be distilled into three categories: lust, attraction, and attachment. Though there are overlaps and subtleties to each, each type is characterized by its own set of hormones. Testosterone and estrogen drive lust; dopamine, apart from norepinephrine and serotonin, creates attraction; and oxytocin and vasopressin mediate attachment.

The experience of romantic love (which includes attraction and attachment) is triggered by three major neurotransmitters: dopamine, oxytocin, and vasopressin. Dopamine is the primary pleasure neurotransmitter of the brain's reward circuitry, which plays an important role in both sexual arousal and romantic feelings. Dopamine is associated with reward, desire, addiction and euphoric states. 'Release of dopamine puts one in a "feel good" state, and dopamine seems to be intimately linked not only to the formation of relationships but also to sex, which consequently comes to be regarded as a rewarding and "feel-good" exercise'. (Zeki, 2007). An increase in oxytocin and vasopressin induces attachment and bonding behaviour.[7]

When one is in love, certain brain areas are activated (they light up) and other areas are de-activated. When looking at our beloved, key areas of our brains decrease activation: the amygdala, frontal cortex, parietal cortex, and middle temporal cortex. The amygdala is concretely implicated in fear and anger, meaning that decreased activation suggests a lessening of fear (Zeki, 2007). This might explain why we feel so safe and happy in our beloved's arms. A decrease in activity of amygdala (which is responsible for fear) makes one feel even better and promotes trust in one's partner. A decrease in the frontal cortex activity makes one overlook one's partner's flaws and be willing to do anything for the love relationship. The frontal cortex is the center of executive functioning, judgement, and logic, all of which get thrown overboard in love. This is due to decreased activation in this brain area, which translates to a "suspension in [critical] judgement or a relaxation of judgemental criteria by which we judge other people" (Zeki 2007). People in love judge each other less harshly because their frontal cortex is drugged by infatuation. Deactivation in the 'mentalizing' areas of the brain provide creates a sense of unity in love in spite of differences (Castro, 2014). There is thus a neural basis not only for saying that love is blind and illogical, but also for the 'unity-in-love'. 'Love is often irrational because rational judgments are suspended or no longer applied with the same rigour. ... Nor are there moral strictures, for judgement

---

7   'The amygdala is known to be engaged during fearful situations and its de-activation, when subjects view pictures of their partners as well as during human male ejaculation, implies a lessening of fear' (Zeki, 2007).

in moral matters is suspended as well. ... And morality, too, has been associated with activity of the frontal cortex' (Zeki, 2007).

Our infatuation produces a decrease in the brain areas associated with mentalizing, namely the prefrontal cortex, parieto-temporal junction, and the temporal poles. These are the structures responsible for being able to identify other people's emotions and ascribing reasons for them. These areas are implicated in the conceptual distinction between the self and the other, therefore their deactivation is necessary for reaching the merging and unity that lovers seek with each other (Zeki, 2007). Zeki says that: 'sexual arousal activates regions adjacent to – and in the case of the hypothalamus overlapping with – the areas activated by romantic love, in the anterior cingulate cortex, and in the other subcortical regions ... [R]omantic love has at its basis a concept – that of unity, a state in which, at the height of passion, the desire of lovers is to be united to one another and to dissolve all distance between them. Sexual union is as close as humans can get to achieving that unity. It is perhaps not surprising to find, therefore, that the areas engaged during these two separate but highly linked states [i.e., romantic love and sexual arousal] are juxtaposed [and are in close geographical proximity in the brain]. Indeed, the desire for unity through sexual union may be a consequence of it [i.e. such juxtaposition]' (Zeki, 2007).

# CHAPTER 3

# Towards a Marxist Theory of Love: Trans-historical Aspects

## 1    Introduction

Things are often different from how they appear. For example, 'A commodity appears, at first sight, a very trivial thing, and easily understood. Its analysis shows that it is, in reality, a very queer thing, abounding in metaphysical subtleties and theological niceties' (Marx, 1887: 47). Similarly, love might seem like a mundane thing. On closer analysis, it appears to be covered with 'mystical' properties.

There is a need for an adequate theorization of love. Such a theorization must avoid the pitfalls in the existing literature. Like everything else, love must be seen at multiple levels: it must be examined at the level of human society (in its relation to nature and in relation to the materiality of human life itself). At this level, the qualities that are common to all human beings – including their emotional and physical desires – are to be stressed. All trans-historical processes are socially mediated, so love must be also examined at the level of class society, and especially at the level of specific forms of class society such as capitalism. This chapter focusses on the trans-historical aspects of love.

The remainder of the chapter has 3 main sections. Section 2 deals with love as an emergent effect of a mental and physical connection. Section 3 argues that love is more than a relation between two individuals. Section 4 discusses love as a conscious 'labour process'.

## 2    Love as a Social-Emergent Effect of a Mental and Physical Connection

In a wider sense, and as discussed in Chapter 2, love refers to strong attraction and a feeling of caring towards others (this is Davidson's concept of 'unbiased love'). It encompasses a relation of friendship where it is the case that: when one friend is happy or sad, the other friend is happy or sad, respectively. Love *is* a relation of compassion, as in Spinoza's thinking (1954: 179) (and also in

Buddhism), which is the opposite of the relation of envy.[1] One form of love is romantic love, which refers to all the forms of love where there are some emotional ties and where there is potential or actual physical passion (So, romantic love as I define it would include all forms of love in Table 2.1 in Chapter 2, except infatuation). Romantic love exists because human beings possess a need for it and they have the causal power to engage in it, i.e., to show warm emotions combined with physical drives. Romantic love, in a philosophical sense, is an emergent effect: it is an emergent effect of warm emotions *and* physical attractions in that it is a product of both while it can neither be reduced to one or the other.

As we have seen, Fisher (1998), who is a biological anthropologist, says that as a biological drive and a survival mechanism, love has three components: lust, attraction, and attachment. Each of these is characterized by its own set of hormones. Testosterone and estrogen drive lust; dopamine, norepinephrine, and serotonin create attraction; and oxytocin and vasopressin mediate attachment. There is scientific basis to suggest that the neurons responsible for warm emotions and those responsible for sex are in close proximity in the brain, and this partly explains how they are inter-related (Zeki, 2007). Or romantic love is an intangible affective compound that is based in those bodily needs, desires and drives, which are 'seasoned with a particularity of orientation that arises out of the condition of our individuality', which is 'itself a historical product' (Arnett, 2011: 82). Or, as Lotz (2015: 132) says: 'love is a form of being social in which the sensual life is as complex as the social world, and not simply an abstraction from the latter'.

If it is assumed that historically, most people are dominantly heterosexual, then Marx's following statement has a lot of relevance to the understanding of love as a social process. Love is a social process, where one person meets the need of another:

> The direct, natural, and necessary relation of person to person is the *relation of man* to *woman* ... [which] is the *most natural* relation of human being to human being. It therefore reveals the extent to which [human beings'] *natural* behaviour has become *human,* or the extent to which the human essence in him has become a *natural* essence.

Marx continues:

---

1  This is opposed to a relation of enmity: when x and y are enemies, when x is happy, y is sad, and when x is sad, y is happy. x and y are strangers when: x's happiness or sadness does not affect y's happiness or sadness.

> This relationship ... reveals the extent to which [human beings'] *need* has become a *human* need; the extent to which, therefore, the *other* person as a person has become for him a need – the extent to which [a person in their] individual existence is at the same time a *social being.*
>
> MARX, 1844a: 43; italics added[2]

People's consciousness is influenced by human beings' social conditions, i.e., the ways in which people live their lives materially or the ways in which they produce 'the immediate material means of subsistence' and consequently attain 'the degree of economic development ... during a given epoch' (Engels, 1883). Ultimately, it is not human beings' consciousness 'that determines their existence, but their social existence that determines their consciousness' (Marx, 1859).[3] This principle of historical materialism applies to love in so far as love is a part of culture, of social consciousness. To the extent that romantic love is based on a sexual drive/need and the need for intimate connections (partly as an anti-dote to loneliness), this drive is impacted by wider social forces, including social relations of production and associated economic development and their politics (these will be discussed in the next chapter).

There is another sense in which love is a social process and not entirely a biologically driven process. The recent discovery in neuroscience indicates that human brains possess neuroplasticity: mind drives the brain, and our brain can change because of how we think and act, and the brain, a physical entity, in turn shapes the mind. Reviewing a wide range of neuroscience literature, Davidson and McEwen (2012), conclude that: the brain – especially, its neural circuits implicated in social and emotional behavior – is constantly changing, that among the influences on brain structure and function that are most powerful in inducing plastic change are social influences, and that social and emotional characteristics of people can be educated and altered just as people's knowledge about the world changes through cognitive learning. Neuroscience research has shown that love for oneself, family members,

---

2  Engels says that there are 'mutual relations based on reciprocal inclination between human beings, such as sex love, friendship, compassion, self-sacrifice, etc', and that in a relation based on sexual love, 'each find[s] in others the satisfaction of [their] own urge towards happiness, which is just what love ought to achieve and how it acts in practice'.

3  Fundamental to society's functioning is 'the totality of relations of production' (or class relations), including people's relations to means of production and how they are used and to the control over the social surplus, as this totality is connected to 'a given stage in the development of [the] material forces of production' (Marx, 1859). On the foundation of the relations of production and attendant economic development operate political processes, to which 'correspond definite forms of social consciousness' (ibid.).

strangers and even difficult people can be cultivated, to some extent, through regular practice. Among other things, such practice involves loving kindness meditation in which an individual intentionally wishes that they themselves and others be happy and enjoy good health (Goleman and Davidson, 2017; Lutz, et al, 2008; Weng et al, 2017; Wong et al, 2022). All in all, neuroscientific research has shown not only that love that one naturally feels can cause changes in the brain (Cacioppo, 2022) but also that practice -- loving kindness meditation -- that consciously cultivates love can produce structural changes in the brain that are in turn responsible for wholesome emotions such as love. It is also proven that romantic love, generally considered blind, can be regulated by a conscious thought process. People can 'down-regulate their love feelings by thinking about negative aspects of their partner and/or relationship and imagining negative future scenarios' (Langeslag and Strien, 2016).

## 3      Love Is More Than a Relation between Two Individuals

Love is a social process in another sense. Love between two human beings raises the following question: what is the essence of a human being? For, 'Any theory of love must begin with a theory ... of human existence' (Fromm, 1956: 7). Marx (1845) says: 'the human essence is no abstraction inherent in each single individual. In its reality it is the ensemble of the social relations'. Indeed, there is no such thing as 'an abstract – isolated – human individual', even if people do feel isolated because of the absence of healthy social interaction. In any type of relation, individuals come to be related but they are not merely individuals. *Before* two *individual* human beings encounter each other in the love-spaces, and begin to develop a relation of love, they are already *social* creatures. An individual absorbs (good and bad) influences from others. Our body, our abilities, activities, etc. are social products, the products of social relations that are supra-individual. People are what/who they are because of their relations with others.

There is no society without individuals. But society is not merely the sum of activities and thoughts of individuals nor is it equal to voluntary everyday interpersonal relations. Society is an emergent effect of the sum total of relations among individuals. Society is a mighty reality independent of individuals who reproduce society, a reality created by the interaction among individuals as bearers (or embodiments) of objective social relations. Individuals possess specific qualities, so they *are* different one from another. But the specificities (or the differences) are not individual because the qualities that distinguish individuals are already social. The fact is that the peculiarity of an individual represents a special combination of basic features of the *general* processes that define society. In other words, society has numerous qualities (which indicate the necessary needs and abilities that people have by virtue of the fact that they live in society), and these qualities are present in given individuals in different combinations. These *combinations* of social qualities – not the specific qualities as such – are unique to individuals, and this is what makes individuals somewhat unique. So, social relations (and ideas about social relations, our views) are differently congealed in, and borne by, different individuals. Each individual is a cell, a microcosm, of society.

Each individual is unique, special. So, their view of love or how they experience it is bound to vary in certain ways. An individual's views on love are influenced by their perception of these qualities in others. One individual loves roses, writing romantic birthday cards, and hates people on welfare. Another individual dislikes all flowers, loves hockey, mingles with the homeless on welfare, and wants to fight against the system of low wages. Loving roses, hating poor people, fighting against low wages, writing romantic birthday cards, all these are deeply *social* qualities which are present in different individuals in different combinations, although they may appear to be traits of an individual as an individual. Individuals are like places on a 'map' that is society. Just because not all individuals have the same characteristics does not mean that these characteristics are not social. All this has implications for understanding love. To paraphrase Fromm (1956): inasmuch as we as members of the working class 'are all one', because we share the same conditions of life, so we *can* love everybody within the class on the basis of that fact, but 'inasmuch as we are all also different' in the sense that, for example, we, as individuals, value different things in the world, romantic love 'requires certain specific, highly individual elements which exist between some people but not between all'. (p. 56–57). From a *class* standpoint, a working class person can love – i.e., show relations of warmth and solidarity towards – all of their working class brothers and sisters, but, from an *individual* standpoint, he/she can fall in romantic love with only of some of them. So, love is an individual act and an act that is shaped by class relations, so it is an intensely social act.

As Marx says, an individual is ultimately an ensemble of social relationships. When I say I love this individual, what I am saying, more or less, is that I love an ensemble of social relationships (and qualities as products of social relations) that this individual represents. When I say I love x, what it means is that I love certain qualities of x, and that these qualities are social in nature and are not just about x as an individual. So, when I say I love x, I really say that I love this or that *social* characteristic of the individual, x, but I may think that I love the *individual as such*, and that the social aspects have nothing to do with

my love. When two individuals fall in love, they fall in love as representatives –
as personifications – of social rules, social qualities and social logics.[4]

Love between two individuals is a deeply *social* process, even if it is also
an *individual* process. 'To have faith in the possibility of love as a social and
not only exceptional-individual phenomenon, is a rational faith based on the
insight into the very nature of [human beings]' (Fromm, 1956: 133). In fact,
'Love is not primarily a relationship to a specific person; it is an attitude, an
orientation of character which determines the relatedness of a person to the
world as a whole, not toward one "object" of love' (p. 46). To paraphrase Fromm
once again, if a working class person 'loves only one other person and is indifferent' to the rest of their fellow human beings, then their 'love is not love but
a symbiotic attachment, or an enlarged egotism' (p. 46).

## 4 Love Is a Conscious 'Labour Process', an Activity

Love in the form of romantic love involves desire and ecstasy. But love is more
than this. It is much less spontaneous than it appears to be. Love is a conscious
material and discursive activity. As a social process, love is a trans-historical
act of labour which can be analyzed by carefully following Marx's approach
(1887: 127–130) to the materiality of life and to the trans-historical nature of
labour.[5] Love can be seen as what Marx (1845) calls a '*sensuous human activity*'.
An act of labour, love between two individuals is, in the first place, a process in
which both human beings, as embodiments of human consciousness (intentionality) and natural drives, participate. This is a process in which human
beings of their own accord start, regulate, and control their natural need for
warmth and sexual contentment. In the process of interacting with the natural impulses inside, human beings change their own nature, own conditions
(more on this below).

To the extent that love involves a material act, an act of labour, it involves
imagination, a discursive act. Love itself involves a mental state. Besides, love
is an action with an *aim* – it is an act of labour which involves conscious awareness and conscious imagination permeated by the spirit of intention. The

---

4  Of course, some social aspects (loving a rose vs loving Marxism) may be more social or more
   important (important from the standpoint of changing the current society) than other social
   aspects.
5  The 'social' in the social character of love exists in two ways: the social as opposed to purely/
   dominantly individual, and the social as opposed to the natural (i.e., biological impulse).

people in love have an intention: they have a sense of what it means to be in love. Marx (1887: 127) says:

> A spider conducts operations that resemble those of a weaver, and a bee puts to shame many an architect in the construction of her cells. But what distinguishes the worst architect from the best of bees is this, that the architect raises his structure in *imagination* before he erects it in reality. At the end of every labour-process, we get a result that already existed in the *imagination* of the labourer at its commencement.

The act of loving is a labouring act, a labour process, or at least an act that is like labour process.[6] It is an act where the loving-architect raises their structure of the love relation in *imagination* before he or she erects it in reality. Love does involve conscious thinking. Love is a material act of labour. It involves bodily activity, as we have seen. 'It is the project, naturally including sexual desire in all its facets, including the birth of a child, but also a thousand other things' (Badiou, 2012: 23).

As a process, love is the act of lov*ing*, the outcome of which is also love. And the act of loving is also an act of *giving*. This is a material act too. Love means giving without the intention to receive. How can I say, 'I love you', if I do not care if you have been eating well while I have been enjoying my food (with silver forks)? How can I say, 'I love you', if I don't care if you have been insulted by a bigot or beaten up by police for picketing or forced to work a 16-hour day by your employer? As Fromm (1956: 22) says: 'Love is an activity, not a passive affect; it is a "standing in," not a "falling for." … [T]he active character of love can be described by stating that love is primarily giving, not receiving'.

There is more to love as an activity than giving. In fact, 'Beyond the element of giving, the active character of love becomes evident in the fact that it always implies certain basic elements, common to all forms of love. These are care, responsibility, respect and knowledge'. (Fromm, 1956: 26). We can express this idea more precisely: when x loves y, that means that: x cares for, shoulders responsibility towards, respects, and understands, y. So, love is hard work, but it is also the most rewarding kind of work. 'People think that to love is simple' (Fromm, 1956: 2). As an art, love actually 'requires knowledge and effort' (ibid.: 1). It has to be accomplished through conscious action.

---

6  Love is not *exactly* a labour process because love has partly an intrinsic value while the aim of labour process is to produce something which in turns meets a need.

An activity is an activity because of its transformative impacts on the conditions in which it takes place. In the process of interacting with the natural impulses towards loving, human beings effect a change in their lives as mentioned above. People in love develop what Marx would call their 'slumbering powers', i.e., new ways of loving and new conceptions of love, beyond those primitive instinctive forms of the labour of love that remind us of the mere animal. Love not only transforms the conditions of the loved because the latter is cared for, understood, respected and so on. But as an activity, love transforms the loving person himself/herself. Love involves giving, and 'In the very act of giving, I experience my strength, my wealth, my power. This experience of heightened vitality and potency fills me with joy' (Fromm, 1956: 23). This is in line with the modern neuroscience literature that says that love makes one happy (Castro, 2014).

The concept of love as an activity draws attention to the fact that the people in love are inter-dependent: one's flourishing or happiness depends on another. This is why: 'If you love without evoking love in return – if through the vital expression of yourself as a loving person you fail to become a loved person, then your love is impotent, it is a misfortune' (Marx, 1844a: 43). Similarly, Giles (1994), a Canadian philosopher and psychologist, says: 'in being in love with another I want that person to love me back. ... [W]hat persons in a social relationship want is that the ratio of their own inputs to outcomes is equal to the ratio of the other person's inputs to outcomes' (p. 341). Thus, to be in love with someone would be to engage in the activity of investing 'a high amount of input into a relationship which, if the other person did not reciprocate to an equal level, i.e., show love back, would naturally lead to an uncomfortable dissonance'. So 'love wants love in return' (p. 341–342). In an authentic love relation, the two people in love recognize (and ensure) that their beloved is a free subject and is appreciated as such (de Beauvoir, 2011). I would express this idea as follows:

$$I_1 / O_1 = I_2 / O_2 \ldots \tag{1}$$

This can be re-written as:

$$I_1 / I_2 = O_1 / O_2 \ldots \tag{2}$$

*Where: I = love input; O = love output; 1 and 2 are person 1 and person 2, respectively.*

Equation 1 means that when two persons are in love, the ratio of one person's own input to the outcome (i.e., 'how much' love one receives) in the relationship be equal to the ratio of the other person's input to his/her outcome.

This can be seen in another way as expressed in Equation 2 above: the ratio of one person's input to another person's input be equal to the ratio of one person's outcome to another person's outcome.

Love as a mental state, of course, encompasses feelings. But this is only a small part of love as an activity. If two strangers 'suddenly let the wall between them break down, and feel close, feel one, this moment of oneness is one of the most exhilarating, most exciting experiences in life' (Fromm, 1956: 4). This feels like a miracle, which 'is often facilitated if it is combined with, or initiated by, sexual attraction and consummation' (ibid.). However, this type of love does not last long. This is because there tends to be an inverse relation between familiarity on the one hand and intimacy based on mere feelings and sexual attraction on the other hand. As two people 'become well acquainted, their intimacy loses more and more its miraculous character' (ibid.). This happens 'until their antagonism, their disappointments, their mutual boredom kill whatever is left of the initial excitement', although they do not know this at the early stage of their relation. At the early stage, they actually 'take the intensity of the infatuation, this being "crazy" about each other, for proof of the intensity of their love, while it may only prove the degree of their preceding loneliness' (ibid.).

When one views love as 'the outcome of a spontaneous, emotional reaction, of suddenly being gripped by an irresistible feeling', one 'sees only the peculiarities of the two individuals involved' (p. 56). As a result, one's love object (who one can love) gets confined to a few. As well, when love is merely a spontaneous act, 'One neglects to see an important factor in erotic love, *that of will*' (italics added):

> To love somebody is not just a strong feeling – it is a decision, it is a judgment, it is a promise. If love were only a feeling, there would be no basis for the promise to love each other forever [or for a long duration]. A feeling comes and it may go. How can I judge that it will stay forever, when my act does not involve *judgment and decision*? (Italics added)
>      ibid.

Love is thus a conscious choice which in its early stages might originate as an involuntary feeling, but which, at a later stage, does not depend merely on those feelings, but rather significantly depends on conscious commitment and will. The feeling of love is thus superficial in comparison to one's commitment to love. The commitment to love is materialized through a series of loving actions. These loving actions occur over space, in 'love-spaces': college campuses, study trips, factory floors, union meetings, theatres, parks, restaurants, street corners, beaches, reading group meetings, playgrounds, prison cells shared by comrades, etc. And they happen over a period of time which includes a series of moments. The act of loving – falling in love and continuing the act – indeed requires a 'duration of time necessary for it to flourish' (Badiou, 2012: 32). There is scientific research to suggest that:

> for long-term romantic love many more brain regions are affected compared to those found among newly in love subjects. Some of these differences may reflect time-dependent changes that occur as bonds develop. Some research suggests that it takes ~2 years for enduring attachment bonds to become established .... thus newly in love individuals may not reflect physiology of full-blown attachment bonds.
>
> ACEVEDO ET AL., 2012

The beginnings of love relation 'are clearly ecstatic, but love is above all a construction that lasts' for a variable duration (p. 32). '[L]ove is a tenacious adventure. The adventurous side [indicating ecstatic feeling] is necessary, but equally so is the need for tenacity [indicating commitment]. To give up at the first hurdle, the first serious disagreement, the first quarrel, is only to distort love. Real love is one that triumphs lastingly, sometimes painfully, over the hurdles erected by time, space and the world' (ibid.).

## 5      Conclusion

Love as an activity happens over time and over space, even if it appears as if it happens at *this* fleeing moment and in *that* little space. Morrison et al say, love is not just historical. It is also 'something that is spatial' and 'cannot be separated out from spatiality' (Morrison et al 2012: 506). '[L]ove can only ever exist within specific spatial and temporal contexts' (p. 513).

And love in the sense of romantic love as an activity involves *conscious* decisions, even if it appears to be just spontaneous, driven by a biological impulse and is blind. Because love is more than biological impulse and because it therefore involves activity which requires conscious thinking, love allows, and entails, decision-making. And if love involves decision-making, it can involve *political* decisions: it is possible – and it will be argued later that it is necessary – to consciously think about who one can be in a love relation over a relatively long period.

We have so far dealt with love while abstracting from the historically changing forms of society. That is, we have discussed love at the level of humanity as such. This approach needs to be now supplemented by an approach which sees love in relation to class society, including, especially, capitalism. An immeasurable interval of time separates the state of things in which human beings equate love to the love between two (monogamous) married people, from that state in which human labour of love was still in its first instinctive stage. Love as a labour process or an activity is human action with an intentionality – i.e., the production of emotional and physical enjoyment, which is a use-value. Love in its romantic form is the everlasting nature-imposed condition of human emotional and biological existence, and therefore is independent of every social phase of that existence, or rather, is common to every such phase of human life. In all societies people develop affection, and people engage in sexual activity with varying degrees of emotion. But the form of love-as-an-activity will be different in different forms of society (e.g., feudalism, capitalism, etc.), as we will see in the next chapter. Indeed, as human social life and culture have changed, 'a web of emotional and intellectual experiences has come to surround the physical attraction of the sexes', making love 'a complex state of mind and body' which is 'separated from its primary source, the biological instinct for reproduction' (Kollontai, 1923).

# Towards a Marxist Theory of Love: Love in Class Society and in Socialism

## 1    Introduction

As a trans-historical process, love in its romantic form does have a natural/ biological aspect (e.g., physical drives), as revealed in the philosophical and scientific literature. But love is also a deeply social process. Love is a social process in at least two ways. One is that it cannot be reduced to, and is more than, the physical drives and neurotransmitters. Human activity and consciousness are involved in love. Another is that love is more than about the relation between *two* individuals. Love is much more than the private matter between two people. Culture/consciousness, an important part of the social life of human beings, is impacted by class relations, including ruling class interests as opposed to the interests of the exploited classes. Love as a form of consciousness is impacted by class relations and is in turn made use of in the reproduction of specific forms of class society. Like consciousness, politics is an aspect of the social life of human beings too. Because love is a social process, it is therefore a political process. Love can have a moderate role in the fight for a class-less society.

As a social process, love is therefore a historical process, dominantly shaped by changing economic forces, including the interests of the ruling classes, and principles of property ownership. Society has always regulated love as well as sexual relations which are connected to it because love and sex play a crucial role in the biological reproduction, control over care-labour (generally of women), social cohesion of a society and orderly transmission of property. As forms of class society change and as 'the cultural and economic base of humanity changes', 'ideas of love have changed' (Kollontai, 1923). Not much more can be said about love at the level of class society as such, so we need to examine love in the context of specific forms of class society (e.g., feudalism and capitalism).

In this chapter, continuing the Marxist theory of love, I discuss love in its historically-specific class contexts, i.e., love in pre-capitalist class society (section 2) and love in capitalist class society (section 3–4). In discussing love in capitalism, I focus on three aspects of capitalist society: capitalist property and commodity relations; alienation, and class consciousness. I also briefly discuss how love is shaped by the ways in which capitalist class relations shape gender and other forms of oppression (section 5). I then turn to the nature of love in the socialist movement within capitalism, and love in socialism (section 6).

## 2        Love in Pre-capitalist Class Society

'In the course of the thousand-year history of human society, love has developed from the simple biological instinct – the urge to reproduce which is inherent in all creatures from the highest to the lowest – into a most complex emotion that is constantly acquiring new intellectual and emotional aspects.[1] Love has become a psychological and social factor' (Kollontai, 1923).
Indeed, to the extent that love and sex are connected, 'a web of emotional and intellectual experiences has come to surround the physical attraction of the sexes' (ibid.).

> Each historical (and therefore economic) epoch in the development of society has its own ideal of marriage and its own sexual morality ... Different economic systems have different moral codes. Not only each stage in the development of society, but each class has its corresponding sexual morality ... [T]he more firmly established the principles of private property, the stricter the moral code.
>
> KOLLONTAI, 1921

In fact, 'each class', at least each ruling class, 'strives to fill the conception of love with a moral content that suits its own interests' (Kollontai, 1923).

At a very early stage of human history, when the state was still in its embryonic form and class relations were being formed, love between two members of the same tribe, linked by mental and emotional ties, i.e., love-friendship, was of utmost importance (Kollontai, 1923). It was more important than love between man and wife. This was because at that time the interests of the society as a whole required the accumulation of contacts not between two married people but between fellow-members (usually, males) in defense of the tribe and its political organization (state). In the dominant ideology of the early form of class society, love was relegated to the sphere of narrow, personal experiences

---

1    This section heavily relies on Kollontai's work. Her ideas were perhaps advanced for her time, but raised important questions (often trivialized by socialists) for a future socialist society (Roelofs, 2018).

with which society was not concerned; marriage was based not on love but for convenience (ibid.).

In feudal societies, love was not the basis of marriage either. Engels (1884: 41) says that:

> For the knight or baron, as for the prince of the land himself, marriage is a political act, an opportunity to increase power by new alliances; the interest of the house must be decisive, not the wishes of an individual. What chance then is there for love to have the final word in the making of a marriage?

Love was contracted according to the interests of the family, which were to be prioritized over individuals' personal feelings. It was not that love between the sexes was neglected. In fact, 'for the first time in the history of humanity it received a certain recognition' (Kollontai, 1923). However, 'Sexual intercourse both within and outside marriage lacked the softening and inspiring element of love and remained an undisguisedly physiological act' (ibid.). This happened in a society where economic exploitation was politically coerced in a direct way, so violence was endemic everywhere. This fact has two implications. One, that Kollontai does not quite explore, is that the fact that class-exploitation requires physical coercion (or its threat) in an immediate sense is not conducive to an overall social environment where soft feelings associated with love can flourish (this point is discussed further in the next section). The second implication, which Kollontai does explore, is as follows: 'In certain situations,... love can act as a lever propelling the man to perform actions [of bravery etc.] of which he would otherwise have been incapable' (Kollontai, 1923). A male member of the feudal ruling class (e.g. a knight) would love a woman from outside of his family: 'Usually the knight [would choose] ... as his lady the woman least accessible', for example, 'the wife of his suzerain, or often the queen', for 'Only such a "platonic" love could spur the knight to perform miracles of bravery and was considered virtuous and worthy' (Kollontai, 1923). Indeed, the class-based rule of love in a feudal society appears to be the following: 'The more inaccessible the woman, the greater the knight's determination to win her favour and the greater his need to develop in himself the virtues and qualities' such as military valor, 'which were valued by his social class'. So, love as a mental state 'could be used to the advantage of the feudal class'.

What about love inside the family? 'Love between man and wife was not valued, for the family ... was not held together by emotional ties' (ibid.). The family was held together firmly by the traditions of nobility and birth. For the exploited classes, such as peasants or artisans, the family was an economic

labour unit; its members were so firmly held together by economic circumstances that bonds based on emotional ties were of secondary importance.

## 3      Love and Capitalist Economy

Love, in its universal form and in its romantic form, requires connection, social
and spatial. The bourgeois system has created means of communication so
people can communicate much more adequately. As stated earlier, time is a
pre-condition for love too: love, as an act, requires a 'duration of time necessary for it to flourish' (Badiou, 2012: 32). Capitalism has created the possibility
for leisure because of the massive development of productive forces that it
has allowed post feudalism. Capitalism has also removed the power of the feudal ruling class to exercise violence against ordinary people, including their
everyday life. It has created a social milieu that is much more conducive to
soft feelings characteristic of love than pre-capitalist system did. Yet, bourgeois
relations restrict the scope of and ability to, love. A contradictory system itself,
capitalism creates contradictions inside the very heart of the loving subject.
The question is: why?

'Capitalist production ... produces not only commodities, not only surplus-
value, but it also produces and reproduces the capitalist relation; on the one
side the capitalist, on the other the wage labourer' (Marx, 1887: 407). As a part
of reproduction of capitalist relation, it is necessary that the wage-labourers,
more or less, accept *ideas* that reproduce capitalism. 'The advance of capitalist production develops a working class, which by education, tradition, habit,
looks upon the conditions of that mode of production as self-evident laws of
Nature'. (ibid.: 521). The working class that capitalism needs is one that has specific cultural traits apart from its abilities to efficiently produce commodities
(on the basis of average socially necessary labour time). Given the importance
of love in life (including its implication for the reproduction of future labour
power and for the confinement of property within the capitalist class), capitalism produces specific forms of love-couples, or people-in-love, in a way that
is broadly compatible with the long-term reproduction of capitalist relation.
Love *in* capitalism must reproduce love *with* capitalism.[2] It is no wonder that
with the rising bourgeoisie, a new moral ideal of relations between the sexes
developed, albeit slowly and gradually. Love is deeply linked to capitalism

---

2   'Far from being a 'haven' from the marketplace, modern romantic love is a practice intimately
    complicit with the political economy of late capitalism' (Illouz, 1997: 22).

which, in terms of its major traits, is a class relation. These traits are structural class-based alienation – property-lessness, commodity production, production of value/surplus-value – and the reproduction of labour power (Das, 2017a).

### 3.1     Capitalist Property Relation, and Commodity Fetishism

An important trait of capitalism that Kollontai fails to draw attention to in her discussion on love is this: the 'separation of labour from its product, of subjective labour-power from the objective conditions of labour [as] ... the real foundation ... and the starting-point of capitalist production' (Marx, 1887: 403). Dispossessed of the access to the means of production, people are compelled to work for a wage: 'The dull compulsion of economic relations completes the subjection of the labourer to the capitalist' (p. 521). 'Direct force, outside economic conditions, is of course still used, but only exceptionally' (ibid.), at least in advanced capitalism (we will return to this theme later). Separation of ordinary people from means of production leads to another separation: the nominal separation of the political from the economic (Wood, 1981). Thus, there is a dual separation under capitalism. This is contrast to feudalism (or pre-capitalist class relations as such) where economic exploitation happens through, and in tandem with, extra-economic coercion. The love relation under feudalism is, more less, consistent with the nature of feudal class relations. Under feudalism, a class-based rule of love appears as mentioned above. As well, love is divided into the sexual act (relations within marriage or with concubines) and spiritual/platonic love (as in the relations between the knight and his beloved) (Kollontai, 1923).

With the dual *separation* under capitalism, a dual *union* (non-separation) happens under capitalism: there is a union between love and marriage, and between mental and physical aspects of love. 'Love and marriage that were kept *separate* by feudal ideology were *united* by the bourgeois class' at least in principle (ibid.; italics added). 'Rejecting platonic love, the bourgeoisie defended the violated rights of the body'. So, the role of violence in daily life and of 'indescribably crude norms of relations between the sexes' in daily life that were characteristic of feudalism declined (ibid.). Capitalism has removed the power of the feudal ruling class to exercise violence against ordinary people, including in their everyday life.[3] But love is narrowly defined under the rule of capital accumulation under private property because its moral code is 'often dictated ... by economic considerations'.

---

3  That does not mean that capitalism is a peaceful affair. It is based on the dispossession of direct producers which is a violent affair; besides, the state acting on behalf of the capitalists is very much a violent institution (we will discuss this later).

*To the extent that* in a society dominated by private property and commodity relations, property depends on family savings, and given the already existing inequality in property ownership between men and women characteristic of a class society, and given the absence of socialized sphere of reproductive activity in class society, a man's savings need to be handled with care and skill, so the woman should not only be a good housewife but also the helper and friend of her husband (Kollontai, 1923). There is also a need to prevent the distribution of capital among illegitimate children. The ideal therefore 'is the married couple, working together to improve their welfare and to increase the wealth of their particular family unit' (ibid.).

In order to remain socially stable and economically viable, 'the family has to be based on the co-operation of all its members which entail 'strong emotional and psychological bonds', so 'new moral ideal of love that embraced both the flesh and the soul' was propagated' (ibid.). The family unit based on marital relations ensures childcare, food, and laundry services, etc. at no cost to the state or to the capitalists, the majority of which is provided for by women and young children, especially, female children. The family 'ensures competition [or selfishness] externally, as well as selflessness internally, particularly in the form of women's unpaid labor' (Cozzarelli, 2018). Not surprisingly, 'modern love as connected to marriage was invented by capitalism' (Cozzarelli, 2018). The married love is important from the standpoint of the need for efficient reproduction of labour power too, through 'necessary labour' performed by women 'in the private sphere' (Vogel, 2013; Das, 2020a; Gimenez, 2019) (I will return to this topic below).[4] Generally, there is a tendency for love outside of marriage to be '*antagonistic* with capitalism' (ibid.). In reality, of course, love constantly escapes 'from the narrow framework of legal marriage relations set for it, into free relationships and adultery', which are condemned (Kollontai, 1923), on the basis of moral values that actually reflect bourgeois society but that are often seen as universal values.

Bourgeois society is a society where not only private property rules. It is also a society where the things we need are available only in the form of commodities. It is a society of what Marx (1887) calls commodity fetishism: this means that things that we need behave as if they inherently – naturally – have the quality of being bought and sold for a profit, while, in reality, that quality is a historically-created social fact. In other words, in capitalism, what is a *social* process appears to be *natural*; what is a *historically specific* process appears

---

4  The new moral ideal serves the interests of those who live off income from property, from labour or from a combination of the two (peasants and artisans also).

to be *universal*. As well, in capitalism, even if the socialness of a process is not overlooked, its importance is *under*estimated. This is partly to fetishize the rugged individualism or the so-called 'sanctity of the individual', in the words of the US Congress (2023).[5] Commodity fetishism of capitalism, and associated bourgeois individualism, cannot but have some influence on everyday life, including love.

The natural desire to love and to be loved is over-emphasized at the expense of its social aspect. Love is seen as a relation only between two individuals rather than as dominantly social, involving many. And what is a historically specific form of the concept of love – the bourgeois concept of love – is considered to be historically universal. Hardt and Negri (2009) say that society's institutions provide individuals 'with formulas for living such that, for example, the desire for love is channeled into marriage and the desire for freedom channeled into shopping' (p. 358). Shopping itself is also a source of enjoyment: 'Modern man's happiness consists in the thrill of looking at the shop windows, and in buying all that he can afford to buy'. People's shopping behavior is transferred to their everyday life outside of buying and selling. They see each other in the way they see commodities. In the context of heterosexual relationships, 'For the man an attractive girl – and for the woman an attractive man – are the prizes they are after. "Attractive" usually means a nice package of qualities which are popular and sought after on the personality market'. (Fromm, 1956: 3).[6] And the package of qualities – the qualities one looks for in another person in a love relation – is narrowly defined in the decision-making that is involved in a love relation. These qualities are not innocent. They are those that support the reproduction of bourgeois society and family, or at least do not challenge bourgeois society and family. Besides, the quality and depth of love are often judged by the commodity form of presents lovers give one

---

5  A recent US Congress resolution says, 'the United States of America was founded on the belief in the sanctity of the individual, to which the collectivistic system of socialism in all of its forms is fundamentally and necessarily opposed' (US Congress, 2023). I would argue that the official concern for the sanctity of the individual is inversely related to the regard and love for the wellbeing of millions of *individuals*, whose lives are wasted, as indicated by millions of avoidable deaths in the US and in the world every year that are caused by the public health crisis, police brutality, poverty, inequality, predatory wars, environmental damage, etc., all of which are the different aspects of one single thing: capitalism.

6  'At any rate, the sense of falling in love develops usually only with regard to such human commodities as are within reach of one's own possibilities for exchange. I am out for a bargain; the object should be desirable from the standpoint of its social value, and at the same time should want me, considering my overt and hidden assets and potentialities. Two persons thus fall in love when they feel they have found the best object available on the market, considering the limitations of their own exchange values'. (Fromm, 1956: 3).

another: the expensive or exotic the present, the better is the love relation, it is often assumed. Love has been commodified. As well: the unmaking of social bonds, unloving, etc. – after all, relationships fade, evaporate and dissolve – is connected to contemporary capitalism that is characterized by practices of non-commitment and non-choice, the practices that enable the quick withdrawal from a transaction and the quick realignment of prices and the breaking of loyalties (Illouz, 2021).

In general, the commodity relations of capitalism as such are against the value of love and benevolence:

> What [Adam] Smith bans most adamantly from the marketplace is the common: only from private interests will the public good result. "It is not from the benevolence of the butcher, the brewer, or the baker, that we expect our dinner," Smith famously writes, "but from their regard to their own interest. We address ourselves, not to their humanity but to their self-love, and never talk to them of our own necessities but of their advantages." Our love for one another has no place in the realm of economic exchanges.
>
> HARDT AND NEGRI, 2009: 185

Marx says in *Capital volume 1* that in the sphere of purchase and sale of 'alone rule' not only 'Freedom, Equality [and] ... Property' but also 'Bentham' (Marx, 1887: 123). There is 'Bentham, because each looks only to himself': the only force that brings the guardians of commodities 'together and puts them in relation with each other, is the selfishness, the gain and the private interests of each' (ibid.). But the principle of love is opposed to the principle of Bentham (more on this in the next section).

## 3.2   *Alienation*

We have seen that capitalism 'produces and reproduces ... on the one side the capitalist, on the other the wage labourer' (Marx, 1887: 407). Capitalism produces/reproduces human beings as alienated. The capitalist class is of course alienated as its members are cogs in the wheel of capitalist accumulation: irrespective of what they want, they must do certain things (invest at a certain rate, hire and fire and exploit people, and so on).[7] For the workers, alienation

---

7   The capitalist 'shares with the miser the passion for wealth as wealth. But that which in the miser is a mere idiosyncrasy, is, in the capitalist, the effect of the social mechanism, of which he is but one of the wheels. Moreover, the development of capitalist production makes it constantly necessary to keep increasing the amount of the capital laid out in a given industrial

begins with the sale and purchase of labour power as a commodity. Capitalism forces the worker to sell their 'labour-power in order to live' and it 'enables the capitalist to purchase labour-power' for the capitalists' own enrichment. 'It is no longer a mere accident, that capitalist and labourer confront each other in the market as buyer and seller' (Marx, 1887: 407). Under such a circumstance, the relation between the worker and the capitalist is not based on solidarity (while the worker wants higher wages and better working conditions, the capitalist's interest is in the opposite, for example). Besides, when all workers are forced to sell their labour power in order to live, there is no guarantee that they will get any work: whether one is hired depends on capitalists' need, not workers'. So, workers compete with one another for work and therefore, there is no solidarity among them. There are separated for one another. Each experiences alienation. They are not connected to fellow human beings from their own class on the basis of solidarity.

There is alienation following the sale and purchase of labour power too. The surplus value that workers produce is appropriated by capitalists. Capitalists convert the surplus value into capitalist property which in turn exploits workers. So, workers remain separated from the surplus value they themselves produce. This is how: 'Capitalist production ... reproduces the separation [alienation] between labour-power and the means of labour. It thereby reproduces and perpetuates the condition for exploiting the labourer' (i.e., workers' property-lessness) (Marx, 1887: 407). Workers' exploitation itself is 'the alienation of the worker [from] ... *the products of his labor*' (1844a: 30). This alienation or 'estrangement is manifested not only in the result [i.e., products of labour] but in the *act of production*, within the *producing activity,* itself', over which people have no conscious collective control, so 'in the very act of production he [is] ... estranging himself from himself'. 'If then the product of labor is alienation, production itself must be active alienation' (ibid.).

At work, which is the most important part of people's waking time and outside of the hours needed for their bodily reproduction (e.g., eating or resting, etc.), people are experiencing alienation (which is manifested as negative emotions). Marx says: people do *not* 'affirm' themselves; they do *not* feel 'content', they do *not* 'develop freely [their] physical and mental energy' but 'mortify' their body and ruin their mind; and they do *not* feel at home. Their work 'is

---

undertaking, and competition makes the immanent laws of capitalist production to be felt by each individual capitalist, as external coercive laws. It compels him to keep constantly extending his capital, in order to preserve it, but extend it he cannot, except by means of progressive accumulation ... [Within the capitalist, there is therefore always] a Faustian conflict between the passion for accumulation, and the desire for enjoyment'. (Marx, 1887: 417–418).

merely a *means* to satisfy needs external to it', but not a joyous need itself, and
their alienated labour is 'a labor of self-sacrifice', and their labour 'is not their
own, but someone else's' and when at work they belong not to themselves but
to another (the capitalist). It is no wonder then that to maintain sanity, people
(as workers) rely on bourgeois relations of love including especially, married
love in the family as a negation of negation. Family, including married love,
or love relations confined to two individuals, become a sphere of life that is
opposite of the competitive labour market within which people are alienated
from one another. The family, including married love, becomes a sphere of life
where: people can affirm, and not deny, themselves; they feel content and not
unhappy; they do not mortify their body and ruin their mind; they do not feel
outside themselves; they feel at home; where they do things for meeting their
needs directly; they do not engage in self-sacrifice; they do not feel they belong
to someone else, and so on.[8] Romantic love is, in many ways, a space of refuge
in capitalism.

   Non- or pre-communist social relations and conditions put objective constraints on human beings' ability to show fine sentiments and display genuine
love. Marx (1844a: 46) touches on this in his *Paris Manuscripts*. He begins by
saying that 'only music awakens in man the sense of music' while 'the most
beautiful music has no sense for the unmusical ear'. 'Only through the objectively unfolded [i.e., developed] richness of man's essential being is the richness of subjective human sensibility (a musical ear, an eye for beauty of form –
in short, senses capable of human gratification, senses affirming themselves
as essential powers of man) either cultivated or brought into being' (ibid.).
This is rue not only about 'the five senses' but also  about 'the so-called mental senses, the practical senses (will, love, etc.), in a word, human sense, the
human nature of the senses'. 'The sense caught up in crude practical need has
only a restricted sense. For the starving man, it is not the human form of food
that exists, but only its abstract existence as food' so much so that 'it would be
impossible to say wherein this feeding activity differs from that of animals'.
Similarly, 'The care-burdened, poverty-stricken man has no sense for the finest play', just as 'the dealer in minerals sees only the commercial value but
not the beauty and the specific character of the mineral' (Marx, 1844a: 46).
Likewise, I would argue, the care-burdened, poverty-stricken person would
have 'no sense' for the love as a part of a web of finest emotions and intellectual

---

8  Alienation is really misery: 'Misery is the condition of being separated from what one can do,
   from what one can become'. (Hardt and Negri, 2009: 380).

experiences.[9] A poor person's love often bears the same relation to the love experienced by a rich person, as the relation between, as Marx (1857) would say in *Grundrisse*, on the one hand, quenching hunger by eating 'raw meat with the help of hands, nails and teeth' and on the other hand, quenching hunger by eating 'cooked meat eaten with a knife and fork'. No matter how much love there is within a family and between families, love – and consequent norm of reciprocity, etc. – is not a solution to poverty/destitution, because lack of love is not the main reason for poverty/destitution. Alienation and other objective conditions are. Indeed, 'with destitution the struggle for necessities and *all the old filthy business* would necessarily be reproduced' (Marx and Engels, 1845: 11; italics), so the beautiful human emotion called love is not possible, except superficially. Within a family, when x fails to meet y's material needs, then the love relation is attenuated. This is especially the case when family relations increasingly are – or depend on -- money relations: 'The bourgeoisie has torn away from the family its sentimental veil, and has reduced the family relation to a mere money relation' (Marx and Engels, 1848: 16).[10]

The sphere of bourgeois relations of love (e.g., married love), as an escape from alienation, represents a negation of the negation of negation, so the sphere of love actually leads to, or signifies, alienation. Negation of negation would be a positive act or accomplishment.[11] Negation of the negation of negation is a negative act. This is because given alienation on multiple fronts, people's private matters – as a negation of negation (=negation of alienation) – remain alienated from the wider society, so the love life does not quite serve as a negation of negation.[12] This point can be represented schematically:

a.   Non-alienation: Human beings' interests lie in meeting their needs through democratic control over means of production, and over

---

9    For example, generally speaking, a poverty-stricken (old) parent cannot deeply and enduringly love his/her grown-up children if he/she materially depends on the children and their spouses, in terms of money and care-labour, etc.

10   Further, 'The bourgeois clap-trap about the family ...., about the hallowed co-relation of parents and child, becomes all the more disgusting, the more ... all the family ties among the proletarians are torn asunder, and their children transformed into simple articles of commerce and instruments of labour'. (ibid.: 24–25). For a recent discussion of Marxist theory of the *Communist manifesto*, see Das (2022b).

11   Capitalist private property is a negation of small-scale scattered private property. Socialist property will be a negation of this negation, i.e., a negation of capitalist private property. This negation will therefore be a positive accomplishment.

12   'Love is a means to escape the solitude of individualism' but people become 'isolated again in the private life of the couple or the family'. (Hardt and Negri, 2009: XII).

production and its results (outputs), and in a pleasure-giving productive activity based on solidarity, where they feel at home.

b.    Capitalist alienation: the first negation of human being's real interests and needs→

c.    Negation of the negation: capitalist love as an attempted negation of the first negation→

d.    Negation of negation of negation: capitalist love itself represents a form of alienation, so it fails to produce negation of negation of capitalist alienation, in everyday life→

e.    Non-alienation needs to be accomplished in the sense of a) above, as the only solution to the problem of alienation in the sphere of love and outside

Alienation in capitalist economy is represented in the sphere of bourgeois relations of love. This explains the importance of the unitary subject of love: two people in love who care for themselves only (and their little children) and no one else. Their concept of love is stamped with capitalism. 'Romantic love is one of the ways of overcoming alienation, instrumentalism and final reification of our work in the factories and organizations, and consumer society' (Mažeikis, 2015: 22). Macfarlane (1987) argues that 'capitalism and industrialism, with connected demographic and social changes, were the causes of the peculiar pattern of romantic love' (p. 6). They say that 'If love can exist without capitalism, it is more questionable as to whether capitalism could have existed, or could continue to exist, without love' (p. 13). In capitalism love is forced to take a specific form: love that is confined to two people-in-love or a small group of people around them, without any concerns for the wider world. '[C]apitalism dictates that we care about our spouse and our children more than other people in our community and significantly more than other people in the world' (Cozzarelli, 2018). This is because: capitalism is based on competition (among capitalists, among petty business owners and among workers) and on (rugged) individualism and the weakening of 'collective consciousness'. Collective consciousness is absent, or exists in very narrow circles, and in an ephemeral manner. For the same reason: friendship has lost its importance as a moral virtue. 'Friendship ... may hinder the achievement of class aims; it is viewed as an unnecessary manifestation of "sentimentality" and weakness' (Kollontai, 1923).

There is an intrinsically human need for belonging and communion (Fromm, 1956). Monbiot (2016) says, 'human beings, the ultrasocial mammals, whose brains are wired to respond to other people, are being peeled apart. Though our wellbeing is inextricably linked to the lives of others, everywhere we are told that we will prosper through competitive self-interest and extreme

individualism'. Each of us is forced to look after ourselves. A major form of
alienation in capitalism is experienced when people freely working in their
self-interests are separated from one another: individuals are 'free among
other things to be constantly at another's throats' (Eagleton, 2011: 86). Such
an alienation – alienation from one another – is a constraint on genuine love.
Given insurmountable alienation, excessive individualism, intense competition, and the decline of community life reinforcing the isolation of individuals, love, narrowly typified by romantic couples, has gained dominance. Once
again, in bourgeois ideology, love is, more or less, confined to two individuals.

## 4     Love and Class Consciousness in Capitalism

But that is not all. It is not just capitalist *economy* that has prompted specific
ideas about love and specific practices of love. Capitalism tends to produce
specific types of social consciousness which impacts love which itself is a form
of consciousness too. There are mainly two kinds of consciousness: one is
proletarian or socialist consciousness.[13] Another is bourgeois consciousness
(which includes, individualism, attachment to private property, competitive-
ness, attitude based in commodity fetishism, etc.). '[I]n a society torn by class
antagonisms there can never be a non-class or an above-class ideology [or,
theoretical consciousness]' (Lenin, 1902: 23).[14] Bourgeois consciousness helps
reproduce capitalism, more or less, as it is. Workers can possess elements of
consciousness of the bourgeoisie. They also possess a trade union (type) consciousness which prompts workers to fight for limited improvements in their
living conditions, which in turn reproduces capitalism in slightly modified
form, with the underlying class relations unchanged. Now, trade union consciousness is more spontaneous than conscious. This is in at least two senses.
One is that it is not quite mediated by *theoretical* – i.e. conscious – reflections
on 'the irreconcilable antagonism of their interests to the *whole* of the modern political and social system' (Lenin, 1902: 17; italics added). Spontaneous
consciousness is shaped by the surface aspects of the capitalist society (e.g.,
lower wages; excesses of capitalism) and not by its underlying durable structures (e.g., capitalist property relations; capitalist state). Another is that it 'represents the working class ... in its relation to a given group of employers alone,

---

13    There is a large amount of literature on this, including by Lukacs and Gramsci: see Levin,
      1980; Milner, 2019; Euzebios, 2018; Mohandesi, 2013; Ollman, 1987; DiMaggio, 2015.
14    On Lenin's views on consciousness, see Das, 2017a: chapter 10; Mayer, 1997; and
      Shandro, 2007.

but [not] in its relation to all classes of modern society and to the state as an organized political force' (Lenin, 1902: 34). The main role of the latter is to keep the masses in check by using coercion including its threat, which is supplemented by consent and concession, and to help the ruling class with its accumulation strategies (Das, 2022c). Having to go to work, experiencing low wages, inadequate working conditions, and without the mediation of theoretical consciousness, produces a consciousness that is spontaneous. These conditions prompt people to join a trade union or some such organization, thinking that trade union politics or the politics of economic struggle, and especially, one that is aligned with one of the liberal-bourgeois or social-democratic type parties, is the ultimate solution to their problems. Spontaneous consciousness *is* political, but it represents a specifically bourgeois form of workers' politics: it is political in a limited sense. Conquering state power is not on the agenda. Spontaneous consciousness is subordinated 'to bourgeois ideology' because it 'is far older in origin than socialist ideology' and 'it is more fully developed' (Lenin, 1902: 24) and it is promoted by various ideological apparatuses of the state (Althusser, 2001) and family, etc. Spontaneous consciousness informs 'the spontaneous working-class movement [which] is trade-unionism' and which 'means the ideological enslavement of the workers by the bourgeoisie' (Lenin, 1902: 23). And in fact, the capitalist system, its various coercive and ideological apparatuses, actively impede the formation of socialist consciousness. If there is too much class anger/hatred, the system at best seeks to confine class hatred to its trade union form: it promotes or tolerates trade union consciousness. Trade union consciousness is a lower form of proletarian consciousness. Associated with proletarian consciousness is democratic consciousness: a consciousness that defends the democratic rights of all and the democratic rights of specially oppressed groups and oppressed nations.

Spontaneous consciousness represents a larger tendency: capitalism's reproduction is guaranteed by people being concerned about, materially and ideologically, with the surface elements of society and not with its underlying structures (relations of production and causes of alienation; class nature of state power, etc.). It is this larger tendency towards spontaneous consciousness or to have a completely 'a-political' consciousness that has potential impacts on the conception of love.

Love as a form of consciousness (embodied in sexual and emotional desires, etc.) can, more or less, either function on the terrain of the socialist consciousness or of bourgeois consciousness. Socialist consciousness could tell a human being what qualities in a person are admirable from the standpoint of the concerns of the wider society, but this sort of thinking is usually not a part of the decision-making that is involved in establishing a love-relation. In the capitalist society, most people lack progressive, let alone socialist, consciousness: they not only lack democratic consciousness (democratic consciousness would not permit hatred against women and minorities and people of oppressed nations); they also lack trade union consciousness.

Outside of private life, and in the sphere of work, people fall for, at best, spontaneous 'class' consciousness. Similarly, in the private sphere, people fall for what I would call *spontaneous love consciousness*: this is when two people are in love based on qualities that are reproductive of capitalism. The choice of qualities in a potential beloved that are important appears to be a natural thing and a private matter but actually it helps reproduce the class society. Without any *class* consciousness, and without the consciousness of the relation between the reproductive sphere (the private sphere) and the rest of society, two people fall in love in a manner that is in line with the consciousness that helps reproduce the current order or at least does not challenge that order.

Spontaneous consciousness keeps separate people's everyday life, including love life, from their conception of, and practical attitude towards, society's underlying structures. Just as spontaneous political consciousness relates the workers only to their employers and not to all employers and to overall society, spontaneous love consciousness relates one lover to her/his beloved and not to whole society. Chance encounters, physical attractions or attractions based on common qualities that are not political in any serious sense (the fact that two people love outdoor picnics, 19th century art, wanting a big family, or that they are physically attracted to one another, and so on), etc. become the spontaneous basis for love, which is separated from the totality of society. When two people are attracted towards one another, to quote Fromm (1956) again, ' "Attractive" usually means a nice package of qualities which are popular and sought after on the personality market' (p. 3). These qualities smoothly reproduce capitalism. Love becomes, more or less, a-political. To the extent that love involves conscious decision-making, it is, or it is compatible with, bourgeois consciousness.

If love is more than a relation between merely two people and if love is a social process, two people falling in love may be racists or blatantly pro-capitalist or pro-imperialist and so on. Such a relation means that backward or regressive consciousness that helps reproduce the capitalist society is uniting people-in-love or that capitalism is encouraging people-in-love to treat their lives (their private matters) as apolitical. After all, love is supposed to be a private matter: just care for your partners and your unmarried kids if you have them or care for some pets and plants and DIY activity. Capitalist alienation leads to an excessive focus on the love-life or married family life, and therefore there is little space for people to do anything – intellectually or politically – to challenge the system. When two people fall in love and when they only care about themselves, and when their love has no relation to the fight for a better world, that love is the love that is spontaneously shaped by bourgeois ideology and provides an 'escape' from the need to develop progressive consciousness. As long as I am in love with my partner, I don't care if Muslims or Blacks are being lynched, if people are denied a living wage, if wars are destroying nations, and so on. Spontaneous love consciousness and socialist love consciousness are inversely related, just as trade unionist consciousness and socialist class consciousness are. Love involves decision-making. Love unites. In the decision involving love, however, serious attention is usually not paid to progressive consciousness of prospective partners, in capitalist society.

Love is 'intricately woven' from many 'shades of emotion' such as 'friendship, passion, [parental] tenderness, infatuation, mutual compatibility, sympathy, admiration, familiarity' etc., which is why 'it becomes increasingly difficult to distinguish direct connection between the natural drive of "wingless Eros" and "winged Eros," where physical attraction and emotional warmth are fused' (Kollontai, 1923). Yet, 'In modern [bourgeois] society, sharp contradictions frequently arise and battles are waged between the various manifestations of emotion' and 'a division of the inner emotional world involves inevitable suffering' (ibid.).

The bourgeois system not only tears apart people as workers from the conditions of production and the product of their labour, and so on. Through the ideology of married love, it also tears apart the inner being of a person. There is no recognition that in a society where two love partners satisfy each other's emotional etc. needs, '[a] deep intellectual and emotional involvement in one's work may not be compatible with love for a *particular* man or woman [italics added]' (ibid.). '[L]ove for the collective' (i.e., the society as a whole) 'might conflict with love for husband, wife or children'. Consider another example.

> A woman feels close to a man whose ideas, hopes and aspirations match her own; she is attracted physically to another. For one woman a man might feel sympathy and a protective tenderness, and in another he might find support and understanding for the strivings of his intellect. To which of the two must he give his love? And why must he tear himself apart and cripple his inner self, if only the possession of both types of inner bond affords the fullness of living?
>
> KOLLONTAI, 1923

Bourgeois ethical code does not recognize all this. Instead:

> Bourgeois ideology has insisted that love, mutual love, gives the right
> to the absolute and indivisible possession of the beloved person. Such
> exclusiveness was the natural consequence of the established form of
> pair marriage and of the ideal of "all-embracing love" between husband
> and wife [or between two sexual partners].
>
> KOLLONTAI, 1923

Overall, 'The bourgeois ideal of love does not correspond to the needs of the
largest section of the population – the working class. Nor is it relevant to the
life-style of the working intelligentsia' (Kollontai, 1923).

## 5      Love, Extra-economic Coercion, and Special Oppression in Capitalism

Marx (1887: 506) says that dispossession of direct producers, the history of
which *is* 'written in the annals of mankind in letters of blood and fire', leads to
a situation where workers, without direct access to the means of production
or subsistence, are economically forced to work for a wage under capitalists'
'barrack discipline' (p. 285) or else they would normally remain hungry. In
this sense does 'dull compulsion of economic relations [complete] the subjection of the labourer to the capitalist' (Marx, 1887: 521). 'Direct force, outside
economic conditions, is ...used...only exceptionally' (ibid.). This is true in the
sense that capitalists do not necessarily – or generally – need physical violence
against workers to exploit them on an everyday basis. Yet, this is rather a san-
guine view on the part of Marx.[15] Violence *is* used more than 'exceptionally'.
Physical force *is* used by capitalists against workers to extract more surplus
value per hour, and especially, against certain vulnerable groups of workers
(Das and Chen, 2019). And violence is used when workers resist exploitation,
as evident, for example, from brutality from the private coercive agencies of
capitalists against striking workers.[16] The corporate soldiers and police are

---

15    It should be, however, noted that Marx's overall intention is to show that *even if* the
      'excesses' of capitalism (i.e. the important accidental/contingent influences – including
      the coercive actions of capitalists and wages falling below the value of labour power – on
      capitalism's inner mechanisms) are abstracted from, capitalism *is* essentially an exploita-
      tive system that fails to meet the needs of the vast majority.
16    Indeed, 'The private security (policing) business is one of the fastest-growing economic
      sectors in many countries'; in fact 'In half of the world's countries, private security agents
      outnumber police officers' (Robinson, 2022a; see also Robinson, 2022b).

'deployed to guard corporate property, provide personal security for executives and their families' (Robinson, 2022a). They also 'conduct police, paramilitary, counterinsurgency and surveillance operations; carry out mass crowd control and repression of protesters; run private detention and interrogation facilities; manage prisons and participate in outright warfare' (ibid.).

Besides, given that dispossession of direct producers is an ongoing affair, as Harvey (2006) correctly says, even if he mis-conceptualizes the process (Das, 2017b), capitalist violence continues to be used against them too. Indeed, many men and women who were hitherto small-scale producers, especially in villages *near* the cities, and who are now wageworkers, do have a memory of violence perpetrated against them and of the trauma that comes with such violence. Things cannot be otherwise because 'capital comes dripping from head to foot, from every pore, with blood and dirt' (Marx, 1887: 536). The fact of the matter is that violence by capitalists, whether against direct producers or against wageworkers, is not conducive to a social milieu where love can flourish.

It is not just the capitalists and their hired agents who are violent towards common people. Indeed, the supreme political organization of the capitalist class, and their official vanguard, i.e., the state, is violent too, as mentioned earlier many times. The fundamental role of the state is to reproduce capitalist relations by keeping the masses in check through a combination of concession, coercion and consent (Das, 2022c). The capitalist state uses coercion when workers resist exploitation, as evident from the brutality from the state's coercive agencies against striking workers (Chappell and Di Martino, 2006; Goldstein, 2001; Lipold, 2014; Smith, 2003). The constant threat of the use of coercive methods and/or their actual use on a regular basis are not conducive to a relation of love in society. Fear and love do not go together. Further, the fact that the state uses cheap concessions (meagre and revocable benefits) as well as various means of deception, lies and mystification, including through education and media, in order to naturalize capitalism and manufacture passivity among common people, is also not conducive to a social environment where love can flourish. A state policy for the common people born out of solidarity for them, or even as a forced response to class struggle from below, is one thing. A state policy for the common people with the aim of getting their votes, and more generally, their consent to the capitalist system, is quite another. Granting concessions with the purpose of controlling the masses goes against the conception of love as caring and genuine solidarity. The state *appears* to represent the common interests of society and, in particular, it appears to look after the interests of common people, while, in fact, it is above all the state of and for the capitalist class. *This* non-transparent – and illusory – character of the state, in part maintained by deception and lies, is against the spirit of love which requires trust and transparency (truth).

The scope of capitalist extra-economic, anti-democratic treatment of the masses, unfavourable to love, does not end here. Class relations in general, and capitalist relations in particular, reproduce and strengthen relations of oppression and exclusion based on gender, religion, race, etc. (Das, 2020a; 2022d; 2023a). There is always a need to protect private property relations and the exploitative accumulation process from opposition by common people by weakening and dividing them. They are divided along the lines of gender, race, religion, etc. in a way that submerges their class identity under various socio-cultural identities. Not only do these identities weaken the working class. The ruling class is able to treat the various segments of the exploited people as second-class citizens because of their social-cultural background, and as less worthy. This inferiorization process allows the ruling class to give them lower compensation. It allows the state to spend less on them. Now, the relations of oppression based on race, religion, gender, etc., crucial to the reproduction of capitalism, do impact relations of love.

Consider gender relations. Class relations and capitalist class relations are fundamentally behind regressive views about, and unequal treatment of, women (Gimenez, 2019; Vogel, 2013). Love is shaped by unequal relations between men and women in class society and in capitalism as a form of class society. Love often occurs in an unequal – patriarchal – relation between men and women (de Beauvoir, 2011). In a context where there is a degree of historically-existing division of labour partly based in biological differences, the reproduction of women as subordinate to men allows the reproduction of labour power[17] on the basis of materially and emotionally unpaid and under-recognized labour of women in the family (the sphere of individualized repro-duction) for which employers do not have to pay for in the same way that they pay for the labour performed in the workplaces. Such reproduction of women as subordinate to men is partly helped by the ideology of men's love for women as well as by deeply patriarchal values concerning the role of women.

Engels (1886) says that there are 'mutual relations based on reciprocal incli-nation between human beings, such as sex love, friendship, compassion, self-sacrifice, etc', and that in a relation based on sex love, 'each finds in others the satisfaction of his own urge towards happiness, which is just what love ought to achieve and how it acts in practice'. According to de Beauvoir (2011: 511) too,

---

17    This is future labour power (children), the labour power of those who are unable to work because of their old age, etc. (the older generation), and the labour power of the currently employed.

the ideal relationship of love is one where 'each human being, perfectly self-sufficient, be attached to another by the free consent of their love alone' and not by material or other constraints. This principle applies to both friendship as well as a relation involving physical love: 'for friendship to be authentic, it must first be free'. This ideal is not realized in practice, however.

'Freedom [in a love relation] does not mean whim: a feeling is a commitment that goes beyond the instant … [F]eeling is free when it does not depend on any outside command, when it is lived in sincerity without fear' (ibid.). But the feeling of fear in a relationship, and especially, for women, is not uncommon: a woman stays in a relationship because the alternative could be the denial to her of access to the things, she needs such as food, housing, transportation, physical safety, healthcare, etc. So, 'The word "love" has not at all the same meaning for both sexes' (ibid.: 683). Men and women of a given class have different mental conceptions and practical experiences of love, and this is because they do not necessarily live in the same situations.

Given unequal gender relations, and under certain conditions, men can 'remain sovereign subjects' while 'the woman they love is merely one value among others; they want to integrate her into their existence, not submerge their entire existence in her. By contrast, love for the woman is a total abdication for the benefit of a master' (ibid.: 683). In a love relationship, there is often an unequal, rather than an equal, exchange. It is often the case that the woman is 'a mere distraction, a pleasure, company, an inessential article for the man', while 'for her [the man] is the meaning, the justification of her existence'. '[T]he two objects exchanged are thus not of the same quality; this inequality will be particularly noticeable because the time they spend together', which is the same for each of them at least in theory, 'does not have the same value for both partners' (ibid.: 758). The general point is that romantic love relationships can be exploitative because of an intersection of norms defining and regulating notions of romance, gender, race, labour, etc. (Gregoratto, 2017). The consciousness that informs the kind of unequal and exploitative relationship between men and women in love (or between two lovers) that we observe is one that is not necessarily democratic. The fundamental reason for this is the class relation of capitalism, central to which is the imperative of biological reproduction of labour power in a way that is compatible with capitalism.

Apart from women, there are other groups who are subjected to social oppression. In a society where Muslims, immigrants, Blacks, indigenous people, and other groups are treated as second-class citizens, the relation of love involving these groups cannot but be impacted. In fact, as capitalism has been in crisis and as the system has increasingly been unable to meet the needs of the people, there is a growing tendency towards the right-wing, post-truth politics aiming to keep the masses divided and in check (see the next two chapters). The right-wing resorts to various ideological and political mechanisms. Consider 'love jihad' (love war). Love jihad as a notion refers to the false and conspiratorial belief among fascistic Hindu groups that when a Muslim man falls in love with a Hindu woman, his purpose is to convert the woman into Islam, as a part of the Muslim effort at the demographic domination over Hindus (Rao, 2011). This means that to the extent that love is consciously politicized, that politicization is informed by regressive consciousness about minorities, a consciousness that is characteristic of a crisis-ridden capitalist political economy and politics.

We have seen that the qualities one consciously looks for in one's partners are the qualities that are generally not a threat to capitalism and that indeed help reproduce capitalism.[18] It is also the case that in a context where there are various significant non-class divisions, and where there are racists, sexists as well as warmongers who do not care about the sovereign rights of nations, and so on, the bourgeois form of love – considered a private matter based on spontaneity – has no difficulty in uniting, for example, an anti-racist and a racist, a peace-activist and a warmonger, a sexist and a person who respects women's rights, and so on. Nor does the bourgeois form of love have any difficulty in uniting, for example, two racists, two warmongers, or two sexists. Capitalists and upper-middle class people (super-rich wage-earners) as a class-stratum fall in love, and marry within that stratum, and thus reproduce themselves as occupiers of their class position, and they also reproduce, unintentionally or not, unequal relations in society between different oppressed groups. Capitalism is behind various relations of oppression, even though the latter cannot be reduced to capitalism. These unequal relations adversely impact relations of love, which, otherwise, could be 'truly symmetric, mutual relationships between people' (Kováts, 2015: 5). The bourgeois form of love does nothing to undermine those relations of oppression.

---

18  Bourgeois love allows a politician who is a spouse and a parent, to love their own children and spouse without worrying about their policies killing millions of children and their parents in a poor country. Consider Madeleine Albright's views on Iraqi children. In 1996, the journalist, Lesley Stahl, asked Albright – then the US ambassador to the United Nations – about the catastrophic effect on the Iraqi population of the harsh US sanctions imposed following Iraq's invasion of Kuwait: 'We have heard that half a million [Iraqi] children have died. I mean, that is more children than died in Hiroshima. And, you know, is the price worth it?'. Albright answered: 'I think that is a very hard choice but the price, we think, the price is worth it'. (quoted in Twain, 2022).

6    Love in a Socialist Society (and in the Anti-capitalist Movement)

The Marxist approach to love cannot be satisfied with a discussion of how existing social relations are producing a concept and practice of love that in turn
help reproduce those social relations. Masses are not just alienated. They do
not just suffer. Nor do they just fall prey to bourgeois consciousness. Sections
of the working class (and small-scale producing class) do possess progressive
consciousness. They also fight to change their conditions, both in a gradual
manner and in a more revolutionary way, even if they do not always succeed
and even if they do not fight under the conditions of their own choosing. The
concept and practice of love in the proletarian ideological form can be a small
part of the struggle against capitalism and the struggle for socialism. If love is
social process, if it is more than about the relation between two people, if it is
more than an impulse, and if it therefore involves a conscious decision, and if
love is affected by capitalism which has used a specific ideology of love, then
there is a particular kind of love that Marxist theory would advocate from the
standpoint of the proletarians. It has to be a love that meets the needs of the
proletarians, in their fight for socialism within capitalism, and when it begins
to construct a socialist society.

Love can be a part of, and carrier of, class consciousness. When a Marxist
says 'I love/respect this individual', he/she is not saying that: 'no matter what,
I will love this individual'[19]: if an individual does not respect the economic
and political rights of, say, poor people in the world, the Marxist will hardly
have much love for that individual, even if she/he might fall in love in the first
encounter. That love may not endure. A class-conscious proletarian lover cannot love someone who supports speculative hoarding, or commercial export,
of food when large sections of humanity, including children, are dying of hunger. A class-conscious proletarian cannot love someone who lynches people or
burns them to death because of their different religious practices. They cannot
love someone who thinks that it is right for America to conduct pre-emptive
military strikes against less powerful nations or use the people and the territory
of one relatively less developed nation to launch a proxy war against another
relatively less developed but resource-rich nation seeking to improve its economic position globally. A class-conscious proletarian cannot love someone
who thinks that people are poor because they breed too many or have black/
brown skin. They can hardly be in an enduring love relation with someone who

---

19    Badhwar (2003) criticizes the idea that once a person loves someone, he/she cannot
      abandon that love no matter who that person becomes.

thinks that production based on capitalist private property is the only form of society people can live in, or that it is acceptable for business owners to pay starvation wages and avoid paying their taxes while they make trips to the outer space or vacation in their expensive yachts, and so on. They cannot love a person who believes in and/or, engages in, the production and propagation of blatant lies for an ideological and political purpose, including the oppression of minorities and the concomitant protection of the majority community and its allied politicians.

Hatred is the opposite of love (Spinoza, 1954: 179;183). But Spinoza deals with love and hatred only at an interpersonal level. It must be stressed that hatred and love both have a class character. There is class love. There is class hatred. Emotions in a class society are ultimately influenced by class relations. Lenin talks about a 'natural hatred of the workers and peasants for the exploiters' (Lenin quoted in Andrews undated). Lenin (1964: 210) also talks about 'a mood of hatred towards' capitalists' on the part of 'the broadest masses'. Hatred on the part of the exploited classes towards the capitalists and landlords and towards their political representatives is a part of class consciousness of the exploited classes.[20] This is a response to the class hatred on the part of the ruling classes and their political representatives.[21] On the class hatred against the masses, Lenin says: 'During the lifetime of great revolutionaries, the oppressing classes ... received their theories with the most savage malice, the most furious hatred and the most unscrupulous campaigns of lies and slander' (Lenin, 1917b: 7).

Like class hatred (or class anger), class love is a part of class consciousness. As far as the masses are concerned, class love exists when a worker shows class-conscious solidarity with another worker and when a peasant does the same for another peasant. Under certain conditions, this solidarity develops into red romantic love between, say, two workers, which is a specific form of class love. Red romantic love is the romantic love between two people when their inter-personal love is based on their socialist consciousness, a consciousness in which the interests of the masses and the interests of the large-scale exploiting property owners are fundamentally incompatible, and a proletarian revolution

---

20   In one particular case, he says: 'The capitalist state evicts a working-class family which has lost its breadwinner and cannot pay the rent. The bailiff appears with police, or militia, a whole squad of them. ... They know that the scene of an eviction arouses such fury ... among thousands and thousands of people who have been driven to the verge of desperation, arouses such *hatred* towards the capitalists and the capitalist state, that the bailiff and the squad of militiamen run the risk of being torn to pieces at any minute'. (Lenin, 1917a; italics added).

21   'The great Russian novelist Leo Tolstoy, who admired Dickens greatly, said of him: "He *loves* the weak and poor and always *despises* the rich."'(Walsh, 2020; italics added).

is therefore necessary to resolve that contradiction and to build a better, more harmonious, society (i.e. socialism). Love indeed implies solidarity. When two people are in love and when one is happy, the other person is happy and when one is sad, the other person is sad too. Kollontai says, "Solidarity is not only an awareness of common interests; it also depends on the intellectual and emotional ties linking the members of the collective', where people are capable of 'love and [other] warm emotions' (Kollontai, 1923). In the proletarian ideology of love, 'every member of the working class [is] to be capable of responding to the distress and needs of other members of the class, of sensitive understanding of others and a penetrating consciousness of the individual's relationship to the collective' (ibid.).

From the proletarian angle, love must be influenced by progressive consciousness, at the minimum. Progressive consciousness, as discussed earlier, includes: democratic consciousness, including anti-landlordism, anti-oppression, anti-imperialism and anti-fascism. It includes: trade union consciousness which supports workers' right to fight for improvements within capitalism and for concessions from employers and from the state. Progressive consciousness at the highest level is class consciousness which supports struggles for socialist democracy, i.e., for a world beyond the dictatorship of capital. Progressive consciousness is needed for a new society. Love life cannot be separated from progressive consciousness if love is not to be separated from the totality of human social existence. If love is a decision and not an impulse, then it means that at least some of the forms of progressive consciousness must have a role in deciding on how we maintain an enduring love relationship while freely a) meeting our physical and emotional needs, and b) exercising the right to enter and exit an emotional relationship without any adverse material consequences. Falling in love romantically can and must intersect with falling in love with the exploited and oppressed masses and being sensitive towards their distress, on the basis of progressive forms of social consciousness.

When I say I love a person xp and not Tp because xp does yq or xp is zq, what I mean is that y and z as qualities of Xp meet *my* individual needs, make *me* happy. If y and z are values (qualities that are valued), then these reflect qualities (and needs) of the current social arrangement (capitalism) which specific individuals such as Xp possess. Contrast the above to the following: I love x because x wishes to contribute to the socialist movement, and I wish to contribute to the socialist movement too. This 'individual' quality of x is a deeply social thing from the standpoint of social consciousness. The 'search' for a romantic partner should be, partly, a political search. A person with progressive consciousness would look for a partner with such a consciousness, or would at least, make an effort to help their partner develop one if it is not in existence during the initial encounter. If a romantic relation becomes a fetter on the development and/or the expansion of progressive consciousness, the relationship must weaken or break.

Love is not merely a physical impulse. It involves a variety of emotions all of which people should be free to nourish and enjoy. 'All these 'warm emotions' – sensitivity, compassion, sympathy, and responsiveness – derive from one source: they are aspects of love, not in the narrow sexual sense but in the broad meaning of the word' (Kollontai, 1923). In fact, 'The existence of love friendship where the element of physical attraction is absent, of love for one's work or for a cause, and of love for the collective [i.e., society as a whole], testify to the extent to which love has become "spiritualized" and separated from its biological [sexual] base'. (ibid.). '[T]he complexity of the human psyche and the many-sidedness of emotional experience should assist in the growth of the emotional and intellectual bonds between people' (Kollontai, 1923). In fact, 'The more numerous these inner threads drawing people together, the firmer the sense of solidarity and the simpler the realization of the working-class ideal of comradeship and unity'. (ibid.).

Recent radical scholarly writings show that love itself embodies flashes of communism or communist consciousness. Badiou (2012) recognizes the communistic character of love, even if partially and at a personal level. If 'communist' means that 'which makes the held-in-common prevail over selfishness, the collective achievements over private self-interest' (p. 90), then 'love is communist in [the] sense ... that the real subject of a love is the becoming of the couple and not the mere satisfaction of the individuals that are its component parts'. Indeed, 'In today's world, it is generally thought that individuals only pursue their own self-interest. Love is an antidote to that' (p. 16). So 'another possible definition of love [is] ... minimal communism' (ibid.).

In the proletarian or communist ideology of love presented here, people give love as per their emotional-biological *abilities* and receive love as per their emotional-biological *needs*. At the risk of some exaggeration, it can be said that spaces of proletarian love are in existence within capitalism as small islands of sparks of communistic practice of love. More generally, 'islands of miniature communism can be found in different love relations with others, with partners, family, friends, or anyone with whom we are happily connected for other reasons than money [or self-interest]' (Gilman-Opalsky, 2021a; also, Gilman-Opalsky, 2020). This is evident when 'we expect from others only what is in line with their ability and desires', and when 'we strive to provide people with everything they need' often at the risk of our own happiness. Consider parental love. 'I do not give my kids food and shelter in exchange for work' or anything else they do for me (ibid.). Take another example. 'If you and your partner', or indeed, if members of a Marxist reading group or a communist or anti-fascist organization, 'measure every chore and favor you do for one another on a spreadsheet to ensure an equal exchange, you'll be on a fast track to resentment' (ibid.). A major characteristic of these islands of spontaneous communistic love, i.e., love with flashes of communistic value, is that these are 'no-go zones for capitalist exchange relations'. Here interaction is not based on the expectation of quid pro quo. This is because 'love relations motivate actions and commitments' in ways other than exchange relations do (ibid.). The motivation is to meet the other person's need, to the extent possible, given all the material constraints imposed by capitalism. The motivation in these no-go zones for capitalist exchange reveals the extent to which meeting the needs of the 'the *other* person has become for us a *need*' (Marx, 1844a: 43). These no-go zones are 'little precarious communes' where love is as close as we may get to a universal communist aspiration to meet other people's needs without bourgeois selfishness. Little communes of family, friendship, comrades, artists, and colleagues shield us from the worst realities of life under the dictatorship of capital' (Gilman-Opalsky, 2021a).

More or less in line with the argument made above is what the philosopher, Frankfurt (2004) says in his *The reasons of love*: 'Loving someone or something essentially *means* or *consists in*, among other things, taking its interests as reasons for acting to serve those interests' (Frankfurt, 2004: 37). One's love 'is not necessarily grounded in the value of the beloved but does necessarily make the beloved valuable to the lover', and this holds true for parental and other forms of love (Frankfurt, 2004: 40). The beloved is valued because of the love of the lover: 'what we love necessarily *acquires* value for us *because* we love it' (Frankfurt, 2004: 39), and it is 'love that accounts for the value to us of life itself' (Frankfurt, 2004: 40). Love 'creates the reasons by which [a person's] ... acts of loving concern and devotion are inspired' (p. 37). Giving love necessarily involves, once again, meeting the needs of the people we love: 'the activity of the lover is subordinated to the interests of his beloved' and 'loving consists essentially in being devoted to the well-being of what [or whom] we love' (Frankfurt, 2004: 59), so 'loving is important to us for its own sake' (Frankfurt, 2004: 59). de Beauvoir (2011: 693) says that 'The supreme aim of human love, like mystical love, is identification with the loved one'. Frankfurt (2004: 61) goes further: because the lover identifies himself with what he loves, 'protecting the interests of his beloved is necessarily among the lover's own interests'. '[H]is life is enhanced when' his beloved's 'interests prevail' and 'he is harmed when its interests are defeated'. The lover is one who 'is invested in his beloved: he profits by its successes, and its failures cause him to suffer' (ibid.: 61). This means that 'for the lover selflessness and self-interest coincide' (ibid.: 62).

Love – the act of loving – itself has an intrinsic value. In some contexts (e.g., a relation between parents and children), one is able to give love just for the sake of it. This also means that no matter how much it tries, the capitalist system cannot completely erase sparks of anti-capitalist thought and action, even at the individual and emotional level.

Love involves reasoned care and commitment. Indeed, love is a 'notable variant of caring' (Frankfurt, 2004: 11). One must therefore be critical of the idea that reduces love to love in its merely romantic form; one must reject its commercialized form too (Evans, 2002; Brooks, 2019). Gilman-Opalsky (2021b) claims that 'love is a practice that socializes a unique polyamory beyond the structure of the romantic relationship', a polyamory that 'is not about having multiple partners, and is not primarily sexual or romantic, but is instead the polyamory of a communist affection for others'. Love activates a sensibility about being with other people for reasons that are antithetical to the reasons for being with others that stem from a system of production based on exploitative private property and profit.

In capitalism, people tend to run towards love in the private sense (married love, etc.) to escape from loneliness and alienation in the wider society. Its motivation is negative. It is running away from. But communist love is positively based. It is based on, and it is running towards, acts of solidarity. In socialism, 'love-solidarity will become the lever that competition and self-love [and individualism are] … in the bourgeois system'. 'Collectivism of spirit can then defeat individualist self-sufficiency' (Kollontai, 1923). And the "cold of inner loneliness," from which people in bourgeois culture have attempted to escape through love and marriage, will disappear'. (ibid.).

By removing feudal obstacles and by developing productive forces, capitalism promotes opportunities for multipronged human interaction in space-time. Yet, it restricts human interaction that does not obey exchange relations and tends to confine the relations of love to a smaller scale (e.g., family scale, etc.). The expansion of the islands of miniature communism, i.e. islands of communism of love, to the extent this is possible within capitalism, can contribute to people's struggle against capitalism and to their preparation for that struggle, which consists of elements of their everyday life (e.g. building relations with people who possess progressive consciousness; expanding one's knowledge about the world from a progressive angle, and so on). Under communism, relations based on love, care, and compassion for *everyone* will flourish. If people wish to confine love to marriage, they will be free to do so. If they do not wish to, they will be free to do so too. The privateness of romantic love is not going to disappear under communism. But there is no necessary imperative to put our romantic partners first before 'the love for your friends, your neighbors, and your family' (Cozzarelli, 2018). '[T]he ideal of the working class at the same time subordinates ... [romantic] love to the more powerful emotion of love-duty to the collective. However great the love between two members of the collective, the ties binding the two persons to the collective [to society as a whole] will always take precedence'. '[M]en and women will strive to express their love not only in kisses and embraces but in joint creativity and activity'. (Kollontai, 1923). In fact, 'The greater the intellectual and emotional development of the individual the less place will there be in his or her relationship for the bare physiological side of love and the brighter will be the love experience' (Kollontai, 1921).

The expansion of love beyond a romantic partner is part and parcel of (love for) socialism, the future of humanity beyond the rule of capital. In proletarian theory, love does not seek to possess anyone. 'No one person can be our other half, fulfill all our needs, and heal all our wounds, despite capitalism's insistence that they can' (Cozzarelli, 2018). The proletarian theory of love directs the multiple forms of love as a complex emotion 'into channels which are advantageous to the [working] class during the struggle for and the construction of communist society' (Kollontai, 1923). It does not matter 'whether love takes the form of a long and official union or is expressed in a temporary relationship. The ideology of the working class does not place any formal limits on love', except that society will restrict any form of love that a) 'involves excesses and therefore physical exhaustion, which lower the resources of labour energy available to society' and that b) 'impoverishes the soul, hindering the development and strengthening of inner bonds and positive emotions' (Kollontai, 1923). Society will also restrict any form of love that reinforces 'an inequality of rights in relationships between the sexes, on the dependence of the woman on the man and on male complacency and insensitivity, which undoubtedly hinder the development of comradely feelings' (ibid.). This is also the view of Simon de Beauvoir according to whom: 'The day when it will be possible for the woman to love in her strength and not in her weakness, not to escape from herself but to find herself, not out of resignation but to affirm herself, love will become for her as for man the source of life and not a mortal danger' (de Beauvoir, 2011: 708). A socialist concept of love cannot at all be based on the oppression of women in any form.

'Comrade love will only be hegemonic in communism, when the family as it exists today is a distant memory and there are material conditions to enter and exit relationships, to experiment, to mess up, to get your heart broken and to fall deeply in love with friends, lovers and everything in between' (Cozzarelli, 2018). As Kollontai argues, already within capitalism, love is not confined to marriage; from friends to extramarital affairs to love triangles, love is bursting at the seams. Demands of capitalist development (including developed means of communication) as well as changes in social relations of gender, and women's struggle for freedom, have made it possible for women to enter public spaces. With all these changes, the boundary of love has outstripped that of the bourgeois family.

Love in the wider sense *requires* socialism/communism. It is as well a part of the process of fighting for communism. The fight for the conditions where one can truly love, the fight for true love, is a part of the fight for socialism. Fromm correctly says: 'important and radical changes in our social structure are necessary, if love is to become a social and not a highly individualistic, marginal phenomenon' (Fromm, 1956: 132). Given how unequal gender relations, caused primarily by class relations, result in unequal love relations, changes in women's economic situation as well as social, moral and cultural changes are necessary for the new women to appear who can be an equal love subject with her partner (de Beauvoir, 2011: 761). As we have seen, 'the direct, natural, and necessary relation of person to person is the *relation of man* to *woman*', even if, one might add, the relations between two individuals of the same sex are not un-natural). About this comment from Marx, de Beauvoir says: 'This could not be better said' and that to enjoy real freedom, 'men and women must, among other things and beyond their natural differentiations, unequivocally affirm their brotherhood [i.e. solidarity]' (ibid.: 766). Kollontai (1911) says that there can be 'more loving and consequently happier relationships between the sexes only if the human psyche is changed radically and man's 'potential for loving' is increased. Such a change inevitably demands the basic transformation of socio-economic relations: in other words, it demands the transition to communism' (ibid.). Only socialism will clear the [obstacles to] the recognition of the value of love as a psychological and social force' (Kollontai, 1923). 'Socialism, if it is worthy of the name, means human relations without greed, friendship without envy and intrigue, love without base calculation' (Trotsky, 1973: 88).

If theory is a form of class struggle (Althusser, 1968), then the Marxist theory of love is an aspect of class struggle. 'It is the struggle to build free and equal relations of love, sexuality and comradeship in which desire is neither simply sexual nor exclusive, but involves a solidarity of multiple connections and interrelations to others as well as to the work and welfare of the collective. These are relations that cannot be developed in a social formation dominated by [capitalist] property relations as the signifier of individual freedom' (Ebert, 1999).

In capitalism, individuals are free 'but free among other things to be constantly at another's throats' while under communism social life is organized in such a way that 'individuals are able to realize themselves in and through the self-realisation of others' (Eagleton, 2011: 86). In other words, under communism, 'Only through others can we finally come into our own. This means an enrichment of individual freedom ... It is hard to think of a finer ethics. On a personal level, it is known as love' (ibid.).

So, 'Working men and women', as well as progressive intellectuals, 'armed with the science of Marxism and using the experience of the past, must seek to discover the place love ought to occupy in the new social order [i.e. socialism] and determine the ideal of love that corresponds to their class interests' (Kollontai, 1923). The bourgeois has tried to use the social character of love – i.e., its uniting and 'organizing character' – and thus create a stable family based on its conception of love (married love) in its own interest 'as a moral virtue' (ibid.). Similarly: 'The proletariat should also take into account the psychological and social role that love, both in the broad sense and in the sense of relationships between the sexes, can and must play, not in strengthening family-marriage ties, but in the development of collective solidarity' (ibid.). The proletariat must reject the modern concept and practice of romantic love because modern love 'absorbs the thoughts and feelings of 'loving hearts' and isolates the loving pair' from the wider society' (ibid.). In other words: just as the bourgeoisie which 'saw love as a "private matter,"' and which 'was able to channel the expression of love in its class interests', similarly, the working class 'must pay even greater attention to the significance of love as a factor which can, like any other psychological or social phenomenon, be channeled' to its class advantage (ibid.). 'Love is not in the least a "private" matter concerning only the two loving persons: love possesses a uniting element which is valuable to the collective' (ibid.).[22]

That love, even personal love, is not unconnected to revolutionary politics, can be evident in the personal lives of great Marxists. It is interesting that the partners of well-known socialists – men and women who have tried to contribute to the emergence of a society that meets people's needs in a deeply democratic and egalitarian manner – were also socialists or politically progressive persons. Marx and his wife, Jenny, and their children, bound together by ties of love, even under very difficult material and political conditions, dedicated themselves to the progressive and socialist cause. In her biography of Marx, called *Love and Capital*, Mary Gabriel (2011) insightfully says: 'The story

---

22    Pagan (2019) explores the different forms of love which appear in a work which is part family memoir, part autobiography, and part literary fiction, Jung Chang's *Wild Swans: Three Daughters of China*, and shows that love is not merely a private matter between two individuals but rather a social and political phenomenon.

I discovered was of a love between a husband and wife that remained passionate and consuming' (p. LVI). 'The Marx family ... ate, slept, and breathed political, social, and economic revolution. That, and a consuming love for Marx, was the steel mesh that bound them together' [LVII]'. Without the loving women in the family (Marx's wife and daughters, and Hele Demuth, the indispensable housekeeper of the Marx family), 'there would have been no Karl Marx, and without Karl Marx the world would not be as we know it' (LVIII).

Engels 'turned to the proletariat for his amours' (Heilbroner, 1999: 140), and he found a long-term partner in working-class women named Mary Burns (for 20 years), and after her death, Lydia (Lizzy) Burns (for 15 years). Mary Burns and Lizzy Burns were fervent Irish nationalists. Mary Burns influenced Engels' thinking about the conditions of the English working class and about the oppression of the Irish by the English. About Lizzy Burns, Engels said: 'She came of real Irish proletarian stock, and the passionate feeling for her class, which was instinctive with her, was worth more to me than all the blue-stockinged elegance of 'educated' and 'sensitive' bourgeois girls'.

Lenin and his beloved wife, Krupskaya, passionately worked together for the socialist cause. Krupskaya was a schoolteacher and active in the revolutionary movement. When Lenin was in prison, she would stand 'for hours on one particular spot of the pavement outside the prison in the hope that Lenin might catch a glimpse of her through a window' (Hill, 1971: 38). This was in 1895. In 1898, she was sentenced to exile, and the two got married in the Siberian prison. She 'shared Lenin's life, in eighteen long years of exile, and for seven years when her husband was head of the state' (p. 39). 'She was Lenin's collaborator and secretary as well as his wife'. Her strength, calmness and understanding were a necessary background to Lenin's political life' (ibid.).

Trotsky and his two spouses as well as his son, Sedov, were all involved in the socialist fight. Trotsky (2007) said this about his first wife in his autobiography: 'Her utter loyalty to socialism and her complete lack of any personal ambition gave her unquestioned moral authority. The work that we were doing bound us closely together, and so, to avoid being separated, we had been married in the transfer prison in Moscow' (124). Similarly, Rosa Luxemburg and her partner, Leo Jogiches, founded a socialist party together, and she and her partner, Kostja Zetkin, fought for socialism together.

Could all this be a mere happenstance? Was the love between Marx and his wife, Lenin and his wife, and so on, merely based on private emotional and physical attractions? And did their *personal* love not make a positive difference to the love for their intellectual and political lives? The answer is yes.

7      Conclusion

This chapter is partly a critical response to the following existing ideas that are problematic: that romantic love is mainly driven by the pleasure-drive, that it is mainly a relation between the two love-partners, that love is therefore a private matter, and that it has little to do with politics. The chapter builds on Marx and Kollontai as well as other Marxists. It puts Kollontai's ideas about the link between capitalism and love on a firmer basis in Marxist political economy and Marxist social theory including of consciousness. It also politicizes love under capitalism in a stronger way than Kollontai's and others' discussion does, in terms of the relation between love and class struggle. In explaining the social nature of love, my thinking did not begin with Kollontai, who wrote extensively about love. I began with Marx. However, I ended up agreeing with Kollontai's ideas about love. And I also show that although Marx did not write much about love directly, his political economy is relevant to a serious examination of love.

In presenting a Marxist theory of love in this and the previous chapter, I examine the conscious aspect of love, and love as a 'sensuous human activity' (Marx's words) and not just as a mental state. I argue that love is a deeply social process and therefore it is a potentially political process too. Love is not the private matter it might seem to be at a first glance.[23] I examine love trans-historically and in relation to historically specific forms of society: love in pre-capitalist society and love in capitalist society (where love is shaped by material conditions as well as certain forms of consciousness promoted by capitalism). Like everything else in society, love is connected to class relations: as class relations have changed, the concept and practice of love have changed. '[T]he practice of love exists in a historical, social and class context' (Kováts, 2015: 12). Love relations can contradict the interests of the ruling class or support these interests, so love relations are regulated by society. I also examine the proletarian conceptions of love that are appropriate for both the fight against capitalism and the construction of socialism.

Trans-historically, love is an emotion that encourages caring and solidarity, and trans-historically, love in its romantic form is based on a biological impulse too, but gradually, its nature has been shaped by social relations, and especially, class relations. The concept and practice of love have changed in

---

23   It is 'an important psychological and social factor, which society has always instinctively organized in its interests' (Kollontai, 1923). '[L]ove is not only a powerful natural factor, a biological force, but also a social factor. Essentially love is a profoundly social emotion' (ibid.).

the past, in accordance with interests of the ruling classes. 'At the tribal stage love was seen as a kinship attachment (love between sisters and brothers, love for parents). The ancient culture of the pre-Christian period placed love-friendship above all else' (Kollontai, 1923). According to Engels, it goes without saying that 'personal beauty, close intimacy, similarity of tastes and so forth awakened in people of opposite sex the desire for sexual intercourse, that men and women were not totally indifferent regarding the partner with whom they entered into this most intimate relationship'. 'But it is still a very long way to our sexual love' (Engels. 1884: 40). 'Before the Middle Ages we cannot speak of individual sex-love' (ibid.).

In fact, 'Throughout the whole of antiquity, marriages were arranged by the parents, and the partners calmly accepted their choice. What little love there was between husband and wife in antiquity is not so much subjective inclina-tion as objective duty, not the cause of the marriage, but its corollary. Love rela-tionships in the modern sense only occur in antiquity outside official society' (ibid.). The feudal world idealized platonic courtly love between members of the opposite sex outside marriage'(Kollontai, 1923). Love is no less regulated in capitalism: 'The bourgeoisie took monogamous marital love as its ideal', and it 'saw love as a "private matter," and 'was able to channel the expression of love in its class interests' (Kollontai, 1923).

It should be noted that the morality about love changed very slowly, and this is consistent with historical materialism which stresses the relative auton-omy of the non-economic and the importance of what Althusser (2005: 114–116) calls survivals (aspects of the old society that continue in the new society for a long time even if the underlying economic conditions have changed). For example, in the Victorian age (1820s–1914), 'love was mostly not a spon-taneous personal experience which then might lead to marriage' (Fromm, 1956: 2).[24]

Under capitalism, economic forces such as commodity fetishism, alienation, property relations and accumulation and the need for cheaper reproduction of labour power have had a deep impact on love relations. Love is also impacted by different forms of social consciousness: progressive forms of consciousness (e.g. democratic consciousness, trade union consciousness, class or socialist

---

24  On the contrary, in practice 'marriage was contracted by convention – either by the respective families, or by a marriage broker, or without the help of such intermediaries; it was concluded on the basis of social considerations, and love was supposed to develop once the marriage had been concluded. In the last few generations the concept of roman-tic love has become almost universal in the Western world' in accordance with the bour-geois ideology of love (Fromm, 1956: 2).

consciousness) have a different impact on love than do the social consciousness the content of which are capitalist values of competition and egoism. The
discussion on the social and class character of love has specific political implications (discussed in the final chapter).

CHAPTER 5

# The Post-truth Condition in Capitalist Society: Its Major Characteristics

## 1　Introduction

Both individuals and societies (civilizations) need truth for their existence and continued reproduction.[1] Civilizations 'cannot flourish if they are beset with trouble-some infections of *mistaken* beliefs' (Frankfurt, 2006: 34).[2] Truths 'consist of', and 'they therefore can provide us with, accurate accounts of the properties (including, especially, the causal powers and potentialities, and I would add, vulnerabilities), 'of the real objects and events with which we must deal with' and on which our lives depend on. So 'Truths have practical utility' (Frankfurt, 2006: 52).

The statement that capitalism does not produce economic and geographical inequality is false. Conversely, the statement that capitalism produces economic and geographical inequality is true.[3] The practical implication of this true statement is that any policy that does not at least control capitalist businesses will make a society more unequal. To take another example, it does matter 'whether or not our industrial practices are precipitating climate change', and it does matter 'whether cutting taxes benefits or further cripples the poor' (Dudiak, 2022: 8). It also matters 'whether a policy of peace through strength really leads to stability or just masks a more subtle form of war' (ibid.). In short, 'truth matters, it matters a lot, and it matters to us all' (ibid.).

Truths are important for the everyday life of individuals too. 'Individuals require truths in order to negotiate their way effectively through the thickets of hazards and opportunities that all people invariably confront in going about their lives. They need to know the truth about what to eat and what not to', for example (Frankfurt, 2006: 34–35). 'No one in his [or her] right mind would rely on a builder, or submit to the care of a physician, who does not care about truth' (Frankfurt, 2006: 24). The philosopher, Blackburn (2018: 11), says, 'the

---

1　This chapter and the next chapter draw on Das (2023b).
2　'Civilizations have never gotten along healthily, and cannot get along healthily, without large quantities of reliable factual information' (ibid.).
3　This does not mean that individual level natural differences are not a reason for inequality. They *are* in capitalism. Marx (1875) does recognize this.

difference between it being true that a mushroom is poisonous and it being false is the difference between death and a good dinner'.

Human beings are by nature rational animals. One can say that humans are truth-seeking animals. Being rational and being truthful are internally related. To be rational is 'a matter of being appropriately responsive to reasons', and 'reasons are constituted of facts' (Frankfurt, 2006: 63). To be rational is to know 'the difference between being true and being false' (Frankfurt, 2006: 63). Let us return to the mushroom example: if it is true that a certain mushroom is poisonous, then it is in our interest – it is rational – to avoid it. Take another example: 'the fact that it is raining in a certain region means that there is a reason for people in that region to carry umbrellas if they wish to avoid getting wet' (Frankfurt, 2006: 63). In other words: only if it is truly a fact that it is rain-ing, there is a reason for someone to carry an umbrella. It follows that: 'False statements provide no rational support for anything; they cannot effectively serve anyone as reasons'. (Frankfurt, 2006: 64). Facts and truths are internally related. 'For every fact, there is a true statement that relates it; and every [true] statement relates a fact' (Frankfurt, 2006: 67).

Certain statements about the natural and social world are true and cer-tain statements are false, even if we can agree that there is no such thing as absolute truth. It is, however, being increasingly recognized that a post-truth phenomenon, a part of the turn towards philosophical idealism, has arrived where lies and deception inform politics and everyday life as a normal state of affairs in capitalist societies (see Harsin, 2018). In the post-truth world, feelings are more accurate and more potent than facts, and lies are constantly told for the purpose of the political subordination of reality. For quite some time now, says Kakutani, an American literary critic, scholars have indeed lamented the death of truth. Kakutani (2019) has said that truth has become an endangered species, where social media, literature, television, academia, and politics have combined to elevate subjectivity over factuality and science. McIntyre (2018), a Research Fellow at the Center for Philosophy and History of Science at Boston University, describes the post-truth condition by drawing attention to the increasing dismissal of science, evidence, facts, and truth itself. The post-truth condition is one where 'facts are less important than feelings in shaping our beliefs about empirical matters' (McIntyre, 2018: XIV).

The remainder of this chapter has 3 sections. Section 2 discusses the various traits of the post-truth phenomenon. Section 3 deals with the postmodernist philosophical 'origin' of post-truth. Section 4 shows how it is that the post-truth phenomenon is a political ideology and a political practice of the Far Right. These sections set the context for a discussion in the next chapter on the political economic origins of the post-truth condition.

## 2 The Truth about Post-truth

Post-truth is connected to what Stephen Colbert, a TV comedian, in 2005, called "truthiness": truthiness is the noun for lies which feel right in the gut. 'Truthiness' refers to a situation where people are 'being persuaded by whether something *feels* true', even if there is no factual evidence (McIntyre, 2018: 5) and even if there is no logic or intellectual examination. In an interview with Rabin (2006), Colbert said that truthiness is where: 'It's not only that I *feel* it to be true, but that *I* feel it to be true. There's not only an emotional quality, but there's a selfish [and narcissistic] quality'. The term was named the Word of the Year in 2006 by Merriam Webster and by American Dialect society.

Then came the term post-truth which, by around 2014, appears to have replaced truthiness, although the term seems to have been first used in this sense earlier. This was when reflecting on the Iran-Contra scandal and the Persian Gulf War, the late Serbian-American playwright Steve Tesich lamented the arrival of 'the post-truth' era in the US (D'Ancona, 2017: 9).[4]

The term post-truth rocketed to public attention in November 2016, when it was named the 2016 Word of the Year by Oxford Dictionaries, following a 2000% increase in its usage over 2015.

According to Oxford Dictionaries (2016), post-truth is an adjective which is defined as 'relating to or denoting circumstances in which objective facts are less influential in shaping public opinion than appeals to emotion and personal belief'. The prefix, 'post', in *post-truth*, means that we live in a time in which truth 'has become unimportant or irrelevant' (ibid.). In a post-truth world, "alternative facts" replace actual facts and feelings have more weight than evidence (McIntyre, 2018). In the post-truth 'condition' there is a rift between evidence and truth (Peters et al, 2020).

I will use post-truth as an adjective. I will also use it as a noun to refer to the post-truth condition/politics itself. I will use post-truthers to refer to those who engage in post-truth. The post-truth phenomenon, or post-truth, for short, has several specific traits which will be discussed below schematically.

### 2.1 *Post-truth on a Spectrum*

Post-truth is on a spectrum of processes in which people subvert truth (McIntyre, 2018: 7–8) (see Figure 5.1). These processes include:

---

4  The use of the term suddenly increased massively between 2015 and 2016, the year of the election of Trump as the US president who has been known to have made numerous false statements (ibid.). Donald Trump had hothoused the seed, that was 'planted by George W Bush over Iraq, by jettisoning the need for his lies to feel even vaguely credible' (Norman, 2016).

1.   Simple ignorance: If one is honestly ignorant, one may be motivated to learn.

2.   Falsehood: One says things that are untrue without meaning to do so; in that sense one is uttering a falsehood but not a lie, for the mistake is not intentional.

3.   Willful ignorance: This is simple ignorance coupled with the decision to remain ignorant. One does not know whether something is true but one says it anyway, without bothering to check the facts when in fact it is possible to do so.[5]

4.   Lying: This is when one tells a falsehood with the intent to deceive and with the full knowledge that what one is saying is not true.[6]

5.   Post-truth: This is when one consciously lies for a political or ideological purpose,[7] and where how one feels about a matter matters more than what empirical evidence says about it.[8]

Lines between these stages are not clear-cut, of course. And the transition from one to the next stage is slippery.

---

5   Willful ignorance, normally, occurs when someone has a firm commitment to an ideology that proclaims it has all the answers – even if it counters empirical matters that have been well covered by scientific investigation. More than mere scientific illiteracy, this sort of obstinacy reflects a dangerous contempt for the methods that customarily lead to recognition of the truth. And once we are on that road, it is a short hop to disrespecting truth (McIntyre, 2015).The strategy of willful ignorance is not to fight theory with theory and statistic with statistic. It is instead to say, 'I refuse to believe this', and then filibuster in the court of public opinion. It is not crackpot theories that are doing us in. It is the spread of the tactics of those who disrespect truth (McIntyre, 2015).

6   'The trouble with lying and deceiving is that their efficiency depends entirely upon a clear notion of the truth that the liar and deceiver wishes to hide' (Hannah Arendt quoted in Popova, 2016). Lying, unlike simple ignorance or falsehood, does have an audience because our intention is to deceive *someone*.

7   The ideological purpose refers to the fact that post-truthers want people to have specific beliefs (wrong beliefs or partly true and partly wrong beliefs) that reinforce the political supremacy of one group over another.

8   Another word associated with all these is 'bullshit' as distinct from lying: Frankfurt, the author of *On Bullshit*, says 'bullshitters ... are fakers and phonies who are attempting by what they say to manipulate the opinions and attitudes of those to whom they speak' (Frankfurt, 2006: 3–4). Then, there are skepticism, disbelief, etc. If we are skeptical, we can continue to search for answers. If we disbelieve, maybe others can convince us. And perhaps even if we are honestly wrong, and put forward a proposition that is open to refutation, we may learn something when our earlier belief is overthrown (McIntyre, 2015).

| | Falsehood | | Lying | | |
|---|---|---|---|---|---|
| Simple ignorance | | Willful ignorance | | Post-truth | |

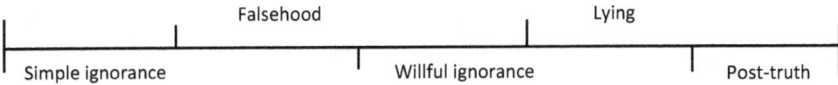

FIGURE 5.1   Post-truth phenomenon on a spectrum

## 2.2   *Lying in Post-truth Condition*

The 'post' in post-truth does not necessarily mean it is 100% falsehood. If it is simply the opposite of truth, i.e., if it is 100% falsehood, it may lose its efficacy. More than ignorance and falsehood, it is lying that is most connected to post-truth. Post-truth includes, but is more than, lying. Indeed, the post-truth phenomenon has a quality of hybridity.[9]

In everyday life, people have always lied.[10] Lying for political purposes, like lying in everyday life, is also nothing new. People and politicians have been lying in what the BBC journalist, Davis, calls the 'pre-post-truth period' (Davis, 2018: xx). Five hundred years ago, Machiavelli said: the ruler of the state must be 'a great liar' (Blackburn, 2018: 5). But post-Truth is not the same as a long tradition of political lies, exaggeration and spin that has characterized modern society (D'Ancona, 2017).

In an article in *Nature,* Higgins, a philosopher, says that post-truth is different from the notion that 'all politicians lie and make promises they have no intention of keeping' in the sense that people still expect 'honesty to be the default position', but in the post-truth world, 'this *expectation* no longer holds' (Higgins, 2016).

The aim of post-truth lying is the political subordination of reality and political domination:

> [Lying has always posed challenges] but never before have such challenges been so openly embraced *as a strategy* for the political subordination of reality. Thus what is striking about the idea of post-truth is not

---

9   'It has hybrid, recombinant qualities that mix in different ways and confuse its recipients – a bricolage of old-fashioned lying, clever quips, boasting and wilful exaggerations' (Bhadrakumar, 2019).

10   And indeed, lying is not always and necessarily bad. Referring to the research done by the psychologist, Belle DePaulo, Henig says that lying is not bad when it can protect someone else's life or feelings. Henig (2006) notes: lying is not bad when, for example, 'a genetic counselor says nothing when she happens to find out, during a straightforward test for birth defects, that a man could not possibly have fathered his wife's new baby'. Lying is not bad when 'a neighbor lies about hiding a Jewish family in Nazi-occupied Poland' or 'when a mother tells her daughter that nothing bad will ever happen to her'.

just that truth is being challenged, but that it is being challenged *as a mechanism* for asserting political dominance'. (Italics added)
MCINTYRE, 2018: XIV

Indeed, lying has taken new dimensions in recent times: its scale and frequency have massively increased. In the post-truth condition, the use of blatant lies is a routine affair across society, where 'politicians can lie without condemnation' as they 'take their right to lie as a given' (Higgins, 2016). This is evident from Trump's America. Consider some of the lies of Trump (see Kessler, 2020). Post 2016 election, he said that he won the popular vote (even if in reality Hilary Clinton had won 3 million more votes than he did).[11] Trump also claimed that he had the biggest election victory since Reagan. He tweeted that the 'concept of global warming was created by and for the Chinese in order to make US manufacturing non-competitive' (D'Ancona, 2017: 45). Referring to the 9/11 terrorist attack on the world trade center, Trump said: 'I watched in Jersey City, New Jersey, where thousands and thousands of people were cheering as that building was coming down'. All these claims are false. Indeed, according to PolitiFact, 69% of Trump's statements are 'mostly false', 'false' or 'pants on fire' (D'Ancona, 2017: 8). Trump lied on an average 18 times a day during his presidency, and his propensity to lie increased over time (Figure 5.2). Trump made as many as 30 573 false or misleading claims during the four years of his office, according to Washington Post. Yet, he has enjoyed much popularity and even won an election.

Trump is not the only US president who is a post-truther, although some call him the first post-truth president and 'the most mendacious president in US history' (Kessler, 2020: x). 'Just about every recent president is associated with one big lie' (Kessler, 2020 x). Consider some pre-Trump presidential lies. Ronald Reagan, a former President,[12] said: 'I told the American people I did not trade arms for hostages. My heart and my best intentions still tell me that is true, but the facts and the evidence tell me it is not' (quoted in D'Ancona, 2017: 25). Similarly, Bush, another former President, lied about the Iraq war (more on this below).

Not only do politicians lie on a massive scale. Large segments of the public openly accept lies by politicians as the norm. In fact, 'Lying is regarded [by

---

11   In a tweet he said, 'In addition to winning the Electoral College in a landslide, I won the popular vote if you deduct the millions of people who voted illegally' (quoted in Barry, 2017).

12   Reagan launched the neoliberal regime of free trade and austerity after crushing the strike by air-traffic controllers (Harvey, 2005).

THE POST-TRUTH CONDITION IN CAPITALIST SOCIETY

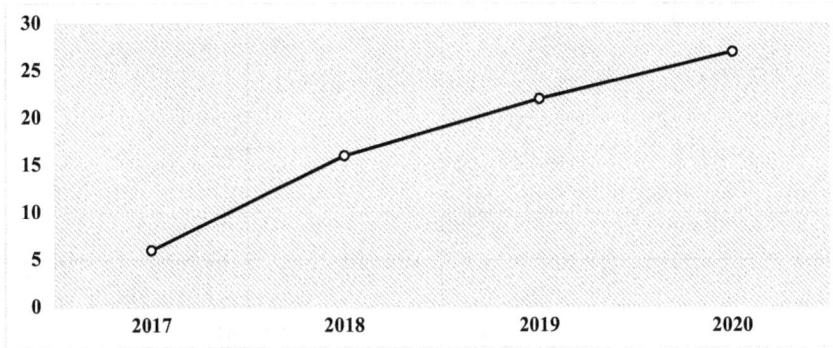

FIGURE 5.2   The number of times Donald Trump lied a day during his presidency
SOURCE OF THE STATISTICAL DATA: SNYDER (2017)

large segments of the public] as the norm even in democracies ... We no longer expect our elected politicians to speak the truth' (D'Ancona, 2017: 26; 27).[13] As Higgins (2016) says: 'Public tolerance of inaccurate and undefended allegations, non sequiturs in response to hard questions and outright denials of facts is shockingly high'. The public's initial response may be 'outrage' but it slowly 'gives way to indifference', partly due to 'sheer exhaustion', and, then indifference gives way 'finally, to collusion' (D'Ancona, 2017: 26; 27).

Indeed, in the post-truth environment, blatant politically motivated lies are told *both* by politicians and the common people. Saddam Hussein had no role in 9/11. This is true. Yet, the US President Bush said that Iraq under Hussein was attempting to purchase the materials necessary to build nuclear weapons.[14] In Fall 2003, a poll showed that almost 70% of Americans thought Hussein played a personal role in the 9/11 attack. It was true that Hussein had no weapons of mass destruction. Yet, according to a survey in 2006, 50% of Americans believed that there were these weapons in Iraq (Manjoo, 2008: 22–23). Consider another example. According to approximately 1000 peer review journal articles published by 2004, the planet is heating up due to human activities. Yet, a 2006 survey showed that only 41% of Americans thought there was solid evidence that humans were changing the climate (ibid.: 23). It is true that 'Democrats ... are twice as likely as Republicans to accept the [scientific]

---

13   D'Ancona (2017: 90–91) is mistaken to think that: what is POMO is to post-truth, Marxism is to communist totalitarianism (Stalinism). There are two conflations here. Marx = totalitarianism. Marxism = Stalinism. Both are simply wrong.

14   And his administration said that whether or not this was true, the war resulted in stability in the region (Lynch, 2005: 1).

evidence', but this only means that 'Even scientific fact isn't safe from politically motivated perception' (ibid.). All in all, the post-truth condition is characterized by political lying from above and from below.

### 2.3    *Facts vs Feelings in Post-truth*

People have always held some wrongheaded or irrational beliefs (e.g., the earth is flat; an illness is because of the wrath of a deity). Such beliefs were later subject to correction by reason and evidence. However, as McIntyre (2018) says, when people profess to know something even in the face of absent or contradicting evidence, that is when people stop looking for the truth, and that is where post-truth comes from. Post-truthers claim they know the truth when in fact they do not. They do so even if their mistake is pointed out, because they have an ideological-political reason to make the false claim. 'Don't bother me with facts' is no longer a punchline. It has become a political stance' (Higgins, 2016). When one believes that there are no facts, 'nobody tells lies or falsehood, just alternative, equally valuable facts' (McIntyre, 2018: 25).

So, with post-truth, we have reached a watershed moment, when people's beliefs are increasingly based on intuition or feelings rather than on facts. Post-truthers do not accept that some things are true irrespective of how we feel about them and that our interests are best served by finding the facts that are true. They aim to knowingly falsify facts, spread fake news and neutralize rational and critical thought by appealing to emotions or half-truths (Joshi, 2021). Reagan had said that 'people believe in something because they want to believe it' and that there's nothing wrong with that. I do it all the time' (quoted in D'Ancona, 2017: 25). When Newt Gingrich, a right-wing American politician, says that how we feel about the murder rate in the US (i.e. we feel threatened), is more important than statistics, he is a post-truther and enabler of post-truth (McIntyre, 2018). He once said: 'liberals have a whole set of statistics that theoretically may be right, but it's not where human beings are'.... 'I'll go with how *people feel* and let you go with the theoreticians' (ibid.: 4). In other words, if facts are not what a right-winger says they are, then facts are *theories*, or the right-winger's facts are facts too (i.e., alternate facts). If the murder rate not rising in the US is a fact, then Gingrich's fact that the murder rate is rising is also a fact. If one goes by Gingrich, i.e. by the principle of post-truth politics, where one's view of the world is driven by one's feelings, and not by facts, then governments should build more prisons if they merely *feel* that crime rates are going up (McIntyre, 2018: 14). Post-truthers believe that 'a crowd's reaction', i.e. the reaction of the people they speak to, 'actually does change the facts about a lie' (ibid.: 9).

Post-truthers have a selective approach to facts. They do not reject all facts. Depending on what one wants to be true, some facts are considered to matter more than other facts. 'The selective use of facts that prop up one's position, and the complete rejection of facts that do not, seems part and parcel of creating the new post-truth reality' (McIntyre, 2018: 34). Their main criterion for respecting facts is what facts suit their pre-existing beliefs. Post-truthers 'only want to accept those facts that justify their ideology' or pre-conceived belief (McIntyre, 2018: 10). This is not the abandonment of facts but the corruption of the process by which facts are credibly gathered and reliably used to shape one's beliefs about reality (McIntyre, 2018). Post-truth is not so much a claim that truth does not exist as that facts are subordinate to our political point of view (McIntyre, 2018: 11). The post-truth politician does not simply pick-and-choose among relevant facts, offer questionable interpretations or avoid inconvenient questions (Lockie, 2016). The post-truth politician *manufactures* their own facts. They assert whatever they believe to be in their own interest, and they continue to press those same claims, regardless of the evidence amassed against them. Unlike in what are only political spin, lying, etc. that have happened before, what is new in the post-truth era is the challenge to the existence of objective reality itself (McIntyre, 2018: 10).

Without evidence, for example, climate change deniers – who are one type of post-truthers – say that the theory of climate change is a conspiracy while they cite most favourable facts that allegedly say that climate change is not happening (ibid.: 11). If today is a cold day, such climate change deniers interpret today's cold weather, which is a fact, as proof that climate change is not real, and if millions agree with this, then the idea of climate change, which is true, is treated as a hoax. If a politician and their followers perceive record attendance at a political rally, then there *is* a record attendance, even if photographs say there were only a few people in the audience (C. Lynch, quoted in McIntyre, 2018: 144–145). Post-truthers justify their alternate facts by saying there are two sides to – two facts about – a given phenomenon. But 'Two sides to a story exist when evidence exists on both sides of a position. Then, reasonable people may disagree about how to weight that evidence and what conclusion to form from it' (Levitin, 2017: x).

## 2.4 *Post-truth Relativism and Attitude to Truth*

Post-truth exists in two modes in terms of its attitude to truth. There is a soft mode. Post-truthers may say that truth exists or that certain things are true, but they do not care about truth if it gets in the way of their personal preferences. In other words, truth exists, but their subjective experience matters more. Post-truth also exists in a hard mode: willingness to propagate blatant falsehoods, knowing they are false because doing so serves a higher political and social agenda (Murray, 2018 13–14). As Arenchibia and Velazquez (2021: 15), say, post-truth:

> refers to the existence of a subjectively distorted truth, which is built according to the perception of each individual, based on the idea that it is possible to consider something as true on the basis of simple emotional presuppositions, without ever taking into account the events that could contradict it.

In the post-truth condition, objective truth *dies* in several ways which can be seen as truth-denial or facts-denial strategies (Snyder, 2017: 66–70).[15] Firstly, there is an open hostility to verifiable reality, a hostility which takes the form of presenting inventions and lies as if they were facts. Post-Truth 'creates' an alternate reality based on an alternative set of facts, and it creates an 'illusion of truth' (Joshi, 2021). This can include even magical thinking.[16] The second process is an open embrace of contradiction. 'The idea of 'doublethink' – 'the power of holding two contradictory beliefs in one's mind and accepting both of them' – is the direct ancestor of post-truth' (D'Ancona, 2017: 102). For example, liberating wealthy people from taxes will not increase national debt. The third process is the shamanistic incantation which depends on endless repetition, designed to make the fiction plausible and the criminal desirable. Post-truthers believe that if we speak a lie and if many people believe it, then it is not a lie. It is a fact.[17] Finally, there is a misplaced faith in self-deifying claims. 'I only can solve it'. 'I am your voice'. 'If the supreme leader is there, everything is possible'. When faith descends like this from heaven, there is no room for 'small' truths of our individual discernment because truth is considered oracular and is treated as oratorial rather than factual as if evidence is irrelevant. Understanding the world is useless. We have faith in our leader.

---

15    This is based on Victor Klemperor (quoted in Snyder, 2017: 66–70).

16    Some say that magical thinking – of the type that is involved in astrology or tarot reading -- is useful so including lying is actually useful. 'The truth might be that your friend looks uncomfortable in his new suit, but if he's on his way to a job interview it is probably more appropriate to say: "You look great! You will win them over!"' (Dukes, 2019: 9). This idea is defended even by critics of post-truth.

17    These three processes closely correspond to what Adler and Drieschova (2021) call: *false speak* (flagrant lying to subvert the concept of facts), *double speak* (intentional internal contradictions in speech to erode reason), and *flooding* (the emission of many messages into the public domain to create confusion), respectively.

A variation of this set of truth-denial strategies is employed by Trump. First, raise questions about some outlandish matter: 'people are talking'; I am saying what I read in the newspapers (about, say Obama's birthplace). But do this without providing any evidence beyond one's conviction/belief. Then say that the press (or intellectuals) cannot be trusted because they are biased. This will make people doubt what they hear from the press (or intellectuals). In the face of such uncertainty, people will be more prone to believing only what fits with their preconceived notions. This creates an environment for fake news (or alternative facts) which will reinforce the above processes. Thus people believe what someone says just because he/she, seen as their ally, says it (McIntyre, 2018: 115) and just because people feel good. Besides, facts that post-truthers do not agree with are treated by them as negative, pessimistic and unpatriotic, seditious and anti-national; any fact that describes the truth about the oppression of minorities is also said to be disturbing social harmony (ibid.).

In the post-truth world, truth appears in fragments: for example, in the US, the truth has dissolved into Trump's truth vs the media truth; liberal truth vs conservative truth; women's truth vs men's truth; my truth vs your truth, and so on. All this means the death knell for the Truth itself (Dudiak, 2022: 19–20). Thus, in the post-truth world, 'you choose your own reality, as if from a buffet. You also select your own falsehood, no less arbitrarily' (D'Ancona, 2017: 56). There is a marketplace of truths from which one can freely choose.

## 2.5    *Post-truth Attitude towards Experts*

The post-truth skepticism and the post-truth belief that there are all sorts of theories about a given object all of which are equally true produce the death of expertise. This is in the sense that ordinary people are unwilling to listen to expert advice (Nichols, 2019: IX). There is indeed a generalized and angry defiance towards established knowledge. (ibid.: XIII; XXI). 'We are witnessing the "death of expertise": a Google-fueled, Wikipedia-based, blog-sodden collapse of any division between professionals and laymen, students and teachers, knowers and wonderers – [i.e.] between those of any achievement in an area and those with none' (Nichols, 2014). The anti-intellectualism that is implied is evident in Trump's claims that 'the experts are terrible' (Nichols, 2019: 210–211) and 'I *love* the poorly educated' (ibid.: 213). Michael Gove, the then Justice secretary on David Cameron's cabinet and himself a major intellectual, says: 'people in this country have had enough of experts' (D'Ancona, 2017: 35).

Democracy, of course, means people's 'equal rights versus the government, and in relation to each other' but democracy 'does not mean that "everyone's opinion about anything is as good as anyone else's." And yet, this is now enshrined as the credo of a fair number of people' (Nichols, 2014). Producing knowledge based on reason and evidence requires years of work. But if anyone can have a theory of everything, then where is the need for experts? Experts are seen as elites, who know only theory and who are out of touch with ordinary people, who apparently know the reality (and who because they are ordinary *people*, like customers in a market-place or of an enterprise, know the best and are above rational criticisms). This is a hallmark of authoritarian 'populism', a component of fascistic tendency

The ordinary people apparently know the reality the best *because* they are ordinary people, so they are considered to be above rational criticisms. Criticisms of the ordinary people – and many of them are followers of post-truth authoritarian populist politicians – by experts are seen by both the groups as insults. Indeed, nowadays everyone feels easily insulted. People 'no longer distinguish ..."you're wrong" from ..."you're stupid." To disagree is to insult. To correct another is to be a hater .... [To] refuse to acknowledge alternative views, no matter how fantastic or inane, is to be closed-minded' (Nichols, 2014). In the post-truth condition, a new epistemological identity seems to have come into existence: the post-truth identity. This is a person who believes whatever feels good regardless of reason and empirical evidence, and if one criticizes their lies/falsehood, one is accused of criticizing their person, their identity. 'It is very difficult to get a [person] to understand something' when their 'tribal identity depends on [their] not understanding it', says Michael Bérubé (quoted in Warner, 2011).

In the scientific world, a fact that is considered to be true today can be refuted in 10 years by scientists when new reason and new evidence come. Post-truthers exploit this legitimate scientific method by disputing the independence and objectivity of scientists and scholars. Scientists 'are dismissed as 'elites' – as one more cog in the establishment machine that allegedly suppresses free speech and imposes political correctness' (Lockie, 2016). Post-truth politics contests scientists' right to act as public intellectuals. Their 'contributions to the public sphere are decried as undemocratic' and their 'words [are seen as] silencing the voices of 'ordinary', 'everyday', 'real' people' (Lockie, 2016: 2). Post-truth's populist worldview is against science.

Post-truthers reject the four following claims (Nichols, 2014). 1) Experts are not always right but are far more likely to be right than laypeople.[18] 2) To be an expert requires years of hard work in the form of education and experience.

---

18    '[D]octors ... do better with most illnesses than faith healers' (Nichols, 2014). Experts on a topic are more right and more frequently right about that topic than laypeople (those who do not spend most of their working life studying nature or society or both), although the experts on a topic $T_1$ are more or less ignorant about topic $T_2$, $T_3$, etc.

3) Having a strong *opinion* about x is not the same thing as knowing x (i.e., understanding its nature, where it came from, and its necessary causal conditions/powers and effects). 4) Laypeople's political opinions have value, but their political analysis has far less value than experts' and is not probably as good as they think. 'To reject the notion of expertise, and to replace it with a sanctimonious insistence that every person has a right to his or her own opinion, is silly'. (Nichols, 2014). Further, 'the perverse effect of the death of expertise is that without real experts, everyone is an expert on everything'. (Nichols, 2014).

## 2.6    *Immorality and Demagogy of Post-truth*

Belief and public debate grounded in the best possible evidence must be ethical (Sokal, 2008: 447). 'Misleading the American people about the reasons for war is immoral. Killing thousands of civilians who have done us no harm is immoral' (Sokal, 2008: 424).

One can truthfully or scientifically determine how many people of a particular religion or ethnicity or race as the target of post-truth politics of hate can be fitted into a car to be taken to a place to be killed, but this is a fact 'that is so utterly a betrayal of every moral imperative, of every decency, of every remote echo of neighbour love, that it cannot with any integrity be called true at all, despite being so very correct. To call such a fact "the truth" is a violation of those to whom we are called to be faithful [i.e. to the common people around us, all of whom share a common interest – an interest in the protection of their life, liberty and dignity]; this fact stands at the antipode of "being true"' (Dudiak, 2022: 42–43; parenthesis added).

Because post-truthers disregard objective facts, the post-truth era is an era of 'willful irrationality' (Levitin, 2017: x). And this goes against the idea that 'Rationality is our most distinctive characteristic' as human beings (Frankfurt, 2006: 62). For a rational person, there is a reasonable amount of harmony between what one says/thinks and what one does. In a post-truth world, there need not be any necessary connection between a thought and action. A post-truther politician can agree, at least, in public, that lynching someone based on the true fact of them eating a certain kind of food (e.g., beef) is not acceptable, but when there *is* lynching, there is often no action, or not even criticism, against it by the politician. A post-truther can say they treat all people equally irrespective of their religions and yet engage in action that discriminates against religious minorities.

Hence post-truth and demagogy go together. Post-truth advantages the demagogue: if you don't know the facts, you can say whatever you wish to (in order to please your audience), and it won't be a lie (Joshi, 2021).[19] Bhadrakumar (2019) says: 'The demagogue employs language to keep thoughts at bay, tapping into the fragile but essential compact based on trust between the government and the citizens'.

## 3    Post-truth's Philosophical Affinity with Postmodernism

In the light of all this, it is easy to agree with Naranjit (2020) according to whom the post-truth era is a complete repudiation of classical philosophy:

> Whereas Plato saw philosophy as leading man out of a cave of darkness, of transcending ignorance of the truth, in the post-truth world, man is led back to a cave of unyielding darkness where no one can see the truth because there is no truth. It is a new age of blindness, a cave that imprisons eternally. It is a cave where the strong can oppress and enslave and destroy with impunity since no one can claim to witness their deeds, since all are blind. The post-truth society is one in which the only truth is the will to power.

The basic distinction in philosophy is one between a materialist view and an idealist view. In his *Materialism and Empirio-criticism*, Lenin (1908a: 99) writes summarizing Engels' view: 'Materialism regards nature as primary and spirit as secondary; it places being first and thought second. Idealism holds the contrary view'.

If we apply this principle to the social world, we can say this: the idea that the social world is dominantly and ultimately created by human thought is idealism, while the view that social world is ultimately created by the interaction between nature and human practice and by the social relations (of production and exchange) that exist independently of human thinking or will, at a given point in time, is materialism, although materialism does not ignore the fact that human thinking also influences the social world. Since the 1970s, however, there has been an ascendancy of idealistic tendencies, especially, in the form of postmodernism, which prioritize the realm of ideas (discourse) over the objective conditions.

---

19    In post-truth environment, statements become true if audiences desire them to be such. That leads to the creation of affiliative truths or ways of knowing that are capable of mobilising audiences (Kalpokas, 2018).

First, a few words about postmodernism. There may be legitimate theoretical questions about our ability to accurately know the objective truth (i.e., what exists objectively such as geographically uneven development across Canadian provinces), but this does not mean that one can completely reject truth and objectivity. But this is exactly what postmodernism does[20] (McIntyre, 2018: 17, 127). According to Papazoglou, Nietzsche, whose ideas are precursor to postmodernism, posits that, "'once we realise that the idea of an absolute, objective truth is a philosophical hoax, the only alternative is a position called 'perspectivism' – the idea there is no one objective way the world is, only perspectives on what the world is like'" (quoted in Lynch 2017).

Postmodernism as a philosophy has been widely popular in academic circles (and among relatively privileged layers of society) (Callinicos, 1991; Eagleton, 1996; Morley and Alizadeh, 2022; North, 2015; Smith, 1993). In postmodernism, there is no such thing as objective truth. Objective truth is an illusion. Postmodernism believes in the doctrine of equal validity: there are many radically different, 'yet "equally valid" ways of knowing the world', and science is just one of them (Boghossian, 2006: 2). Further, science is seen as a western and an imperialist tool of oppression.

The reality has a qualitative dimension as well as a quantitative dimension. Facts of economic development, rainfall, climate change, frequency of imperialist wars, and so on can be all measured and analyzed, and Mathematics as a universal language of humanity plays a useful role here. Because state-sponsored racism has utilized mathematical numbers, Mathematics itself is seen as inherently racist, so there is a push for ethnomathematics, i.e., Mathematics for, and of, the people of color (Costa and Hanover, 2019). So, the disregard for facts becomes a disregard for Mathematics.

'[T]ruth is just another name for power' (Lynch, 2005: 2).[21] Any profession of truth is a simple reflection of one's political ideology, so knowledge claims are merely assertions of authority (McIntyre, 2018: 126). The epistemological status – the truth status – of a statement depends on extra-epistemological criteria, i.e., who is making the claim, what sorts of institutional support it receives and so on. Even if he appears to be critical of some postmodernist claims, Bruno Latour says: 'No attested knowledge can stand on its own. ... Facts

---

20  It is as if 'epistemologists and critical theorists do not go to a physician when they get sick' (ibid.: 13).

21  The response of the physicist from New York University, Alan Sokal, was provocative: 'anyone who believes that the laws of physics are mere social conventions is invited to try transgressing those conventions from the windows of my apartment. I live on the twenty-first floor' (Sokal and Bricmont, 1998: 269).

remain robust only when they are supported by a common culture, by institutions that can be trusted [and so on]' (Latour, 2018: 23; see also Kofman, 2018). Postmodernism indeed believes that since there is no truth, or since there is no distinction between what is true and what is false, anyone who says they are telling the truth is really oppressing us, not educating us.[22] Postmodernism has led to 'the systematic disparagement of modern science' (p. ix). It stands for 'infectious spread of pernicious relativism disguised as legitimate scepticism' (D'Ancona, 2017: 2).

Postmodernism, as a philosophical tool for post-truth, used consciously or not, is wrong in many ways. To say that all metanarratives are wrong is a metanarrative. Why should one believe a postmodernist when they say that there is no such thing as truth? (Wilber, 2017: 7). Is it universally true that there is no universal truth? Postmodernism is contradictory in another sense. It is obsessed with questions of identity and with the social construction of reality, which amounts to mainly the mental construction of reality, while denying the objective character of reality. This idealistic approach to the reality fails to answer the question of how it is that I can know who I am unless I differentiate myself from who I am not, i.e. from the objective reality *outside of myself*. And can I really create reality as I wish to? The 'concept of reality ... is essentially a concept of what limits us' (Frankfurt, 2006: 99). 'When certain aspects of our experience fail to submit to our wishes ... it then becomes clear to us that they are not part of ourselves' or our identity (Frankfurt, 2006: 99). '[O]ur recognition and understanding of our own identity arises out of, and depends integrally on, our appreciation of a reality that is definitely independent of ourselves' and that 'there are facts and truths over which we cannot hope to exercise direct or immediate control' (p. 100–101). Postmodernism wrongly denies facts and truths. 'If there were no such facts or truths' and if 'the world invariably and unresistingly became whatever we might like or wish it to be', then 'we would be unable to distinguish ourselves from what is other than ourselves and we would have no sense of what in particular we ourselves are' (Frankfurt, 2006: 101).

Postmodernist idealism has indeed no basis in life, in its materiality and in its objectively social character. Postmodernists are like those idealists whom Marx and Engels (1845: 3) once mocked: they were those who conflated the objective force of gravity with the theory of gravity and who thus 'fought

---

22   Latour acknowledges this when he says: 'Entire Ph.D. programs are still [teaching] that facts are made up, that there is no such thing as natural, unmediated, unbiased access to truth ... while dangerous extremists are using the very same argument ... to destroy hardwon evidence that could save our lives' (Latour, 2004: 227).

against the illusion of gravity, of whose harmful results all statistics brought [them] new and manifold evidence'. The fact is that: ideas about the objective world are not the same as that world itself. When people lose their jobs, it is not because of the idea of capitalist financial crisis but because of the very objective reality of crisis. This crisis is more or less independent of how we think about it at a given point in time. There is thus a mistaken practical implication of postmodernism. What *does* need to be changed is the objective reality (e.g., increasing commodification of education or the crisis-proneness of the economic system or climate breakdown) that is preventing men and women of different races, ethnicities and religions from meeting their social-ecological needs. If this is true, then how can a new and better world be produced merely in, and through, the world of ideas, and that too, the ideas about one's own identity? Postmodernists are like the idealists of Marx's time just referred to above who 'forget…that they are in no way combating the real existing world when they are merely combating the phrases of this world' (Marx and Engels, 1845: 5).

There *are* facts. Facts signify the truth about something. There can be different interpretations of a given fact. And there are personal beliefs driven by emotions. However, facts and personal beliefs are not necessarily the same, and certain interpretations of a given fact are truer (that is, they are more in line with the objective reality and are more practically adequate) than other interpretations. That capitalism is not a harmonious, crisis-free system is objectively true. This is the case no matter how much revisionists wish to characterize it otherwise (Lenin, 1908b; Das, 2022e). And this is the case even if interpretations of 'forms, the sequence, the picture of particular crises' can vary as can the interpretations of the reasons and the frequency of crises (Lenin, 1908b). If there is an objective world, more or less independent of how we think at this moment, then the information about that world must be factually true. A true statement is one that more or less correctly reflects the world in our mind. A false statement is an incorrect reflection of the world, as it, more or less, fails to correspond to the world.

Now, one of the saddest roots of the post-truth phenomenon, where feelings or personal beliefs matter more than facts and truths, 'seems to have come directly out of colleges and universities which are spreading postmodernist ideas' (McIntyre, 2018: 123). '[U]under the banner of postmodernism, cynicism about truth and related notions like objectivity and knowledge has become the semi-official philosophical stance of many academic disciplines' (Lynch, 2005: 1). What a person considers to be true depend on 'the person's individual point of view or is determined by what the person is *constrained to regard* as true by various complex and inescapable social pressures' (Frankfurt, 2006: 21).

The postmodernist idealist tendency is where the reality is reduced to ideas/opinions about the reality and where ideas about the reality cannot be assessed in relation to an independent objective reality. If ideas do not have to be assessed against an independent reality, one idea is as good as another, so the distinction between a true statement and a false one is immaterial. The 'post-truth' phenomenon has affinity with postmodernist idealism which sees no difference between 1) 'x claims that the statement S is true' and 2) 'S is true'. If a statement feels true, for 'post-truthers', it must be true, even if it is completely false. If ideas create reality and if ideas determine things in the world in abstraction from the reality, as in postmodernism, then there is an ease with which the elite can create and disseminate false ideas in support of their interests, a process that common people accept. This is the post-truth phenomenon. This makes any critique of capitalists and their politicians on the Far Right, difficult: capitalists and politicians constantly produce false ideas, but they cannot be exposed by denying any difference between truth and falsehood.

Postmodernism has supplied, directly or indirectly, the philosophical basis for post-truth, whether or not 'the post-truthers' have read the postmodern texts or are aware of postmodernism. A large number of thinkers say this, and I agree. There is much textual evidence for this. 'The epistemology of post-truth is no more than the postmodern idea [advanced by the postmodernist, Rorty] that 'Truth is what my colleagues will let me get away with' (quoted in D'Ancona, 2017: 98). Professor Daniel Dennet, an American philosopher, says: 'postmodernists ... are responsible for the intellectual fad that made it respectable to be cynical about truth and facts' (quoted in Cadwalladr, 2017). Postmodernism is a precursor to post-truth, and it is the godfather of post-truth (McIntyre, 2018: 126; 150). As the literary critic, Michael Bérubé noted: postmodernism has helped create a culture of skepticism towards objectivity and facts whereby 'now the climate-change deniers and the young-Earth creationists are coming after the natural scientists', and 'they're using some of the very arguments developed by an academic left [postmodernists] that thought it was speaking only to people of like mind' (quoted in McIntyre, 2015). Postmodernist pernicious relativism has 'paved the way for Post-Truth' and indeed Trump's rise based on lies is the 'ultimate post-modern moment' (D'Ancona, 2017: 96–97). 'To the extent that postmodernist ideas are widely disseminated in the culture, even in watered-down form, they create a climate in which the incentives promoting the rigorous analysis of evidence [that requires time and skills] are undermined' (Sokal, 2008: 344). The philosopher, Grayling, identifies postmodernism and relativism as the intellectual roots of post-truth. If 'Everything is relative' and if 'stories are being made up all the time' then 'there is no such thing as the truth' (quoted in Coughlan, 2017). He says that this sort of ideas has filtered its way indirectly into post-truth politics, which is a type of politics that is untroubled by evidence (ibid.).

Mike Cernovich, one of the leading online personalities of the alt-right, says: "Look, I read postmodernist theory in college. If everything is a narrative, then we need alternatives to the dominant narrative" (in Lynch 2017). Promoters of Brexit said: they spread information (for example, about Britain giving 350 pounds to EU a week) which they knew were false; they said there really were no facts and what really counted was that they truly believed this. And one of them said 'I have read my Lacan – it's whoever controls the narrative that counts' citing Lacan, a leading postmodernist (Wilber, 2017: 25). So, the Right, including those who reject evolutionism and the material origin of life, has managed to successfully adopt a postmodern style of politics, where alternative facts counter objective truth, and alternative narratives create a new, paranoid picture of the world.[23]

While postmodernism has contributed to post-truth, they are not exactly the same, however. The post-truth is more dangerous than postmodernism. While postmodernism is generally used by oppressed minorities and their intellectuals/politicians, post-truth is used by the majority community and its intellectuals/politicians. Also, unlike postmodernism, to the extent that the post-truth mindset at all acknowledges objective truth, it subordinates it to personal or group preferences. That is, according to post-truthers, if evidence fits their preference (i.e. what they wish to believe), then it is well and good, but if not, then the evidence is in-admissible (Murray, 2018: 14). The post-truth mindset is like bacteria that have mutated to become immune to anti-biotics. We can combat postmodern bacteria with the aid of truth, logic and evidence, but these tools seem powerless to arrest post-truth's infectiousness (Murray, 2018: 14–15).

Political domination by fascistic forces, which are growing stronger in liberal democracies such as the US and India, requires the rejection of truth by ordinary people. It is interesting that according to postmodernism, 'If there are many perspectives [on an issue or a fact], then insisting that we accept any particular one is a form of fascism' (McIntyre, 2018: 126). In other words, according to postmodernism, insisting on objectivity – which effectively amounts to being anti-postmodernism – would be fascistic. But, as we see below, being fascistic is a trait of post-truthers who are directly or indirectly inspired by

---

23 Intelligent Design Creationists reject the naturalism of modern science in favor of a pre-modern supernaturalist worldview. An irony is that they try to advance their premodern view by adopting (if only tactically) a radical postmodern perspective (Pennock, 2010).

postmodernism. 'Post-truth amounts to a form of ideological supremacy, whereby its practitioners try to compel someone to believe in something whether there is good evidence for it or not. And this is a recipe for political domination' (McIntyre, 2018: 13). 'Part of what fascist politics does is get people to disassociate from reality'. Fascist intellectuals and politicians get common people accept a 'fantasy version of reality, usually a nationalist narrative about the decline of the country' and consequently, about 'the need for a strong leader to return it to greatness, and from then on their anchor isn't the world around them – it's the leader' (Stanley, 2018). Commenting on the 2021 storming of the US Capitol by right-wing forces, Timothy Snyder, a Professor of history at Yale University,[24] says: 'In its philosophy, post truth restores precisely the fascist attitude to truth' whereby 'Fascists despise small truths of daily existence and preferred creative myths to history or journalism' (Snyder, 2017: 71). The whole phenomenon of alternative facts and post-factuality is pretty familiar to the 1920s fascist situation about which Orwell had written this: 'It is quite possible that we are descending into an age in which two and two will make five when the Leader says so. Mr. [Bertand] Russell points out that the huge system of organized lying upon which the dictators depend keeps their followers out of contact with reality and therefore tends to put them at a disadvantage as against those who know the facts' (Orwell, 1939).

## 4 Post-truth's Political Implications and Fascistic Tendencies

Ideas, true or false, are always connected to objective interests and have practical implications. Lenin famously (1908b) said: 'There is a well-known saying that if geometrical axioms affected human interests attempts would certainly be made to refute them'. Truth – or its absence – has political/practical implications. Post-truth-ism serves the right-wing political agenda.

Fascists are always telling a story about a glorious past that has been lost, and they tap into this nostalgia. The power of such a narrative comes from the fact that while 'the truth is messy and complex, and the mythical story is always clear and compelling and entertaining. It's hard to undercut that with facts' (Stanley, 2018). Post-truth's vision is indeed very similar to the central premise of the fascist vision of the 1920s. The rule of law presupposes facts, and

---

24    Snyder is the author of the book *On Tyranny*, which is about America's turn toward authoritarianism and what is to be done about this.

democracy presupposes the rule of law, so without facts there will be no rule of law or democracy (Snyder quoted in Illing, 2017).

Kakutani (2018) says that the absence of commonly agreed-on facts (as opposed to so-called alternative facts) is not conducive to rational debate over policies or to the evaluation of specific leaders for political office, nor does such absence help citizens to hold elected officials accountable. So, without truth, democracy – the opposite of Far Right politics – is endangered. In the post-truth era, the art of lying is shaking the very foundations of democratic politics, and, it thus supports authoritarianism (D'Ancona, 2017; see also Baron, 2018).

In fascistic conditions, authoritarianism from the top is (unevenly) combined with authoritarian conduct/thinking from below (i.e., on the part of common people who includes segments of the working class, lumpen proletarians and distressed small-scale producers). This is how the post-truth phenomenon works too. Ordinary people believe in lying even if it leads to authoritarian politics. Tesich writes the following about America, where right-wingers are gaining ground:

> We [Americans] are rapidly becoming prototypes of a people that totalitarian monsters could only drool about in their dreams. All the dictators up to now have had to work hard at suppressing the truth. We, by our actions, ... have freely decided that we want to live in some post-truth world.
>
> quoted in KREITNER, 2016

In the context of the 2021 storming of the US Capitol by right-wing forces, Snyder (2021) writes:

> When we give up on truth, we concede power to those with the wealth and charisma to create spectacle in its place. Without agreement about some basic facts, citizens cannot form the civil society that would allow them to defend themselves. ... Post-truth wears away the rule of law and invites a regime of myth. ... Truth is to be replaced by spectacle, facts by faith.

Fake news makes us doubt if any source can be trusted. 'Once we don't know what to believe any more, we can be exploited: perhaps true propaganda comes later ... because we already know who is in charge' (McIntyre, 2018: 117). In post truth politics, a supreme leader (along with a coterie around them) presents themselves as 'the single source of truth' and any information that is critical of

them is dubbed by them as 'fake news' (Nazis' lying press'), or worse, as ideas
that are created by the elitist 'enemies of the people'.

## 5      Conclusion

The post-truth phenomenon, or simply, post-truth, is when one consciously
lies for a political or ideological purpose, and where how one feels about a
matter is more important than what empirical evidence or reason says about
it. Post-truth is on a spectrum which includes: simple ignorance; falsehood;
willful ignorance and lying. Post-truth not only privileges feelings over facts
but also does it reject objectivity truth. It is very critical of experts and scientists. Postmodernism is a precursor to post-truth which is turn associated with
the right-wingers (Far Right).

For a rational person, thinking must be based on reason and evidence.
The right-wingers avoid conducting any serious thinking that is based on reason and evidence. Hitler said that broad masses of a nation readily fall victims to the 'big lie' than to the small lie as they would not believe that one
could deliberately distort the truth so much. In the hands of the powerful,
the post-truth technique goes beyond winning votes or dealing with political
foes (Bhadrakumar, 2019). It has a sinister effect: it disorients and destabilises
people, destroying their capacity to make judgments and turns them into play-
things of power, so post-truth is regarded as the harbinger of a new totalitarianism (ibid.). Once again, as Snyder says, post-truth is pre-fascism. So 'maybe
fake news is merely an early tactic, whose purpose is to soften us up for what
comes later' (McIntyre, 2018: 117).

# CHAPTER 6

# Towards a Marxist Theory of the Post-truth Condition

## 1    Introduction

It is important to ask: where has the post-truth condition – the massive scale of lying for the ideological and political purpose that we see today – come from? The aim of this chapter is to explain the post-truth phenomenon in terms of the mechanisms of class society, especially, the contradiction-ridden capitalist economy and capitalist politics.

Lying is a relatively universal phenomenon, of course. But lying has a specific connection to class contradiction. As a part of culture, lying is shaped by its material conditions in all forms of class society, pre-capitalist and capitalist. Reasons for lying in pre-capitalist class society and in capitalism are similar and different. In both forms of society, class relations prompt the need for ideological-political lying, and the latter helps reproduce the class relations. In pre-capitalist society, the under-development of productive forces caused by pre-capitalist class relations, and consequent development of religious mythology, are a source of lying. Capitalist societies, especially, during the progressive stage of capitalism, have fought against religious mythology, but have also refined the technique of secular (non-religious) lying. There are definite reasons for this. Capitalism has certain contradictions (including one between political 'equality' and economic inequality, and contradiction between capital and labour), the justification for which requires lying. Capitalism develops into imperialism, which also requires justification through lying. If capitalism inherently produces conditions which are a threat to life and to the life-supporting environment, and if these conditions must be *at least* regulated by the state, such regulation will hurt the capitalist class. This means that regulation must be resisted. To do this, the relevant scientifically-established facts that support regulation must be denied. So, lying is resorted to.

Just because there is a structural need for lies, a need that is created by the contradictions of capitalism and imperialism and by the capitalist state, does not explain how lies are produced and disseminated. Capitalists (and capitalist politicians) have specific strategies in which they produce lies. Production of lies requires a network of liars and an enterprise of lying. Lies have become a capitalist commodity produced for profit. Capitalism also produces opportunities – via capitalist media – whereby lies could be spread and magnified. The media (social media or conventional media) that spreads lies is itself a capitalist commodity.[1] While capitalism needs lies and produces means of lying, why do common people accept the lies? One answer is that lying has become an opium in their lives over which they have limited control. If capitalism is behind the massive political lying – post-truth – that we are experiencing, this conclusion points to the fact that only socialism can gradually create conditions for a truthful public sphere, where the structural need for ideological-political lying ceases to exist.

The remainder of this chapter is split into 8 sections. The next section (section 2) briefly discusses some existing views on lying, and critiques them. It then presents some ideas about the relatively universal character of lying. Among other things, this section lays the foundation of treating lying as a class phenomenon. The successive sections deal with lying in relation to capitalism.

Section 3 discusses the political lying, or the post-truth condition, as a justification for the foundational contradictions of capitalism as well as the contradictions of capitalism that concern the 'negative' use-values that happen to be produced under capitalism. Section 4 discusses imperialism, a major capitalist contradiction, as the source of political lying. Section 5 shows how the capitalists' need to avoid any regulation of their activities makes them resort to lies (including the lies that are used in the process of lobbying which is illegal bribing) about the facts that support the need for regulation. Capitalists (and politicians) devise specific strategies to produce lies; capitalist production of lies requires liars, a network of liars and an enterprise of lying. This is the topic of section 6. How capitalism uses the media to disseminate lies is the focus of section 7. Section 8 explains why common people believe the lies told by politicians. The last section summarizes this chapter and the last chapter.

## 2    Historical Materialism and Political Lying

According to some, the failure of institutions/authorities that defend truth forms the social basis of the post-truth era (D'Ancona, 2017: 36). 'If we lose the institutions that produce facts that are pertinent to us, then we tend to wallow in attractive abstractions and fictions' (Snyder, 2021). Dudiak (2022), a Christian philosopher, says that post-truth is because of 'a deeper breakdown

---

1    Elon Musk bought Twitter for $44 billion in October 2022. *The New York Times* writes: 'The world's richest man closed his blockbuster purchase of the social media service, thrusting Twitter into a new era' (Conger and Hirsch, 2022).

of social trust' (vii). People trust their guts and intuition and personal preferences rather than any outside authority's attempts to provide us with the truth,
so my truth is as valid as any other's, and that lack of shared trust on the part
of a society in the authorities causes many to question the validity of truth
altogether (ibid.: 5). Thus, post truth is not only because of the collapse of trust
in the institutions that defend truth but also because of an inadequate conception of truth itself. In another explanation, 'A certain number of people seem
to hold views not because they think the evidence supports them, but because
they feel that professing a belief in them can serve as an expression of group
allegiance and loyalty' (Davis, 2018: XXVI). Then there are explanations that
blame the post-truth politics on the Far Right. Here the idea is that Far Right
politicians lie, and spread false ethno/religious nationalist claims, to get votes.

   In a slightly different approach, but one that is not unconnected to the idea
about the inadequate conception of truth mentioned above, *the current crisis in truth is said to be the effect of an impoverished sense of truth*' (Dudiak,
2022: 9). Dudiak says that one meaning of truth is faithfulness. When one says
at the wedding 'I pledge you my troth' [I promise you my truth], it means that 'I
will be faithful to you'. When we say X is our true friend, we mean X is a faithful
friend. Truth as faithfulness is broader than truth as facts. When we promise
to be faithful, it is not a fact: it is not about what is the case but about what is
not yet the case. '[R]educing truth to facts at the expense of an idea of truth
that includes the idea of faithfulness ... is the impoverishment of truth that lies
behind our current crisis in truth, and that therefore lies behind the post-truth
era' (Dudiak, 2022: 13–14). Truth as facts is a sub-category of truth as faithfulness. Truth as facts is one kind of faithfulness, the faithfulness of a statement
of fact to the facts themselves (p. 14).

   These (inter-related) explanations of the post-truth politics do capture certain aspects of the contemporary condition with respect to the commitment to
truth. But they are inadequate. Their basic assumption, which is problematic,
is that we can understand politics (or culture) mainly in terms of political (and
cultural) processes. When economic mechanisms are discussed (for example,
how specific companies and institutions promote lies, the analysis is at the
level of the *parts* of society rather than society *as a whole*, in terms of its driv-
ing logics). We need explanations of the post-truth era that are less idealistic
and that do not explain the post-truth phenomenon merely in political terms,
or in terms of the action of this or that businessperson, or merely in terms of
a cultural attitude, i.e., an impoverishment of the concept of truth. Post-truth
is a *systemic* issue: society-wide objective mechanisms need to be unpacked.
A dialectical approach is needed that unpacks both economic and political

mechanisms, and their internal connections, and that shed light on the contradictions of the system.

In *Capital* volume 1, Marx makes a significant point about the political and the cultural life of people. He begins with the idea that in certain time periods (e.g., the Middle Ages and ancient times), politics and religion, and not 'material interests', are said to reign supreme. But then, he says that '[T]he middle ages could not live on Catholicism, nor the ancient world on politics. On the contrary, it is the mode in which' people living in these societies 'gained a livelihood that explains why here politics, and there Catholicism, played *the chief part*' (Marx, 1887: 9; italics added). For Marx, indeed, 'the economic structure of society ... is the real basis on which the juridical and political superstructure is raised and to which definite social forms of thought correspond' and for him, 'the mode of production determines the character of the social, political, and intellectual life generally' (ibid. 58). Of course, the political and the cultural processes react back on the economic. The major reason for the post-truth phenomenon, I will argue, is the crisis of bourgeois economy and politics.

Lying has a universal character. But like everything that is universal, it has a historically specific social form. As a fact of life, lying exists in pre-class and class societies. And the nature of lying also changes between the forms of class society (e.g., pre-capitalist society vs capitalist society). So, lying as a part of culture is influenced by universal conditions of human existence (e.g., biological struggle for existence) and by the conditions that characterize all class societies. Lying is also influenced by the qualities of specific forms of class society (e.g., capitalism).

Lying is observed in the animal world: 'Animals ... show cunning and deceive others in the struggle for existence' (Trotsky, 1973: 247). Lying is resorted to by human beings at all stages of their social evolution. Lying is indeed 'older than class society': '[a] considerable part was played by deceit ... in the life of primitive tribes [communities]', a fact that stemmed 'more or less directly from the zoological struggle for existence' (ibid.). But the nature of lying changed with the emergence of class society: 'from the time when ... class society appeared, lying became frightfully complicated' (ibid.). This is in the sense that 'it became a social function, was refracted along class lines, and also entered into the body of human "culture." ibid.). So, 'Lying [or]... deceit is [or becomes] not merely an individual sin but a function of the social order' (ibid.). 'Lying is a method of struggle, and consequently is derived from the contradiction between interests. The fundamental contradictions result from relations between classes' (ibid.).

In pre-capitalist class societies, given their limited knowledge about the natural and social worlds and given the limited development of productive forces, there were widespread superstition, magical thinking, irrationalism. The use of religious mythology had a powerful influence on people's thinking and action:

> The highest expression of serf-owning ideology is religion. The internal relations of feudal-monarchical society were based on blind tradition and were elevated into the form of religious myths. Myths are imagined, false interpretations of natural phenomena and social institutions and the connections between them.
>
> TROTSKY, 1973: 247

The interesting thing about pre-capitalist myths is that both those who lie and those who are lied to believe in the lies: that is, 'not only the deceived, ... the oppressed masses, but also those in whose name the deception was carried out, the rulers, mostly believed in the myths, and were honestly guided by them'[2] (ibid.).

Capitalism fought against the feudal era superstition and lying. In its heydays, capitalism *was* indeed a progressive mode of production. 'The bourgeoisie, wherever it has got the upper hand, has put an end to all feudal, patriarchal, idyllic relations. ... It has drowned the most heavenly ecstasies of religious fervour' (Marx and Engels, 1848: 15). Under the bourgeois rule, 'All fixed, fast-frozen relations, with their train of ancient and venerable prejudices and opinions, are swept away, all new-formed ones become antiquated before they can ossify' (ibid.: 16).

To expand market and to increase profit, capitalism needed the development of technologies which demanded the development of scientific knowledge and attitude. According to a historian, Mary Poovey, commercial practice was essential to increasing value assigned to verifiable information (D'Ancona, 2017: 101). As just suggested above, capitalism did weaken the force of the lies and the mistaken beliefs.[3] That process helped reproduce the pre-capitalist

---

2  'Only in proportion as social relations become more complicated – that is, as the bourgeois order develops and religious mythology comes into ever-greater contradiction with it – does religion become a source of greater and greater trickery and deliberate deception' (ibid. 247–248).

3  Capitalism weakened these and other qualities of pre-capitalist societies a little less comprehensively than Marx at times thought: to him, unlike the pre-capitalist times, the bourgeois epoch is characterized by 'uninterrupted disturbance of all social conditions, everlasting uncertainty and agitation,' so much so that 'ancient and venerable prejudices and opinions ... are swept away, all new-formed ones become antiquated before they can ossify' (Marx and Engels, 1848: 16). I would say that these *are*, of course, the tendencies emanating from the structure of the relations of capitalism and attendant economic development, but that the actual outcomes of the operation of these tendencies 'are not characterized by the finality

forms of exploitation and subjugation of the masses. But lies and mistaken beliefs are also needed to help reproduce the capitalist form of class rule. So, capitalism, and especially, in its more developed stage, has been conducive to lying and an anti-science attitude. Why? There are several reasons for this, all of which concern the contradiction-ridden capitalist system.

## 3 Contradictions of Capitalism

### 3.1 *Fundamental Contradictions*

All inegalitarian and exploitative regimes rely on certain ideological techniques. One is lying, or deliberately making claims that are totally or mainly false. Lies are a tool to get common people to accept the contradictions that capitalism necessarily creates. Some of the contradictions are fundamental: they are essential to the very existence of capitalism and to its functioning, if not to the effects of its existence and functioning.

Capitalist social relations tend to further the development of productive forces in a systematic manner. This creates a necessary condition for the elimination of nature-imposed scarcity and of avoidable suffering. Yet, the majority of humanity suffer as they are deprived of one or more of the things that they need such as food, shelter, healthcare, transit, etc., while a small minority (top 1-10%) enjoys the wealth created by the majority's labour (mainly in the form of wage-labour but also in the form of non-exploitative self-employed labour). People also suffer because of the contradiction between capitalist social relations and the development of productive forces. On a regular basis, capitalist social relations of production and exchange fetter the further development of productive forces. Production and exchange as well as investment in productive sectors slow down causing unemployment and low wages, etc. A particular form of the contradiction between capitalist relations and the development of productive forces is expressed in the long-term tendency towards the average rate of profit to fall relative to the rate of exploitation, which happens due to the faster rise in the organic composition of capital; a fall in profitability, that is *expressed as* the crisis of over-production or over-accumulation, slows down investment, and consequently employment and wealth production, etc.

---

that is suggested here by Marx' (Das, 2022b: 222). There are indeed residues (or remnants) from the past that are combined with modern capitalist development and social relations as the latter exist in specific times and places. But overall, 'capitalist culture dominates pre-capitalist (type) culture' (ibid.). So one might say that the capitalist culture of lying tends to dominate the pre-capitalist culture of lying, within modern capitalist society.

(Roberts, 2016). To resolve the problem of profit, capitalism resorts to austerity and to globalization, the adverse outcomes of which must be justified through lying, as we will see below (Closely connected to globalization is imperialism, a fundamental contradiction of capitalism, which is dealt with in a separate section).

Lying is a specific example of non-transparent action, which partly or fully hides the reality by producing mistaken appearances and wrong ideas. Yet, capitalist production is the most non-transparent act: even if workers are paid at the value of their labour power (i.e. even if workers are paid a wage that allows them to meet their average needs), capitalists appropriate a part of the net product that they produce in the form of surplus value, without any necessity for extra-economic coercion and without any law (of exchange, etc.) being violated. Yet, capitalism has to be presented as non-exploitative, and capitalist wealth is seen as produced by capitalists, by their hard labour, by their ability to save and to innovate, and so on. The wealth that is socially produced by the cooperation of labour (i.e., the large majority of humanity) is treated as individual wealth in the hands of the capitalist class which is seen as wealth producer. People are free to work for one property-owner today and another property-owner tomorrow. This freedom did not exist before capitalism and is therefore a positive trait of capitalism. Yet, people are generally not free not to work for a wage for the capitalist class, which controls a large part of common people's working life (through its control over the workplace). People are also not free to demand that they take home the product of their own labour after deductions for social expenses. In spite of the contrary appearance, the capitalist class also controls a large part of people's life at home (in the sphere of reproduction), through its control over what they consume and how. Yet, on the basis of lies, capitalism is presented as a society of freedom (and socialism is counterposed to freedom). Further, capitalism is about the production of commodities for sale for profit. But capitalists produce things for profit, including education, healthcare, transport, etc., which *can be* alternatively produced by the state on a non-profit basis. So, lies must be told that the production of these things by the state and the state making them available to people for free or at a subsidized rate are necessarily inefficient and ultimately against the interests of people.

In bourgeois-democratic countries, people are led to believe that everyone is equal and that through their freedom to buy and sell, they can be whatever they want to be, but there is actually a massive economic inequality, including between capitalists and workers. All individuals are equal in the political sphere, i.e., before the law and the state. But this supposed equality contradicts real 'inequality' in the economic sphere, society's productive resources are concentrated in the hands of a few who control the lives of the vast majority.[4] Lies are objectively necessary to make common people ignore this contradiction between the content of the exploitative capitalist economy and its democratic political shell or form.

> Developed bourgeois ideology is rationalistic and directed against mythology. The radical bourgeoisie tried to get on without religion and to build a state upon reason, not tradition. This was expressed in democracy with its principles of liberty, equality, and fraternity. Capitalist economy, however, created a monstrous contradiction between everyday reality and democratic principles. In order to make up for these contradictions, higher-grade lying was needed. Nowhere is there such political lying as in bourgeois democracies.
>
> TROTSKY, 1973: 248[5]

But such lying is not necessarily of the religious or mythological type. Of course, the latter type of lying *is* resorted to (see the next chapter), which points to an uneven and combined development of a culture of lying whereby religious/mythological lies coexist with, and support, more secular (non-religious) type lies about the nature of the existing political-economic system:

> This [lying] is now not the objective "lying" of mythology, but consciously organized deception of the people by means of a combination of methods of exceptional complexity. The technique of lying is cultivated no less than the technology of electricity. The most lying press is found in the most "developed" democracies, in France and the United States.
>
> ibid.

---

4  I am not suggesting here that in a class society, including capitalism, there can ever be equality between property-owning exploiters and property-less direct producers, in a *qualitative* sense, i.e. in terms of the logic of production, control over property, the power of property-owners to appropriate surplus labour, their control over the state, and so on. Of course, the actual quantity of surplus appropriated, or of concessions from the state, can change from time to time and from place to place, partly due to the impact of class struggle. However, the fact that such a quantitative diminution of surplus appropriation or increase in state support *can* at times happen *within* the logic of capitalism is made use of to produce lies not only about the possibility of good capitalism, which is variously seen as 'democratic capitalism', 'conscious capitalism', etc. (Tomasi, 2014; Mackey and Sisodia, 2013) but also about the supposedly pro-people character of lesser evil parties (e.g. Democratic party in the US).

5  'Political Freedom without economic equality is a pretense, a fraud, a lie; and the workers want no lying' (Bakunin, 1870).

This sort of contradictions at the heart of capitalism – the contradictions that are not about the *excesses* of the system (e.g. wages falling much below the value of labour power) but that define the *essence* of the system as a whole – cannot be resolved within capitalism: basic interests of capitalists (and allied large landowners) and those of common people (workers and small-scale producers, including the peasantry) are fundamentally incompatible, given the two opposed class positions (Das, 2017a). Lies must be told to imply that these contradictions do not exist, or that they are being, or can be, significantly and durably resolved on the basis of: liberal democracy protecting the right to capitalist private property (as a human right), adequate state regulation (and/or conscientious actions of some ethically responsible businesspeople).

There is capitalism and there are its consequences (e.g., suffering). Lies have to be also told and mistaken claims must be deliberately made to minimize the extent of suffering: consider how farmers' suicide, hunger deaths, poverty-count, Covid-19 deaths, etc. are all deliberately under-estimated. Governments knowingly under-report the actual deaths from these events.

Capitalism as a whole is justified on the basis of the lie that it is in line with human nature or human condition (it is human nature to buy and sell and to be selfish, to own private productive property etc.), that capitalism is the only guarantee of freedom, that capitalism is a free society, that it believes in the power and dignity of the individual and that it ultimately promotes environmental sustainability, whereas socialism is against human nature as such, is inherently anti-democratic and totalitarian and is destructive of the environment. While lies must be constantly told to help reproduce class rule, capitalism must also make use of science to develop the productive forces in order to increase the efficiency of production and exchange and to increase the rate of exploitation, among other things. So, the political culture of lying must attack science too because the scientific temper is against lying (as we will see below) even science is in the immediate economic interest of capitalists.

### 3.2    'Conjunctural' Contradictions

Apart from the fundamental contradictions that characterize capitalism as a whole as noted above, there are other contradictions of capitalism that are more conjunctural and that concern the 'negative' use-values produced. The justification for these contradictions also requires lying.[6] Common people

---

6  On an excellent discussion on the various contradictions of capitalism, see Harvey (2014). But he does not treat these contradictions from the standpoint of their political implications, i.e., from the standpoint of the ruling class need for covering them up. So, Harvey's approach is more objectivist than materialist. I will return to this in the last chapter.

earn money to buy the things they need, so the things they buy (e.g., food, shelter, software, etc.) have intrinsic use-value. In contrast, capitalists invest money to produce commodities for sale to make more money. The usefulness of the commodities is not capitalists' intrinsic interest. For capitalists, commodities are important primarily *because* they bear exchange value. Their primary purpose is not to produce commodities to meet their own or other people's needs. In *Capital Volume 1*, Marx (1887: 107) says: 'The capitalist knows that all commodities, however scurvy they may look, or however badly they may smell, are in faith and in truth money, ... and what is more, a wonderful means whereby out of money to make more money'. But capitalists end up producing commodities that are *harmful* to individuals and to society even if the production of such commodities (negative use-values) benefits only the capitalists who produce them, and not the whole capitalist system. There are at least four categories of these commodities.

a)     Some capitalists produce commodities that are needed by people but are produced in such a way that they are more harmful than they are said to be, so lies must be told that there is nothing wrong with these commodities. Consider the medicines and vaccines that are more unsafe and/or inefficacious than advertised (Das, 2014: Chapter 9). Here what is in doubt is not the scientific method itself but the corruption of that method in the hands of profit-seeking capitalists. Similarly, capitalists produce food that is not healthy but lies must be told to suggest that they are. Capitalists also produce unsafe houses which result in much avoidable harm, including deaths. When an earthquake happens, lies must be told to suggest that deaths are due to a natural event even if it is the case that an earthquake, like a pandemic, *is* a natural event, but its effects on human lives is anything but natural.

Capitalism has been known for cutting costs at the expense of workers' health and wellbeing (Das, 2022f). This tendency has been particularly strong under neoliberal austerity and globalization. To temporarily resolve the problem of falling rate of profit, austerity – including de-regulation of business activities and reduction of welfare benefits – has been resorted to domestically and internationally (economic globalization). If, in order to cut costs and increase profit, houses are constructed by capitalist enterprises with scant regards towards the necessary safety measures, which is what happens when austerity is in place,[7] there will be many avoidable deaths when an earthquake strikes.

---

7    To the extent that some safety rules *are* in place, politicians/officers look the other way as they get a share of the above-average profit through secret deals with capitalists.

Similarly, if the necessary healthcare is not in place to treat the victims because capitalists impose austerity, then there will be many avoidable deaths when a pandemic hits. The effects of austerity get worse under economic globalization, which effectively is a euphemism for the spread of capitalist market relations and logic to all parts of the world. Globalization, which causes a race to the bottom in terms of labour condition, living standards and environmental quality, etc., is presented as a process that would benefit all from rising prosperity. Yet, globalization has brought or intensified absolute or relative poverty and inequality (Rodrik, 2012; Stiglitz, 2018). The facts advanced in defense of globalization are half-truths.

Austerity (along with globalization) is, as mentioned, a response to the contradiction between the 'expected' (or average) rate of profit and the actual (low) rate of profit, a contradiction that is due to a fundamental contradiction between capitalist social relations and the development of productive forces under those relations. And austerity as a contradiction in turn results in the 'contradiction' surrounding its outcomes – i.e., 'contradiction' between, say, the number of actual deaths and the number of un-avoidable deaths (the deaths that can be attributed to a natural event at the current level of economic development, and assuming that state intervention is as good as it can be in any form of society). Therefore, political lying must be used to justify this contradiction.

Such lying takes four forms. The first two are naturalization and under-estimation, as already mentioned.[8] The third is individualization: if poor people consume unsafe food, etc., society falsely blames them for their lack of judgement, bad habits, etc. The fourth is superstition: when people feel powerless in the face of these events, to get illusory relief, they voluntarily resort to superstitions (e.g., worshipping deities) or they believe in lies (Covid-19 is not a serious threat or that it is going to end soon), and this is encouraged by Far Right post-truth politicians.

b)   Capitalism produces means of subsistence (e.g., food and shelter, etc.) and means of production (e.g., tractors to produce food). The third type of commodity is arms (and luxuries). Arms are not items of consumption to meet any individual need: people cannot eat bullets or tanks. And arms generally are not used to make things that people need. Thus, arms are neither means of subsistence nor means of production. They are simply means of destruction: the destruction of the means of subsistence

---

8   Naturalization is when earthquakes, pandemics, etc. are seen as purely natural events and/or as the outcomes of the wrath of gods, etc. Under-estimation refers to the under-estimation of the extent of suffering.

(e.g., food, shelter, roads, etc.) and of the means of production (e.g., factories, etc.) and of human lives. Money is spent on arms production *at the expense of* the spending that can directly meet the needs of people. The contradiction between welfare spending and military spending is resolved in favour of the latter in the interests of the imperialist countries' military industrial complex and in the interests of their capitalist class as such (especially, the monopolies); the interests of these monopolies are in the general conditions (e.g. access to natural resources, markets and cheap labour, etc. in foreign countries) for capitalist accumulation at the world-scale. So, lies need to be constantly told that increased funding for the military-industrial complex is good *for the nation*, and concomitantly, lies need to be told that the situation with respect to the working, living, and environmental conditions within the nation are nothing much to worry about. Lies are manufactured about the threat to national security when in fact there is none or none that people need to worry about. Lies are also told by imperialist governments that they go to war to save democracy and national sovereignty in other countries (more on this below).

c)    A by-product of all forms of production, capitalist or not, is a certain amount of environmental damage.[9] This by-product is controllable to various degrees in all societies. Under capitalism, there is an excessive amount of environmental damage. Environmental damage is a class issue: the problem is basically caused by the competitive pursuit of profit at the expense of environmental quality which in turn adversely affects human lives and livelihood (Das, 2018). But to hide the class character of the environmental damage, it must be falsely attributed to excessive population growth or a large size of the population (Oreskes, 2023), or to the normal process of economic development or industrialization (which is often described as *human* action, abstracted from its capitalist form), and so on. A most important form of environmental damage is climate breakdown (or, global warming). Its level has now reached life-threatening proportion. It requires a massive amount of lying to hide its true magnitude and class-origin. Indeed, against all scientific evidence, climate change is denied, or when its existence is not denied, its anthropogenic origin is denied, and when its anthropogenic origin is

---

9   In capitalism, even the environmental damage and the strategy of mitigating it have been commodified, as the introduction of carbon markets indicates.

not denied, its 'capitalocenic' origin is denied or under-emphasized.[10] Big lies are manufactured to paper over the fundamental contradictions between capitalism and nature. (I will have more to say about this later below).

d)   Then there are certain commodities used by individuals that *are* inherently harmful to their active or passive users and yet their harmful character is hidden on the basis of deliberate lies. Tobacco (or cigarettes) is a prime example. These commodities are different from food and shelter, etc.: food and shelter are not inherently unsafe but are *made* unsafe, given the competitive pursuit of profit. These commodities (e.g., tobacco) are also different from, say, arms which are not for individual consumption. Because the commodities such as tobacco are harmful, post-truthers must deny science to tell lies to make people believe that they are not after all bad for health. I will have more to say about this below.

## 4    Contradictions of Capitalist Imperialism

Imperialism, as a fundamental contradiction of capitalism in its advanced stage, is a significant fact (Lenin, 1977), even if there is a tendency among some Marxists to deny its significance because of the flow of capital across the world.[11] It represents a major contradiction of advanced capitalism: the contradiction between the globalized character of capitalist economy (accumulation) and nation-state centric political framework of capitalism. In other words, the development of productive forces under capitalism has spilled over the nation-state boundaries. That imperialism leads to predatory wars (including in their proxy form) is also a fact. Imperialist exploitation leads to suffering of the masses in the South. Imperialism-driven wars cause suffering both in imperialist and imperialized nations. So imperialist economic actions (e.g., economic sanctions) and wars are justified on entirely false ground. The idea propagated in the West that Russia began its special military operation in

---

10   While the concept of 'Anthropocene' recognizes human beings as a geological force with a massive impact on the natural environment, this concept does not treat human action in its capitalistic form which is the main 'anthropocenic' reason for destructive environmental changes, including climate breakdown. So, scholars such as Moore (2016; 2017) have correctly suggested naming the current epoch as the 'Capitalocene'.

11   There is also a mistaken analysis of imperialism which describes countries such as Russia as imperialist, when in fact it is a low-income country that relies on export of natural resources (King, 2021; Roberts, 2022).

Ukraine unprovoked.[12] It is also widely believed that Russia's aggression represents a battle between what is called a rules-based order, and one that is governed by brute force, is a lie (Damon, 2022). One must ask: whose rules, and when has the US refrained from using force when using force is in its interest? One must ask: what changes have been happening in Ukraine since 2014 and what role has western imperialism played in these? The Ukraine war (which, more or less, is or has become a proxy war by the US-led NATO against Russia) is falsely justified on the ground of defending democracy in, and sovereignty of, Ukraine.[13] Ukraine is a nation which is dictated to by imperialist forces. Such forces actually do not recognize sovereignty rights of any country that comes, or that is seen by imperialist powers as coming, in their way. The real motive of the decades-long engagement on the part of US/NATO forces in Ukraine and surrounding countries is their long-term goal of encircling and weakening Russia and then China, in order to gain access to the resources of the two nations, and to remove them as commercial and geopolitical competitors by balkanizing them (Black, 2022). Lies need to be told to hide this naked truth. The cost of the lies are the entirely avoidable deaths and suffering in the war zones, including in Ukraine, where common people, as elsewhere, are interested in a decent livelihood and peace rather than in war. Similarly, Iraq had no weapons of mass destruction, but Iraq has/had a very important commodity: oil. As well, Iraq's threat to bypass dollar in international trade in its oil was too big to be allowed to succeed. So, came the imperialist war against Iraq. This means that imperialism is creating conditions where falsehood is being treated as true. In April 2008, New York Times reported that many retired generals, who were paid employees of the military industrial complex or of the state, said that Iraq war going on fine, when it was not. They appeared on TV as independent commentators, but they were a part of the state's propaganda war (Oreskes and Conway, 2011 243). When China is perceived by imperialist powers as a threat to them because of its massive economic success (in terms of economic growth/development, technological progress, and success in poverty alleviation) enabled by its state playing an active role, including protecting the domestic economy to some extent from the global law of value. China

---

12    Chomsky says: 'it's quite interesting that in American discourse, it is almost obligatory to refer to the invasion as the 'unprovoked invasion of Ukraine…Of course, it was provoked. Otherwise, they wouldn't refer to it all the time as an unprovoked invasion' (quoted in Baroud, 2022).

13    During an unannounced visit to Ukraine in February 2023, Mr. Biden reaffirmed America's 'unwavering and unflagging commitment to Ukraine's democracy, sovereignty, and territorial integrity' (The White House, 2023).

is also a threat because of some of the positive consequences of its economic success such as its enormous modern military power, its resistance, however weak, against imperialism, and its wide acceptance in the Global South due to its developmental role there. So, lies are created about China, that it manipulates it currency, that it oppresses minorities (e.g., Uighurs), and so on. All this is done to create a preparatory condition for attacks on the nation in the name of democracy and human rights and in the name of a rule-based global order or liberal international order (which is, effectively, another name for America's global hegemony).[14]

An advisor to President Bush said to a commentator, Ron Suskind: there are people from 'the reality-based community' as opposed to 'the faith-based community', and the former 'believe that solutions [to society's problems] emerge from your judicious study of discernible reality'. The advisor added: 'That's not the way the world really works anymore ... We're an empire now, and when we act, we create our own reality. And while you're studying that reality – judiciously, as you will – we'll act again, creating other new realities, which you can study too, and that's how things will sort out. We're history's actors ... and you, all of you, will be left to just study what we do' (Suskind, 2004). The American empire creates its reality on the basis of force ('when we act, we create our own reality'), which is, of course, justified on the basis of lies which are in turn converted into truth by force. This is exactly how Far Right post-truth forces operate: they try to resolve their differences with democratic and left-leaning forces and with minorities by resorting to a combination of raw force and blatant lies. Thus, they engage in a process where force and lies justify, and feed into, each other.

There is another way in which capitalist imperialism creates conditions for massive political lying. We have seen that post-truth is rooted in the postmodernist doctrine of equal validity (all views on a topic are equally valid). 'Ideologically, the appeal of the doctrine of equal validity cannot be detached from its emergence in the post-colonial era. Advocates of colonial expansion often sought to justify their projects by the claim that colonized subjects stood to gain much from the superior science and culture of the West' (Boghossian, 2006: 6–7). Now, concludes Boghossian, who is a professor of philosophy, 'In a moral climate which has turned its back decisively on colonialism, it is appealing to many to say not only – what is true – that one cannot morally justify subjugating a sovereign people in the name of spreading knowledge, but that

---

14    On the rule-based international order, see Fujii, 2021; Ikenberry, 2018; Parmar, 2018; Sloss, 2022.

there is no such thing as superior knowledge only different knowledges, each appropriate to its own particular setting' (Boghossian, 2006: 6–7). This sort of ideas – i.e., equal validity doctrine – fuel post-truth politics.

## 5      Opposition to Regulation, and Capitalist Politics

If capitalism inherently produces conditions (sometimes as by-products) where there is a threat to life and to the life-supporting natural and built environments, and if these conditions can be, and must be, *at least* regulated by the state, such regulation will hurt the capitalist class. This means that regulation must be resisted, and that the market and the animal spirits operating within it must be given a free reign. To do this, the facts behind the necessity for regulation – the facts that correctly identity/describe and quantify the harmful effects of capitalism – must be denied. If facts indicate that climate change or inadequate access to healthcare causes illness and that therefore the state should act (e.g., state-provided care; state control of emissions), then those facts must be negated. The opposition to regulation characterized both the right and the center of bourgeois politics.

It is not just that contradictions of capitalist production and exchange necessitate political lying. The contradictions of the entire capitalist political system (especially, the state), also require political lying. Political lies must be told to hide the class nature of the state, including the gap between the appearance of the state as democratic and the reality which is the opposite. In this sense can one say that: the whole culture is lying everyday (Wilber, 2017: 30).

If capitalism and imperialism, both of which all bourgeois parties including those on the Far Right are wedded to, are producing conditions for politically motivated lies, then it is false to say that only Far Right is responsible for post-truth. The entire capitalist system is. It is indeed the failure of the center (liberals, left-liberals, etc.) to defend democracy and protect lives and livelihood that creates conditions for Far Right with which post-truth is most associated. Capitalism's attacks on common people's lives and livelihood lead to potential/actual opposition from masses. Those attacks require lies and deception to hide their class origin; the authoritarian response of the state to, and the need to weaken, such opposition, also require lies and deception, including those aimed to divide them along racial, religious, etc. lines.

The fact that one party (from the center or 'center-left') rules today and another party (from the Right) rules a few years later hardly makes any difference to the exercise of democratic rights of people or to their material needs being met, because the different parties are actually the different political factions (or, representatives) of the same class, the class of the bourgeoisie. This means that the capitalist state – which effectively represents the dictatorship of the bourgeoisie, misnamed as Democracy – is actually managed by *one* party.[15] When all parties have turned themselves into peddlers of policies in the service of (neoliberal) capitalism (and of imperialism), there is a need for a party – a faction of a party of the bourgeois dictatorship – that distinguishes itself from others. It is necessary therefore to manufacture (demagogic) lies to tell the voter that Party x is better than Party y and that Party x will do many good things (e.g., massive increase in employment; eliminating corruption; substantial increase in farmers' income, etc.) when in fact it has no intention of doing any such thing. The right-wing – as a relatively newcomer in the history of bourgeois politics in the post-1950s period seeking to displace or undermine the 'democratic' factions of the bourgeoisie – for example, says that 'our party is different from that party', when in fact the right-wing party and the other bourgeois parties are, more or less, equally pro-business and pro-imperialist.

The fundamental interests of the masses (the majority) are in a good life and livelihood; their interests are need-based. The fundamental interests of capitalists are in the endless pursuit of wealth in its abstract form (i.e., money for the sake of money) and in the reproduction of a political order that ensures this. There is a definite incompatibility – i.e., contradiction – between the fundamental interests of the masses and those of the capitalist class (and its allied managers of the state, i.e., politicians, etc.). This contradiction in turn means that there is a long-term tendency towards the failure of capitalism and its state (whether it is managed by one party or multiple parties) to meet the needs of the masses. This is more so when capitalism is in its terminal decline as it is now: given the recurrent economic crises, capitalism's ability to win consent by giving *material* concessions gets increasingly limited. So, there is always a need to grant non-material or ideological concessions (e.g., national pride, racial or religious supremacism, etc.) based on falsity, manufactured illusions, etc., in response to the potential for mass anger which is expressed from time to time in actual struggles of the people in support of their material needs.

There is thus a structural need to keep the masses in check by coercion and deception, including blatant and repetitive lies. The capitalist state rules, of course, ultimately, by coercion (actual or threatened). But too much coercion is expensive and can threaten its legitimacy. So, the state also resorts to consent and concession, i.e., ideological compensation or benefits such as false

---

15    In a recent poll, approximately 67% of Americans do *not* have a positive view of either of the two parties (Choi, 2022).

national pride, etc., and cheap revocable material benefits, respectively. The state indeed rules by 'deception, flattery, fine phrases, promises by the million, petty sops, and concessions of the unessential while retaining the essential' (Lenin, 1917c).

Deception, etc. are connected to political lying directly. Economic promises made are often false. When petty sops *are* given under pressure from below, they make little difference to people's lives but lies must be used to say otherwise: just as big capitalists often resort to lies to get their stock price index artificially inflated thus to exaggerate the gains to shareholders,[16] the capitalist state resorts to lies to falsely exaggerate the benefits it confers on the common people. And ideological benefits also requires lying, as just mentioned. The other side of the coin is: masses' 'unreasoning trust' in capitalists, politicians and top officials, a trust that is not based on reason and evidence and that is fueled by capitalist propaganda and lies.

Political lies are at the heart of the capitalist state. All this is normal. However, when capitalism is in deep crisis because of which its ability to win consent by giving material concessions gets increasingly limited, and when there is (consequently) excessive economic inequality, this situation fuels the emergence and strengthening of Far Right or fascistic forces. These forces acting on behalf of the sections of the capitalist oligarchy to seek to control the masses and to save the capitalist system. Lies, big lies, become a tool especially in the hands of the bourgeois-fascistic forces/politicians to a much greater extent than in the hands of the liberal center (as does physical coercion too). As Desai (2016: 20) notes:

> the possibility of fascism lurks in all capitalist societies in which mass politics has arrived. To be sure, it is not the "normal" form of capitalist rule. However, along with dictatorship – military or civilian – and "Bonapartism," it is one of the authoritarian forms of capitalist rule that have become possible and necessary for capitalism at times when existing forms of rule either no longer sufficed or were seen not to suffice.

The Nobel laureate, Harold Pinter, once said that majority of politicians are interested not in truth but in power and in the maintenance of that power.

---

16    Consider the Adani case. A report by the US-based Hindenburg Research reveals the 'brazen stock manipulation and accounting fraud' on the part of the richest Indian capitalist (Mr. Adani) and his empire that has driven up the price of the Adani companies (by as much as 85%), and inflated his net worth; the report states that this is the "biggest con in corporate history" (Barrett and Ellis-Petersen, 2023; People's Democracy, 2023).

To maintain that power -- and he should have said that their power basically serves the interests of the capitalist class -- they consider it essential that common people remain in ignorance. This means that the use of lies plays a crucial role. In his Nobel prize acceptance lecture in 2005, and this was before the term post-truth became popular, he said: "What surrounds us therefore is a vast tapestry of lies, upon which we feed" (quoted in Bhadrakumar, 2019). So capitalist governments are increasingly based on the enterprise of lying in the interests of big enterprises supported by politicians, setting the stage for post-truth politics. Indeed, by the turn of the last century, government was already less about the "truth" than about how "truths" could be spun. Not surprisingly, only 38% of Britons said they trusted the governments to place the needs of the nation above the interests of their own political party, and by 2014, this number was down to 18% (D'Ancona, 2017: 38). In the US, in 2020, barely 20% of Americans trust that their government does what is right just about always or most of the time (PEW, 2022). And governments may resort to lying to counter the declining trust in them. If, as some scholars say, the collapse of trust in the institutions that are expected to defend truth leads to post-truth, then there are obvious material reasons for that as we have seen.

## 6      Capitalist Production of Lies as a Commodity

We have seen that there is a structural need for lies, a need that is created by the contradictions of capitalism and imperialism and the capitalist state. But this fact itself does not explain how lies are produced and disseminated. We need to move from the level of class-structure to that of class-strategies or class-strategic action. Capitalists (and politicians) have specific strategies in which they produce lies. Production of lies requires liars (a network of liars) and an enterprise of lying.

*Much before* post-truth arrived, big tobacco companies recognized early on that even the most well-documented scientific claims (for instance, the claim that smoking causes cancer) could be eroded by skillful government lobbying, bullying the news media, and pursuing a public-relations campaign (Oreskes and Conway, 2011. This is a part of a wider post-truth strategy called 'tobacco strategy'[17]: keep the debate alive; and maintain controversy by fostering claims that are contrary to the mainstream scientific evidence (ibid.: 241). The industry utilized a few scientists to sow doubt about the links between smoking and

---

17     This term is not to be understood in its literal sense.

health risks by juxtaposing the scientific consensus with pure or semi-pure lies (ibid.: 6).

Consider the energy companies in the US. Their main interest is in profit, and not necessarily in denying science, but denying science (e.g., the science of climate change) is a necessary condition to maintain their profit. This explains why politicians who are supposed to make policies concerning energy to protect the environment say that the government does not need to regulate greenhouse-gas emissions: these politicians are financially supported by the energy companies (Warner, 2011). But the corruption of bourgeois democracy does not end there. The objective profit-motive behind the denial of science works along with a major subjective force, religion which is also used as a threat to science in the hands of the Far Right. To help energy or carbon companies which make money from carbon emissions, and thus to deny the science of climate change, politicians who are funded by the same carbon corporates and who are aided by some scientists who are also funded by these corporates, go against the governments regulating emissions. Politicians in the US do so by making false claims such as: 'God said the earth would not be destroyed by a flood' (Warner, 2011).

There is indeed a strong link that unites the capitalist industries producing harmful commodities, conservative thinktanks, and the scientists who are on the payroll of these industries or who receive research funding from them. This link is the defense of the market (Oreskes and Conway, 2011: 248). There is an objective logic to this. If consuming tobacco causes cancer, or indeed, if global warming is happening and if it is happening because of 'human action' under capitalism, and if the market dominated by big capitalist businesses cannot stop all this, then the state must intervene to at least regulate the capitalist market. But that cannot be allowed by capitalists, so lies must be spread by them to make people believe that there is no causal link between smoking and cancer and that global warming is not happening or that it is not anthropogenic, and so on. Similarly, imperialist wars must be defended on the basis of lies, and this requires (corporate- and/or state-sponsored) liars.

What the post-truthers are fighting for is *not* free speech as such (the idea that all sides on climate change or on smoking, etc. should be heard). Their interest is in the promotion of free markets (ibid.: 248), both within a given country and at the world-scale. The lies are propagated not just in the name of protecting the profit of companies but in the name of protecting the holy cow of the market. The fact is that in the interests of the moneybags, scientists are utilized as *merchants of doubt,* who are backed by corporate-friendly politicians. These scientists misuse the scientific method to produce their 'facts'

in support of corporate interests. They use their status as scientists to disseminate their spurious science.

The road that begins with the capitalists' fight against the regulation of markets is slippery and long. If politicians are anti-government, they are likely to
be anti-facts. They are often anti-governments *because* government action will
deprive big enterprises of profit-making opportunities.[18] The fundamental role
of politicians as state actors is to protect those opportunities, and the corporates financially support the politicians (secretively or not). Policies in support
of the big business and policies that restrict/deny benefits to common people
are effectively commodities bought and sold in the political market. If scientific
facts about smoking's relation to cancer should be negated, then why not other
facts? If these facts and those facts must be negated, the best way would be to
negate *all facts* altogether. This leads society to post-truth. Post-truthers oppose
government regulation not just because such regulation restricts the freedom of
business (to harm the freedom of society from want) but also because such regulation is seen as being against life and human freedom as such. For example,
the opposition to abortion and similar such issues can be justified on the basis
of the argument that they expand the reach of the government and therefore
against human freedom. It does not matter that those who are against abortion do not care about millions dying every year because of lack of healthcare
or proper nutrition or other essential items. There is therefore more at stake
beyond the defense of the unregulated market dominated by the big businesses.

The slippery road continues. A few corporate-funded scientists or scientists
with pro-corporate views, and post-truth politicians who deny anthropogenic
climate change under capitalism view regulations of the market 'as the slippery slope to socialism, a form of creeping communism' (Oreskes and Conway,
2011: 249). So post-truthers' resistance to truth and to objectivity is ultimately
the ideological and political *resistance* against socialism/communism, and it is
the ideological and political *defense* of capitalism. Some scientists such as Fred
Singer indeed believe that those who worry about climate change have hidden
agendas, 'not just to save the environment but to change our economic system'
and these 'coercive utopians are socialists'. (Oreskes and Conway, 2011: 249).
However, the fact that the scientists denying climate change have themselves

---

18    Their anti-government action tends to coincide with that of a large number of common
      people who see that while they pay taxes, they receive limited benefits from the govern-
      ment which is focussed on assisting big businesses, which, in turn, fatten the pockets of
      the political-bureaucratic layers.

a hidden agenda (i.e., supporting free market) is not raised by post-truthers.[19] For post-truthers: claims that support capitalism are inherently true, and claims that support the interests of people or the claims in support of socialism are not.

The slippery slope of science-denial (and the denial of the necessity for government regulation of businesses) is indeed a fact. What is called the tobacco strategy, as the broad strategy of science denial, is used by thinktanks. Consider the Discovery Institute. This Seattle-based organization advocates that 'intelligent-design theory' be taught in the public schools as balance for the 'holes' in evolutionary theory. Another is the Heartland Institute, which bills itself as 'the world's most prominent think tank promoting skepticism about man-made climate change' (McIntyre, 2015). So, science denial – which is a part of the postmodern agenda – is a precursor of post-truth, and science denial is rooted in corporate interests in the continued reproduction of capitalism and in the fight against socialism. Indeed, corporate lobbying and lying on a range of topics have influenced political positions on climate change, gun control, immigration, healthcare, as Ari Rabin-Havt says (quoted in McIntyre, 2018: 21). Science-denial is only a stop on the slippery road that today leads to post-truth (ibid.: 25).

All this points to the existence of the capitalist industry – capitalist production – of lies. Lies are indeed a profitable commodity, albeit an 'immaterial' one.[20] There is 'a growing industry that exists to create and disseminate fictitious public policy "facts" [which are actually lies] on behalf of business and ideological interests willing to pay for them'. And, 'These lies are part of a coordinated, strategic assault designed to hide the truth, confuse the public, and create controversy where none previously existed'; the goal of these lies is 'halting progress' on issues that their clients oppose wither either for financial or ideological reason (Rabin-Havt, 2016: 5–6). The industry of lies has many inter-connected players: 'lobbyists, PR companies, media lackeys, unethical "experts", and unscrupulous think tanks' (ibid.). Recognizing 'the combination

---

19    This situation is akin to the following mistaken claims. Support for capitalism is normal, while opposition to it is ideological and utopian. Democracy in capitalist society is democracy, while a socialist society is inherently dictatorship, regardless of common people exercising any amount of democracy. And, education about the ways in which capitalism works and benefits people and the environment is education, while education in Marxism, which scientifically exposes the irrationality, unjust and anti-nature character of capitalism, is just propaganda. Not only must lies be produced to make the first set of claims but also must lies be produced to refute the second.

20    One can say that lies as a capitalist commodity are produced by a form of 'immaterial labour' (on the concept of immaterial labour, see Lazzarato, 1996)

of deception and the for-profit motive', Rabin-Havt calls this industry 'Lies, Incorporated'. Those who participate in this industry make millions by manipulating public policy and helping generate billions in corporate profits (ibid.). Indeed, 'Wherever there's money to be made, there'll be someone willing to twist the truth to make it' (Phillips, 2020: 213). So, a part of modern capitalist accumulation is the accumulation by falsification, i.e., accumulation by the production and propagation of lies.

## 7       Media of Lies as Capitalist Commodity

Not only does capitalism create problems that produce the need for lies to hide the true nature of capitalist economy and the state. Not only do capitalists produce lies as a profitable commodity. Lies have to be sold too. So, capitalism produces opportunities – via capitalist media – whereby the lies could be spread and magnified.[21] The media is under commercial pressure to increase its ratings by achieving balanced reporting or balanced TV shows, by including views provided by partisans who wish to move the reporter or anchor towards falsehood. This gives undue credibility to fringe opinions: so-called balanced coverage has allowed a small group of skeptics about global warming or ancient 'history' of a nation, immigrants, etc. to have their views amplified and thus denies science and facts. 'If you make a recipe with just one rotten ingredient, the whole dish will taste rotten' (McIntyre, 2018: 84). The media has become a site for multi-billion-dollar capitalist industry of misinformation.

For serious outlets and especially, in the print media, circulation numbers are falling, and with this, revenue from sales and advertisements. 'Less money means fewer reporters, each doing more work than ever with lower budgets, making regurgitating what politicians say a much more cost-effective

---

21    The media itself produces lies and must be treated as a part of 'Lies, Incorporated' (see Chomsky, 1989; Herman and Chomsky, 2002). Of course, the capitalist media does more than lying. Various media organizations 'inculcate and defend the economic and social and political agenda of particular sectors...that dominate the domestic society', and 'they do this ... by selection of topics, by distribution of concerns, by the way they frame issues, by the way they filter information, by the way they tell lies, ...by emphasis and tone' and so on (Chomsky, 1989). Of all these ways, Chomsky says, 'the most crucial... is just the bounding of debate': that is, they say 'here's the spectrum of permissible debate, and within that you can have...great controversy, but you can't go outside it' (ibid.). Chomsky is right to stress the bounding of debate by media, i.e. the fact that it sets limits on what is possible to debate. I would add that the bounding of the debate is partly justified by lies or half-truths and mistaken assumptions about society.

proposition than digging into what they're saying' (Ball, 2017: 10). This has the following implication: 'if a story is going to be unchecked, or exaggerated, why not make it up entirely and reduce the costs even further' (Ball, 2017: 11). Since the media depends partly on state-sponsored advertisements (which often present half-truths about governments' achievements), what we hear from the media is what the state wants us to hear.

Because post-truth is (political) lying on a massive scale, it requires a 'proper' media for dissemination. In the 1920s, it was radio. Now, it is e-media, including social media, which are supported by the rise of alt-right outlets (Fox news, Infowars and Breitbart, etc. in the US, and Republic TV and other such channels in India). Never before have massive political lies been so quickly transmitted and on such a large scale as we see now. New technologies of communication, including social media can manipulate, polarise, and entrench public opinion (D'Ancona, 2017). There are now internet-created bubbles in which people live their everyday lives. These bubbles are the spaces where algorithms feed people's prejudices and misconceptions in a manner that confirms whatever they have selected for their bespoke truth (McIntyre, 2018). In social digital networks, viral media can generate and circulate information irrespective of its truth value (Peters et al., 2018). It is an ideal medium for hype, exaggeration, falsehood, lies and gossip that are characteristic of the age of post-truth (ibid.).

The Internet facilitates the spread of truth. It also enables 'the proliferation of crackpots, ideologues, and those with an ax to grind' (McIntyre, 2015). With no editorial gatekeepers to vet information, outright lies can survive on the Internet. Worse, those who embrace willful ignorance are now much more likely to find an electronic home where their marginal unscientific views are embraced (ibid.). 'The web is the definitive vector of Post-Truth precisely because it is indifferent to falsehood, honesty and the difference between the two' (D'Ancona, 2017: 53). On the whole, 'there are more and better liars today because lying is simply easier', and this is partly thanks to the modern means of communication (Manjoo, 2008: 224) that operate on the basis of private corporate profit.

## 8      Lying by the 'Victims' of Capitalism

Why do common people – victims of capitalism (workers and petty producers) – 'voluntarily' believe in the lies told by the ruling class and its politicians? Why do the masses' have an 'unreasoning trust' in capitalists, politicians and top officials, a trust that is not based on reason and evidence? There are specific reasons.

When scientists have been used by corporates to engage in bad scientific practice and transform facts into lies, and when the public realize this, their trust in science as such diminishes, thus creating a general condition of distrust of science and scientists as such. Denigration of science and experts also fuels false pride in the common sense of ordinary *people*. When jobs are disappearing, healthcare is in crisis, life appears to be out of control, lying is an imaginary source of control. As the orphanage doctor in John Irving's The Cider House Rules says: 'When you lie, it makes you feel in charge of your life ... When you lie, you feel as if you have cheated fate – your own and everybody else's' (quoted in D'Ancona, 2017: 86). Lying becomes the opium of the masses.

When none of the major political parties offers any significant and durable solution to common people's problems, if a party offers some imaginary benefit (e.g., national pride), then sections of the exploited and non-exploiting petty bourgeois layers fall for the soothing lies. One type of lies is about the past (or 'another time') and another type of lies is about 'the other', in a geographical and/or social sense – for example, that country, that religious group, etc.

When the Far Right tells people the story of a once-great society – whether it is that of ancient India, or of an America of the past that needs to be made great again – that is said to have 'been destroyed by liberalism' or by some form of socialism, this story makes, and is meant to make, 'the dominant group feel ... resentful about the loss of their status and power'. (Stanley quoted in Illing, 2017). That story fuels what Stanley calls 'politics of eternity'. The politics of eternity is 'a self-absorbed concern with the past, free of any real concern with facts. ... a longing for past moments that never really happened during epochs that were, in fact, disastrous' (ibid.). As well, 'An eternity politician seduces the populace with a vision of the past in which the nation was once great, only to be sullied by some external enemy' (e.g., immigrants or Muslims) (ibid.). Politically backward layers, irrespective of the level of formal education, fall for politics of eternity.

When the poor people of the dominant social-cultural group mistakenly identify themselves with rich people of that group on the basis of false claims about the superiority of a given race or religion, it gives them a sense of satisfaction, almost like a compensation for their objective suffering which the capitalist economic-political system and the dominant social-cultural group do little about.[22] Thus unscientific beliefs (about the other) get stronger. When

---

22    It is like the poor white people identifying themselves with rich whites for a type of compensation as Du Bois (1935) had explained: whiteness serves as a 'public and psychological wage', a kind of compensation that is delivered to poor whites, who are exploited by capitalism. The compensation comes from the poor white people's slightly better access

there is an artificially created shortage of the things that people need (in part thanks to austerity imposed by the capitalist class), the situation is falsely blamed on a given religious or immigrant or racialized minority group or an outside enemy country. The philosopher, Grayling, says that with economic inequality growing between the rich and the poor, there is a deep sense of grievance including among middle class people who have faced a long stagnation in earnings. Where there is so much economic resentment, it is not difficult to inflame emotions over issues such as immigration and to cast doubt on mainstream politicians (quoted in Coughlan, 2017). Lies, and not a commitment to truth about fellow citizens, and hatred, not a commitment to love, for fellow citizens come together. According to D'Ancona (2017), vilification of immigrants, among other issues, has been based on the power to evoke feelings of hatred and not facts (contemporary or historical). Furthermore, the dominant group is made to feel resentful and victimized on the basis of the false claim that society has followed a policy of appeasement towards minorities. All this is happening as fascistic forces are becoming more powerful.

## 9     Conclusion

We live in a world where 'we are caught between opposing forces of truth and falsehood, fact, and rumour', 'between the open platform of the web … and the gated enclosures of Facebook', and between 'an informed public and a misguided mob' (Viner, 2016). But ideas do not fly in the air. If large segments of people deny facts, science, reason and objectivity, the reason for this ultimately is in the material interests of the capitalist class and its ideological and political backers. It is ultimately capitalism that is behind the production of political lies (the phenomenon of post-truth) even if the relation between the two is mediated by many contingent factors.

The post-truth condition is one where politicians as well as laypeople, who increasingly have limited control over their lives, engage in blatant lying for their ideological and political interests. When all political parties fail to meet the needs of the masses and practice austerity to help the capitalist class resolve its contradiction (the main aim of austerity is to create the general conditions

---

to state institutions. The compensation is also psychological in the sense of a valuable social status derived from them being treated as 'not-black'. Of course, this idea about compensation to the low-income people belonging to the majority racial or ethnic or cultural group does not explain why workers from minority groups such as Blacks do fight capitalism on a regular basis *along with* their white brothers and sisters.

for increased profitability, including countering the tendency for the average rate of profit to fall), some political formation emerges that engages in lies to claim their superior electoral value. Lies must be manufactured and spread in order to naturalize and justify the problems and contradictions of capitalism, to counter any resistance to capitalism and its state, and thus to present the problems created by the capitalist system as those created by God or nature or by the actions/thinking of 'unwanted' minorities or by experts, etc. To paraphrase Trotsky (1973: 88), the culture of lying and hypocrisy of the ruling class 'develops everywhere and always as the square, or cube, of the social contradictions. Such approximately is the historic law of ideology translated into the language of mathematics'.

But truth matters. When politicians supporting corporate interests pronounce that global warming is a hoax, and when, influenced by discredited research, common people stop giving their children routine vaccinations, when lies about national interests lead to increased war spending at the expense of spending to save children's lives, and so on, we have the negative proof of the fact that truth matters, and that truth serves human interests.

There is a price for playing with accurate ideas. The price is the positive outcomes of truth for society and environment. When the entire edifice of science is now under attack, it is the poor and disenfranchised, who will probably bear the brunt of not only disbelief in such things as global warming (McIntyre, 2015). They also suffer because of the mistaken acceptance of unregulated markets dominated by big businesses, austerity and predatory wars, and many other things that are justified on the basis of lies. To manage 'to be even minimally functional' a society 'must have ... a robust appreciation of the endlessly protean utility of truth'. Indeed,  no society can flourish 'without knowing enough about relevant facts to pursue its ambitions successfully and to cope prudently and effectively with its problems' (Frankfurt, 2006: 16–17).

My analysis suggests that the post-truth phenomenon is only partly because a specific kind of bourgeois politics (Far Right) and that the phenomenon is ultimately and dominantly rooted in the crisis-ridden bourgeois system of production and exchange, i.e., in bourgeois class relations. This analysis points to a specific political proposal for the fight against the post-truth condition, which I will return to in the last chapter.

CHAPTER 7

# Post-truth Phenomenon: a Concrete Study with a Reference to India

## 1    Introduction

In a large number of countries, the right-wing movement (or fascistic movement) is gaining ground (Albright, 2018; Banaji, 2006; Blee and Creasap, 2010; Beiner, 2018).[1] As we have seen, a major characteristic of this movement is post-truth, which refers to a condition where politicians tell blatant lies (or half-truths) on a massive scale for an ideological and political purpose. With politicians turning to post-truth, their followers do not remain far behind. The post-truth condition is not just about the production and propagation of blatant lies on the part of politicians and their followers. It is informed by an anti-scientific epistemology. Post-truthers are extremely skeptical of scientists/experts. Post-truthers believe that all perspectives on a topic are equally valid, that one can believe anything one likes irrespective of reason and evidence, that feelings (including religious feelings) are more important than factuality in determining what is true, that there is no distinction between facts and falsehood, and that facts do not have to correspond to anything objective. In other words, the philosophy of post-truth is postmodernist idealism. And, the post-truth condition, as already mentioned, is most closely associated with the Far Right, even though those who are not a part of the Far Right do engage in lying for an ideological and political purpose.

India's right-wing movement (RWM) has been led by the RSS (Rashtriya Swayamsevak Sangh, or National Volunteer Organisation), a fascistic organization established in 1925, the year of the birth of India's undivided communist party. It is the soul of the BJP (Bharatiya Janata Party), the political arm of the RWM. With the ideological-political help of the RSS and with financial support from large sections of the business world, the BJP came to power in 2014.[2] India's post-truth politics appears to have really begun in earnest around this

---

1    This chapter draws on Das (2023c).
2    It had earlier come to power in 1998 for 5 years and for brief periods earlier. It returned to power in 2019 (see Das, 2019a on how this happened and with what implications).

time at the national scale, just as it began in the US with Trump's presidential campaign and his win in 2016.[3]

Aiming to create a nation for Hindus only, the RSS/BJP combine is blatantly against the rights of non-Hindu minorities (Das, 2021a; Vanaik, 2017). It is also blatantly anti-people and anti-communist. It relies on Hindutva (politics of Hindu supremacism). Desai (2013) says that: 'Hindutva ... [is] the ideology of India's New Right' and that 'Like the New Right [ideology] everywhere, ... Hindutva combines neoliberal economic policy and authoritarian social and cultural policy and politics'. A major strategy of India's RWM is post-truth: deliberate lying on a massive scale for an ideological and political purpose, especially, about the inherent superiority of Hindu society and necessary inferiority of other religious groups. Such lying has resulted in the mobilization of Hindus against Muslims and Christians.

The most dangerous effect of its post-truth politics is when it fuels religious conflict based on lies in order to get votes. Indeed, the high point of its post-truth politics was when a Hindu fanatic mob, egged on by fascistic leaders, destroyed a 16th-century Muslim place of worship in 1992 which was claimed by the RWM to have been built on the birthplace of a Hindu god.[4] Such an anti-democratic and anti-secular illegal act along with the massacre of more than 1000 Muslims in riots in the western Indian State of Gujarat by Hindu mobs, helped the transformation of BJP from a political non-entity in the pre-1992 period to the most powerful political force now.[5] The BJP has indeed been

---

3    Modi actually supported Trump's campaign. The two politicians emerging from the post-truth political environment have had a friendly relation, not surprisingly. At a 2019 mega-event called Howdy Modi organized in his honor in Texas, Modi expressed his admiration for [Trump's] "sense of leadership, a passion for America, a concern for every American, a belief in American future and a strong resolve to make America great again ... Modi also claimed, with false optimism, that Trump had "already made the American economy strong again ... Modi championed Trump's candidature by repurposing his own winning 2014 slogan: "Ab Ki Baar Trump Sarkar," "This time, a Trump government"' (quoted in Rao, 2021).

4    'The BJP did not have a majority of its own in any state in India from the time that the party (as Jan Sangh) was founded till 1990 ... It had a national vote share in single digits for four decades till it suddenly doubled to 18 per cent, and then doubled again. What happened in a short time for the party to become nationally popular? Of course it was the movement [based on lies about minorities and ancient India, etc.] that mobilised Hindus against the mosque in Ayodhya [a city in northern India] that was destroyed, triggering pogroms across the country' (Patel, 2022).

5    In the 2002 three-day riots in Gujarat under the BJP'S RULE, at least a thousand Muslims were killed by Hindu mobs. This could not have happened without the support of the elected BJP government at the time. Roy (2023) writes: 'the 2002 anti-Muslim pogrom... raged through Gujarat after Muslims were held responsible for the burning of a railway coach in which 59 Hindu pilgrims were burned alive'. The pogrom saw 'the open slaughter and mass

gaining electoral support by: advocating hyper-nationalism; stoking hatred against non-Hindus based on lies; making false promises of development for all; giving meagre material concessions (assistance in cash or kind) to the poor while spreading false or exaggerated claims about what it has done for the people. The reality is this: as far as the well-being of the masses is concerned, there has been little change since the arrival of the BJP government in 2014 (Das, 2019b; Das, 2021a). If anything, India's situation has been getting worse in terms of a variety of indicators of human and social development, including the hunger index. To the extent that the government can make a difference to people's living conditions, the worsening situation of India is largely because its current right-wing government is wedded to pro-business interventions, including support for crony capitalism, and because a large amount of its energy has been spent on the unproductive post-truth politics, including Hindu majoritarianism.

The following discussion is divided into 4 sections. Section 2 describes India's post-truth phenomenon. Section 3 explains it in terms of the contradictions of India's class society. Section 4 critiques the right-wing's post-truth strategy. The final section is a summary.

## 2      Traits of India's Post-truth Politics

### 2.1    Ideological and Political Lies/Half-Truths
India is experiencing an undeclared emergency since 2014 when the BJP came to power with an absolute majority on the basis of a pro-corporate and divisive political agenda. The undeclared emergency is in the form of persistent attacks by hyper-nationalist fascistic Hindu-supremacist forces, which are well supported by their government at the national level and in selected provinces, on the basic democratic rights of ordinary citizens (unless one is a right-winger) and of religious minorities, progressives (those who value democracy, secularism and a degree of economic equality) and communists. Religious minorities, especially, Muslims, have become the 'near-exact equivalent of the Jew' (Sarkar, 2006: 143). It is no accident that in post-independence India, for the first time, the ruling party does not have a single directly elected Member of the Parliament from the Muslim community which represents about 15% of the nation's population, and there is no Muslim minister either in the Union

---

rape of Muslims that was staged on the streets of Gujarat's towns and villages by vigilante Hindu mobs seeking "revenge". (ibid.).

cabinet (Agha, 2022). The right-wing forces are indeed bent on creating a Hindu state, where religious minorities remain subservient to Hindus, and where the caste hierarchy and patriarchal values will continue. To materialize its political vision, the right-wing forces, including their government, are resorting to the post-truth strategy: at the altar of lies and half-truths, ideas/claims based on reason and evidence are regularly sacrificed.

The RWM *is* deficient in defensible/scientific ideas. To the extent that it has any ideas, there are three types. Firstly, the movement uses what are generally discredited (neoliberal type) ideas of right-wing pro-business economists, CEOS, business-owners and their philistine 'ideologues'.[6] Secondly, there are the ideas borrowed from, or inspired by, academic discourses on postmodernism/post-colonialism. These ideas do not agree with the scientific method and they advocate for local knowledges, folk knowledge, etc. Based on magical and associative thinking, promoters of these ideas see the ancient Indian (Vedic) view of the world as being superior to, and surpassing, modern science.[7] Thirdly, connected to the second type of ideas are many of the right-wing ideas that consist of myths, lies (or half-truths) and slogans which have no basis in reason and evidence (the main topic of this chapter).

The RWM truly believes in telling blatant lies. It excels in peddling falsification. Telling lies to hide its truly pro-business and anti-democratic nature is a part of its identity. Its lies are of two types: foundational and conjunctural. Consider the foundational lies first that are peddled by the RSS and its various affiliates and followers:

> The RSS is not only not interested in truth in any form, it wants Hindus to seek the lies it is producing for them. There are some foundational lies that serve as the basis for all the lies that are woven constantly. The foundational lie is that the first people of India are the Hindus. That Muslims and Christians are intruders and do not constitute the core of Indian culture. That we had all the knowledge of the world at one time. That Sanskrit is the mother of all Indian languages. That we have been modern since eternity.
>
> JAFRI AND APOORVANAND, 2021

---

6  They include: Swaminathan Anklesaria Aiyar, Jagdish Bhagawati, Arvind Panagariya, Gurucharan Das, Ashok Desai, Arun Shourie, Surjit Bhalla, Amitabh Kant, Vivek Debroy, etc.

7  These ideas are even promoted by scientists and engineers allied with the Hindutva movement such as Subhash Kak for whom sacred texts of Hinduism are scientific texts (Nanda, 2002).

Foundational lies also include the claim that 'we have been modern since eternity' (ibid.), that everything that modern science, including about atoms, says is already in Hindu religious scriptures (Nanda, 2002).

The foundational lies help the RWM engage in what Stanley calls 'politics of eternity' discussed in the last chapter. As applied to the Indian context, politics of eternity is one that is based on the story of an India that was once great. *That* India – the ancient India before the Muslims arrived – needs to be made great again because it has been harmed or sullied by liberalism, by pseudo-seculars and by bad non-Hindu foreigners. This story has a contradictory view of Hindu-national identity: supremacism and victimhood. Hindus are inherently superior to others, but Hindus are also victim of non-Hindus. The story is meant to make the dominant group, i.e., Hindus, feel resentful about the loss of their status and power. Treating imaginary stories about deities – mythologies – as true, the politics of eternity is devoid of any real concern with facts, historical or contemporary. It is preoccupied with a longing for past moments that are extremely unlikely to have happened during the epochs that might have been actually disastrous for the majority of Hindus (and not just Hindus). Consider the thousands of years of oppression of lower castes by the upper castes, or of exploitation of Hindu masses by Hindu propertied strata with their monopoly over political power.

Conjunctural lies follow from the foundational lies and are manufactured according to the demands of contemporary times and places. Conjunctural lies are told mainly to promote communal (i.e., religious-sectarian) polarization to garner votes and to promote cultural-political unity among Hindus based on a false consciousness that all Hindus (the rich and the poor) have the same interest. These lies are false statements that 1) praise Hindus, Hindu kings, and anyone, including businesspeople, who supports the RWM, and 2) denigrate non-Hindus, non-Hindu kings of pre-colonial times, and liberal or left critics of the RWM as well as Pakistan, the main Muslim neighbour.[8]

Consider some recent examples of conjunctural lies. In 1992, as mentioned earlier, a 16th century mosque was demolished on the basis of lies that a god was born in that place and that there was a Hindu temple beneath the mosque. If Hindus *believe* that there was a temple, one must accept that falsehood, because not to accept it would hurt Hindu sentiments. So, a mosque was not only destroyed in front of all the apparatuses of the state in broad day light.

---

8   A new book by two Indian academics shows how the emerging trend of the crisis of truth, fake news and manipulated information leads to unnecessary ideological and ethical conflicts (Abraham and Mathew, 2021).

As per a 2021 Supreme court judgement, the government would facilitate the construction of the temple in the birthplace of the deity.

In 2017, without providing any evidence, the prime minister, who has grown in the RSS milieu and who is from the BJP, made up the story that two Congress party leaders (one was a former prime minister, and another was a Muslim leader), had met, and conspired with, the Pakistani high commissioner and former foreign minister at another congress party leader's house to win the elections in an Indian province, Gujarat (Ali, 2019). Kulkarni (2017), a former ideologue of the BJP, writes: the intent behind the lie 'was to create, and exploit anti-Muslim and anti-Pakistan sentiments among voters, hoping that such polarization would boost the chances of the BJP's victory in the elections'.

Under Article 370 of Indian constitution, the Muslim-dominated province of Jammu and Kashmir used to enjoy a degree of autonomy granted under a given historical condition. In 2019, the BJP government took away Kashmir's constitutional autonomy for its own Hindu-communal agenda, but justified this by saying that it was good for Kashmiris and that it would wipe out decades of armed rebellion in the province, and usher in peace and economic development. Not only is that not much economic development has happened contrary to the promises made. People there live in fear. In 2016, the BJP government introduced a Citizenship Amendment Act which assigned citizenship based on religious identity. To say that the Act is compassionate towards minorities is a half-truth. While the Act allows prosecuted minorities from neighbouring countries to become Indian citizens, what the BJP leadership does not say is that its Act excludes Muslims. Besides, the BJP has repeated the lie that 'only BJP cares for Hindus' in neighbouring countries while all other parties are opposed to it; the real intent of this lie is to try to 'win over Hindus' (Varma 2020). In fact, at least partly as a reaction to militant Hindus' attacks on innocent Muslims in India, militant Muslims are attacking innocent Hindus in Bangladesh.

In 2016, the government announced the demonetization of all ₹500 and ₹1,000 banknotes.[9] The BJP's justification of the policy was a lie: that it is good for the poor and that it helps to fight corruption and capture the corrupt money that people had secretly kept. There was no objective basis for such a policy. Indeed, following demonetization, nearly the entire value of the demonetized notes returned to the central bank. The government-enforced demonetization helped the banks starved of cash (in part because the pro-business

---

9  On 8 November 2016, the Indian Prime Minister gave a surprise address to the nation, announcing demonetization of these notes and saying that those holding onto untaxed 'black money' in the form of these notes will be caught.

government has been writing off loans from the banks owed to the big companies), to replenish their reserve. The policy helped IT companies that deal in online transactions. It also helped corrupt money to be converted into legal income. According to a journalist:

> [India's Prime Minister] said the purpose of sudden demonetisation [of all ₹500 and ₹1,000 banknotes] was to destroy black money [i.e., corruption money] but when that didn't work, his government kept changing goal-posts. Many lies to hide one truth: that demonetisation had failed. Electoral bonds make political donations opaque, but the Modi government says they bring transparency.
>
> VIJ, 2020

In 2018, the government introduced the electoral bonds scheme to make political donations: anyone can buy a bond from a government-bank (State Bank of India) and sell it to any party. The government says the scheme brings transparency, but the exact opposite is the case. Un-surprisingly, the scheme has allowed the BJP to garner a large amount of funding from the business world in a secretive manner; indeed, most of the money through the scheme – and the business world is the source of such money – has gone to the BJP.[10]

During the 2020–2021 farmers' movement which demanded the withdrawal of the government's pro-big-business anti-farmer laws, at least 700 farmers died, including some under the vehicle of a BJP leader who was a critic of the farmers' movement. Yet, a BJP Minister said in the parliament that there was no record of the protesting farmers' death and hence compensation could not be paid to their families.

The Covishield vaccine used for about 88% of all vaccine shots administered in India was developed by the British-Swedish pharmaceutical concern Astra Zeneca (till October 2021). But the Indian government said at the time that India had achieved vaccine self-reliance. The Indian government has heavily undercounted Covid deaths too: the actual death counts are up to 10 times higher than the Indian government's official death toll (Pathak et al., 2021). Further, in 2019, the government knowingly suppressed the unemployment

---

10    'The anonymity of electoral bonds is only for the broader public and opposition parties. The fact that such bonds are sold via a government-owned bank (SBI) leaves the door open for the government to know exactly who is funding its opponents. This, in turn, allows the possibility for the government of the day to either extort money, especially from the big companies, or victimise them for not funding the ruling party – either way providing an unfair advantage to the party in power' (Misra, 2022).

data before the national election, because unemployment reached a 45-year high in 2017 (Gettleman and Kumar, 2019).[11] It told lies about the actual level of employment.

A journalist, Vij (2020), has said this about the lying habit of the RWM. The government itself openly lies, the lies 'that are obvious and blatant'. Vij concludes: 'The full list of the [BJP] government's lies could fill a library' (ibid.).

India's post-truthers, as post-truthers elsewhere, engage in double-speak. They can say a half-truth in the morning, spit out a complete lie in the afternoon, state some banal fact[12] in the evening, and conspire to criticize the criticism of lying after dinner. They can say something today and do the opposite tomorrow. People can openly call for the genocide against Muslims and yet hardly any strong action is taken against them. The right-wing can agree, at least, in public, that lynching someone based on their eating habit is not acceptable, but when there *is* lynching, there is no action, or not even criticism, against it. Some elements *within* the RWM lynch or hurt the minorities, while others say that doing such things is bad or that the bad things are done by fringe groups with which the RSS/BJP combine or the government has little link, and there are still others (including elements inside the police, judiciary, etc.) who protect the perpetrators. So, there is a perfect division of labour within the RWM as a system. This system is reproduced on the basis of lies as well as coercion (anyone, inside the government or outside, speaking the truth will face trouble, even death or physical harm).

### 2.2      *Accumulation of Lies by Means of Suppression of Dissent*

The right-wing post-truth practices effectively double down on what Marx (1887: 542) calls 'the negation of negation' (as shown in Figure 7.1). Far Right's massive political lies are a negation of truth (or, truth-telling). This is the first negation. And, when there is opposition to these lies (second negation), such opposition is negated by Far Right through the (ideological and forcible) suppression of the right to dissent/oppose. This is the third negation. And in suppressing the right to dissent, and more generally, freedom of speech, more lies are told (people who expose or raise questions about the lies are falsely branded as criminals and anti-nationals or as bearers of a colonial mentality,

---

11      While the government suppressed the data, a financial newspaper leaked findings from the unemployment report. 'While the leaked 2017 unemployment rate, 6.1 percent, may not sound so gloomy, it is roughly triple the rate of five years earlier, the last time a comparable national survey was conducted'. (Gettleman and Kumar, 2019).

12      One of the facts can be as banal as this: an unclean street is not good for health.

if they are from a foreign land), so the third negation reinforces the first negation, as shown below.[13]

In a typical fascistic fashion, facts are treated as unpatriotic, while the exposure of lies is seen as disturbing harmony. It is no wonder then that in the right-wing post-truth world, it is alright to criticize Muslims and Christians (who are considered outsiders and invaders), but one cannot criticize Hindus *qua* Hindus, as they are inherently superior and are the real/original inhabitants of India, even if the historical fact is that the ancestors of present-day Hindus have come from outside of what is now India, just as those of Muslims have.[14] If one criticizes any ideas of action of an individual or a group which happens to be Hindu or if one criticizes any aspect of 'Hindu society' (e.g. caste), then one should leave India, according to the right-wingers. Within a circle of conversation (e.g., a forum, a meeting, a university discussion, etc.), if one criticizes Hindus, or India, then one does not have a place there either. If one criticizes right-wing policies, one is considered to be 'compulsive contrarians', i.e., the people who are consistently critical of a government no matter what it does. Their criticisms are automatically criticized as falsehood or distorted or biased. Criticisms of the right-wing government, as well as of businesspeople allied with it, are treated as the criticisms of India as a whole and as criticisms of Hindus as such.

---

13    The most recent case of the suppression of the opinions that are contrary to the government's occurred when the Indian government invoked emergency laws in January 2023 to ban a BBC documentary, 'The Modi question', which 'implicates Modi in the abetment of mass murder', i.e. the 2002 anti-Muslim pogrom, referred to earlier (Roy, 2023). The documentary cites 'an internal report commissioned by the British Foreign Office in April 2002, so far unseen by the public', which called the massacre a preplanned pogrom that bore 'all the hallmarks of ethnic cleansing' and said that 'the police had been ordered to stand down' (ibid.). Yet, in countering the views presented in the documentary seen by the government as contrary to its own, it described the documentary as 'a propaganda piece designed to push a particular discredited narrative' and as one that lacked 'objectivity' and suggested 'continuing colonial mindset' (these were the words of Arindam Bagchi, spokesperson for the foreign affairs ministry). Right-wingers' or the right-wing government's views peddled to hide the truth about their action are not propaganda, but anything said by anyone to raise questions about such views is immediately called propaganda, or worse. The Indian government indeed ordered Twitter and YouTube to take down dozens of accounts that had been sharing the clips of the documentary by saying that it was 'undermining the sovereignty and integrity of India' (Kanchan Gupta, an Indian government official, quoted in Ellis-Petersen, 2023). So, engineering riots against minorities on the basis of false claims is not a threat to 'the sovereignty and integrity of India' but any questions raised about the riots and the forces behind them are.

14    The Hindus who stand for democratic rights of *all* can be, and are, criticized by the RWM.

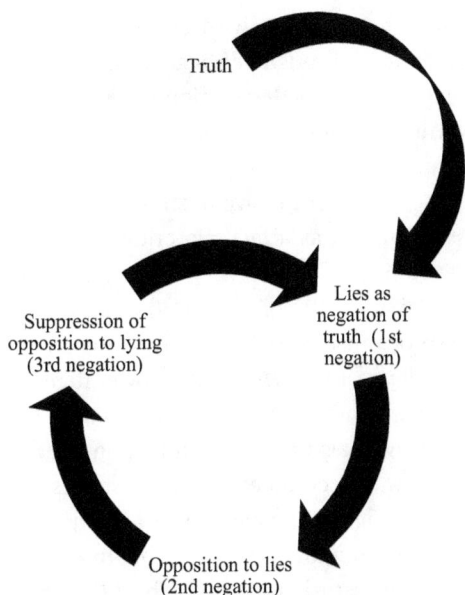

FIGURE 7.1 Cycle of negation of negation in the post-truth world

It often happens that in an incident of violence involving people from different religions, if those who get killed or hurt/raped are Hindus and if the perpetrator happens to be a Muslim, then the right-wing emphasizes the religious identity of the perpetrator, saying that the perpetrators are *necessarily* Muslims, and that the incident is necessarily based on religious hatred. Any statement to the contrary would be interpreted as a pseudo-secular act. But if Muslims get killed in an incident, any possibility of a communal act is minimized, or it is justified on the basis of lies. For example, the right-wingers say the perpetrators against Muslims are just criminals so the incident is not communal, or that, if Hindus are the culprits, it is a necessary spontaneous – natural – reaction on their part, so the communal character is not a bad thing, or that it is a minor incident committed by a fringe, so the incident can be easily ignored. In contrast, any sectarian act on the part of *a* Muslim necessarily represents religious sectarianism of *all* Muslims. In either case, a Hindu is necessarily good (= patriotic, etc.), and a non-Hindu is not.

A right-winger complains that there are too many Muslims in a workplace, and when it is pointed out that such a complaint is communal (religious-sectarian), then the right-winger counters by saying that their complaint is actually based on the fact that Muslims are involved in a scam, when in fact

there is no such scam. Indeed, a scam, or association with drugs, or involvement in violence, can be easily manufactured through political-administrative
power, just as Iraq's non-existent weapons of mass destruction were invented
by the conservative American government, and 'facts' about the torture of
Uyghers in China are being manufactured by western imperialists.

If one of the gods is *believed* by a right-winger to have been born in a particular place, then that belief must be *treated* as a fact. No criticism of the
claim is allowed on any ground because such criticism will hurt religious sentiments of Hindus. If a claim hurts religious sentiments of Hindus, according
to the RWM, that claim must be false or must be treated as false. Based on
claims un-supportable by reason or evidence, the RWM has the power to make
gods become humans and be born and die. India's right-wingers also have the
power to convert gods into juridical individuals in whose name: non-Hindus
can be killed/hurt; property can be held and accumulated; certain spaces can
be defended against; court cases can be fought/won; and courts are expected
to give favourable judgements as any unfavourable judgement might disturb
harmony between religious groups (where 'disturb harmony' = 'hurt the sentiments of Hindus').[15]

If a statement (about, say, the existence of a river mentioned in some holy
scripture) is criticized by progressives as a lie, the RWM ignores it or counterat-
tacks it by saying that what the critics describe as a fact is their (right-wingers')
belief (= majoritarian belief). *Their* beliefs are *their* facts. Of course, they are
not always anti-facts: if certain facts conform to *right-wingers'* beliefs, then
facts are facts. If, however, facts do not conform to their beliefs, then facts are
false or distorted or biased against them.

If a person/group tells a lie or peddles a religious myth to deliberately
deceive people and tell it repeatedly, then they will never tolerate their critics.
In the RWM, the penchant for lies goes side by side with the attempt to crush
all dissent, and to do so physically, if necessary.[16] Similarly, if a statement about
the real world or in a fiction/movie/painting makes a critical comment against
an aspect of the majority-society or its history/culture, then apparently it hurts
the sentiments of the majority, and therefore does not have the right to be.
A belief does not need proof even if a belief can have true material effect, i.e.,
even if it can kill. No one can think critically, or say anything critical, against a

---

15   Disturbing harmony, more or less, means hurting religious sentiments of the majority, the
     Hindus.

16   This is especially possible because of 'unflinching police support for the Right-wing
     forces that has contributed enormously to the growth of fascism in India' (Gonsalves and
     Hashmi in IPT, 2018).

right-wing person/group, a right-wing nationalist government, or indeed, the region or language or religion which the right-wingers identify themselves with.

In the RWM, a criticism of its government and its laws is considered illegal and anti-national. This is the case even if, as Justice D.Y. Chandrachud of the Indian Supreme Court has said: 'The blanket labelling of dissent as anti-national or anti-democratic strikes at the heart of our commitment to protect constitutional values and the promotion of deliberative democracy'.[17]

The post-truthers in India, like post-truth adherents in the US, often justify their opposition to intellectuals by saying that the intellectuals know only theory,[18] while the 'populist' politicians know the real thing (i.e., what people really want). And they also justify their opposition to intellectuals by counterpoising 'Harvard' (which signifies intellectual work) to 'hard work' (right-wing politicians' hard work, which effectively consists of electioneering and engaging in divisive politics).[19] *Because* the academic system is expected to encourage critical thinking, the right-wing movement seeks to destroy the autonomy of the academia. Consider the situation in prestigious institutions and universities such as Jawaharlal Nehru University (JNU). Commenting on the Indian situation, a student activist who has been arrested because of his anti-right-wing democratic-secular political views, Umar Khalid, says: 'It's worse than the McCarthy era in the US' and that 'All critics are simply being branded as anti-national' (quoted in Wu, 2017). In fact, according to an international report, India has plummeted from B grade in 2014 to D Grade now on the International Scale of Academic Freedom, as 'India's respect for academic freedom has dropped steeply since 2014, the year the current BJP-led government took control of Parliament' (Murti, 2020; see Figure 7.2 below). 'The description of India as an elected autocracy and a partially free country

---

17    Justice Chandrachud adds: 'The attack on dissent strikes at the heart of a dialogue-based
       democratic society and hence, a state is required to ensure that it deploys its machinery
       to protect the freedom of speech and expression within the bounds of law and dismantle
       any attempt to instill fear or curb free speech' (The Wire, 2020).
18    Theory is wrongly seen as abstract ideas which say nothing about the real world.
19    So-called 'hard work' effectively consists of a) introducing/implementing policies to ben-
       efit corporates, and especially, those that support the government, and b) electioneering
       where votes are asked for, covertly and overtly, on the basis of religious identity and a
       divisive politics.
           In response to Amartya Sen's comment that demonetization (currency note ban) was
       a despotic action that has adversely affected the economy, the Indian Prime Minister,
       Narendra Modi said: 'On the one hand are those (critics of note ban) who talk of what
       people at Harvard say and on the other hand is a poor man's son who through his hard
       work is trying to improve the economy'. He added: 'In fact, hard work is much more pow-
       erful than Harvard' (quoted in The Hindu, 2017).

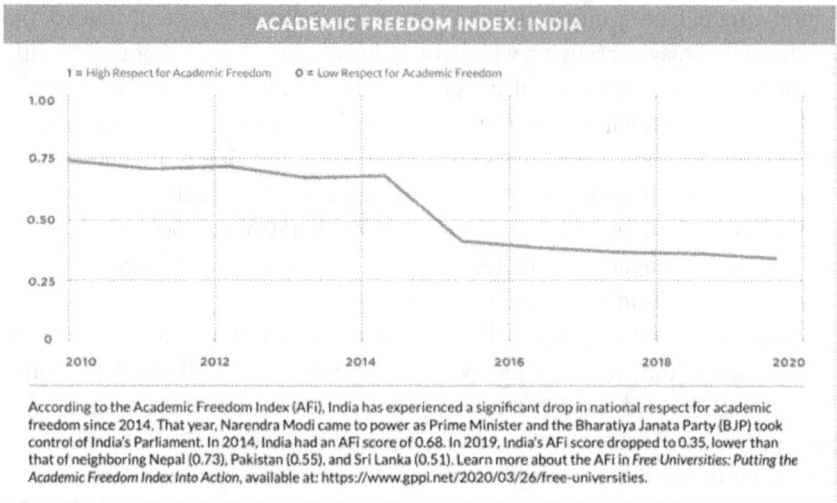

ACADEMIC FREEDOM INDEX: INDIA

1 = High Respect for Academic Freedom    0 = Low Respect for Academic Freedom

According to the Academic Freedom Index (AFi), India has experienced a significant drop in national respect for academic freedom since 2014. That year, Narendra Modi came to power as Prime Minister and the Bharatiya Janata Party (BJP) took control of India's Parliament. In 2014, India had an AFi score of 0.68. In 2019, India's AFi score dropped to 0.35, lower than that of neighboring Nepal (0.73), Pakistan (0.55), and Sri Lanka (0.51). Learn more about the AFi in *Free Universities: Putting the Academic Freedom Index Into Action*, available at: https://www.gppi.net/2020/03/26/free-universities.

FIGURE 7.2    Level of academic freedom increasingly falling in India
SOURCE: MURTI, 2020

by international think tanks demonstrates the extent to which people's fundamental freedom to interrogate political regimes has been compromised with impunity' (Sahu, 2022; Roy, 2022).

## 2.3    Class-Blindness of Right-Wing Post-truthers

Armed with a materialist perspective, Marxists view capitalist society as one that is divided into antagonistic classes on the basis of their objective interests (Das, 2017a). In contrast, in RWM's idealistic worldview, such a view is wrong: an implication of the idealist post-truth view, in which what is true is what one personally believes irrespective of reason and evidence,[20] is its class-blindness. India's right-wing thinks that it is wrong to see Indian society as class-divided. The second chief of RSS and a major ideologue within the RWM, M.S. Golwalkar says in his *A bunch of thoughts*, a key 'scripture' for the RWM:

---

20    This view is reinforced by an ideology of individualism, the view that individuals – or groups of individuals united by loyalty to a religion and religious nationalism – create their own destiny, only if they have the right moral values derived from religious scriptures. The focus on the *individuals*, especially in terms of their *subjective* being (how/what they think), and/or the focus on the groups of individuals formed on the basis of subjective traits, are a recipe for class-blindness and overlap with the post-modernist philosophy, allied with post-truth fascistic politics as discussed earlier.

> Merely because the various ... organs ... appear different and play their own specific functions, should we call them different 'classes' and ... remove them all to make the body a 'classless' entity? If we do that, will that be evolution or murder?
>
> GOLWALKAR, 1960

In his introduction to this book of Golwalkar's, Dr. Rao, a right-wing ideologue, approvingly explains this class-blindness:

> [An] advantage of the Indian view of society is that it eschews classwar. It postulates social harmony as a potentiality .... The destructive idea of class-war or irreconcilable antagonism between different functions and classes is therefore, successfully avoided in the Indian scheme.
>
> RAO, 1960

For the RWO, society has divisions and conflicts, but these are based on cultural (=religious) identity. In India, according to RWM, the main division is between Hindus and non-Hindus. Hindus are superior. Non-Hindus may be allowed to live in India but only as second-class citizens. They are considered acceptable if their thinking/action is Hinduized – i.e., they think and act like Hindus, and/ or if they do not contest Hindus' cultural-political superiority in any way.

Following is the nub of RWM and its post-truth politics. The RWM says that a) there is only a (Hindu) *nation*, a homogenous community that is defined on the basis of faith (a set of ideas), and b) there are no classes in the sense of antagonistically related groups, whose existence is based on objectively verifiable material conditions (e.g., workers, landlords, capitalists, peasants, etc.). This class-blindness of the RWM is a tool to unite the common people *with* their oppressors and to protect the latter (the economic elite) from any potential struggle against them and against the state that protects the economic elite's fundamental interests. In fact, the very origin of the BJP is dominantly traceable to the need for a political party that peddles pro-business, economically conservative ideas/policies, using the politics of religion to implement that agenda. This is because such a conservative agenda would not have – and did not have – many takers otherwise in the first 40 years or so of post-independent India. Contrary to a massive amount of theorization of the Indian state, within Left and Marxist circles,[21] the RWM says that 'The State is not a class agent of the upper class, according to Indian shastras [scriptures]

---

21    See: Das (2021b); Patnaik (2010); Sathyamurthy (1994); Vanaik (1990).

or political and social science. Nor it is an exploiting agency. It is an agent of morality or dharma [moral duty]. It precludes socialism in the sense of adding economic to political power' (Golwalkar, 1960). Just like post-truthers in the US who, in order to fight against any government regulation and ultimately social-ism, criticize the science of climate change or scientific claims that smoking causes cancer, the ideological project of the post-truthers of India is ultimately anti-socialist too.

Therefore, if people fight for class-based interests, if they fight for the work-ing class and the rural poor, the right-wing calls them *tukde tukde gang* (a gang of people that divides the nation). The RWM's class-blindness and its attempt to unite its followers on the basis of loyalty to Hinduism (and Hindu national-ism), as a part of its post-truth politics, prompts the production of its conjunc-tural lies for ideological-political domination. The question is, how does one explain this?

### 3      Explaining India's Post-truth Phenomenon

Gurcharan Das (2003), a former CEO reincarnated as a neoliberal-capitalist ideologue, says, 'Whereas economics is at the centre of China's agenda, poli-tics continues to dominate our debate in India's Parliament, in the newspapers and on the street'. According to the Hindu Right, for which Das has sympathy, Hindu culture is central to India with its 5,000 years of history. According to Hedgewar, the founder of India's Hindu-fascistic organization, 'The Hindu cul-ture is the life-breath of Hindusthan [Indian society]. It is therefore clear that if Hindusthan is to be protected, we should first nourish the Hindu culture' (quoted in Roy, 2021). In his famous footnote in Chapter 1 of *Capital volume 1*, Marx (1887) might have summarized these views of the Hindu RWM like this: the idea that the mode of production generally determines the social, political, and intellectual life is very true for modern-day materialistic China, but not for India in which Hindu religion and politics reign supreme. Marx would not, of course, agree with these views. Marx would then present his own alternative approach by saying that: Indians during the ancient period under Hindu kings could not live on Hinduism nor could Indians during medieval times under Muslim kings live on Islam. Nor can Indians now live on Hinduism under the rule of Hindu politicians who espouse Hindu supremacism. It is the mode in which Indians – and Chinese and other nations – gain a livelihood that, ultimately, governs their political and cultural life, even if culture and pol-itics appear to be independent of the latter. To criticize the RWM and its post-truth politics, one must know where it comes from. The post-truth politics and ideas do not float in thin air. They are solidly based in material conditions (Das, 2021a).

The failure of the bourgeois economy and the bourgeois state to meet the needs of the masses is the context in which fascistic forces have gotten stronger across the world. India's situation illustrates this process very well. The multiple inter-connected processes behind the fascistic tendencies in the world are present in a unique combination in India where the form of the general processes could also be specific. The development of fascistic tendencies is a capitalist class project, even if it is not just that. There are four notable processes here (for details, see Das, 2021a).

### 3.1    *Economic Misery*

India's bottom 70% faces numerous pressing problems: low wages, un/under-employment, insecure employment, limited and shrinking government's welfare, forcible loss of access to land or other means of livelihood, crisis of rural production, ecological degradation, lack of quality health care, education and shelter, and so on. These problems are fundamentally caused by the nature of capitalist class relation and exacerbated by its neoliberal form to which the illiberal BJP (like its 'liberal' cousin, the Congress party) is wedded. While the masses have not been doing well, the top 1–10% of the wealth-owning class began has been doing extremely well, especially, since the late 1980s. The share of the top 10% in country's income has risen over time, while that of the bottom half has been falling (Figures 7.3–7.4 below). The top 10% in India had a share of 64.64% in total household wealth of India, the highest since 1995, the earliest year for which this data is available, while the share of the bottom 50% of Indians decreased to its lowest level since 1995 to 5.9% (Jha, 2021). The percentage of people below $5.50-poverty line has remained stagnant.

The impoverishment of the masses is due to the capitalist economic system's failure to provide employment at a decent wage. It is also due to the state's inability to adequately help them. The state has been implementing an austerity regime imposed by the capitalist class and its collaborators abroad (e.g., institutions such as the World Bank and IMF broadly representing the interests of the US and western imperialist monopolies and their powerful states). As elsewhere, and other things constant, the more the masses consume to enjoy a better quality of life, the less is the money in the pocket of the capitalists, other things constant.

### 3.2    *Countering Political Action by the Masses*

When capitalism and the state fail to significantly and durably meet the needs of the masses, there is a potential for mass anger – mass opposition – which is

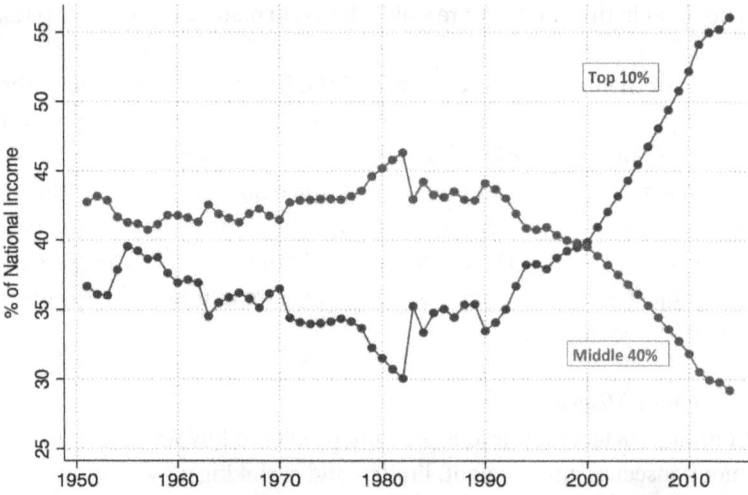

FIGURE 7.3   Top 10% versus middle 40% national income shares in India 1951–2015

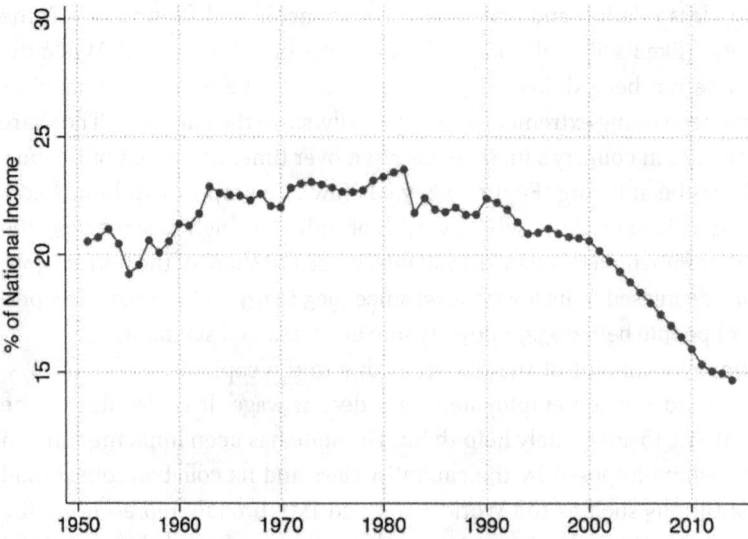

FIGURE 7.4   Bottom 50% national share income in India 1951–2015
SOURCE: HTTPS://WID.WORLD/DOCUMENT/CHANCELPIKETTY2017W
IDWORLD/

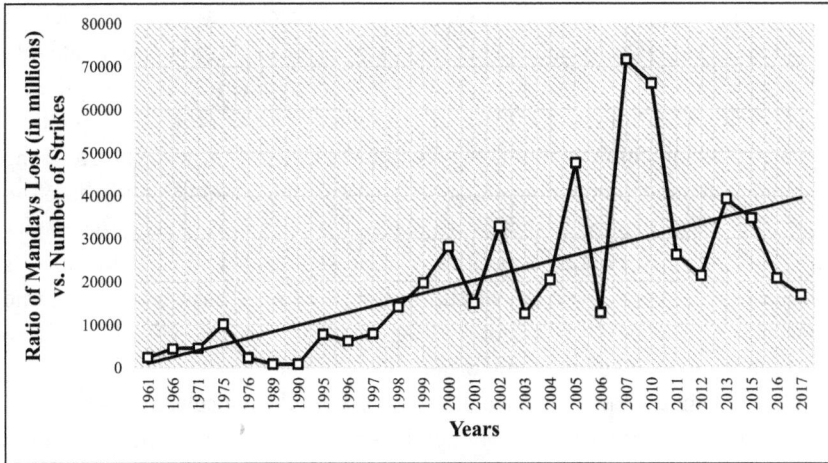

FIGURE 7.5   Intensity of labour strikes increasing in India
             SOURCE: DAS, 2021A

expressed from time to time in actual struggles and national-wide shutdowns. Indeed, millions of men and women, mainly organized by the Left parties, are engaged in recurrent protests and struggles against exploitation, oppression, dispossession and immiserization/inequality. Since the BJP's arrival, India has seen the world's largest strikes where more than 150–250 million people have participated in each. As well, the intensity of labour strikes (e.g., 'man-days' lost per strike) is actually increasing (see Figure 7.5 above).

Strike is a top risk factor for Indian business associations. So, there is a pressure on the enterprise-owners to reduce not only wage-costs of workers but also the possibility of strikes which do inflict an economic cost. To reduce these costs, they need help from political parties. This help comes in the form of repression and through consent-production via deception, which involves lies and half-truths, etc. The need for repression is often expressed as admiration for authoritarianism and for a strongman who could solve problems. Such administration is based on half-truths and lies. The deception works in part through the mental creation of 'an enemy within' (e.g., 'anti-nationals', including Muslims, and indeed, anyone who criticizes the BJP and the RSS), or of 'an enemy outside' (e.g., Muslim-dominated Pakistan; progressive elements in the diaspora critical of the BJP and the RSS), and this is also based on falsehood.

### 3.3    *Crisis of Bourgeois Politics*

The Congress Party (and its various provincial-scale offshoots/allies) and the Communist parties (which are social-democratic *in practice*, if not in words) constitute the combined forces of the 'Center' and the Left. Together, they can be called 'reformist democracy'. The latter has, more or less, failed to meet the masses' economic needs and to protect democracy including demo-cratic rights of minorities.[22] When *all bourgeois* parties in the entire political system pander to, or fail to challenge, neoliberal capitalism, and when a strong socialist left movement, domestically or globally, is absent,[23] and therefore there is no need to provide significant material concessions to keep the masses in check, identity politics – politics of representation and recognition – is played to win votes. The party of Hindu-fascistic forces has played this game most successfully, with the support of big business. The right-wing forces have become stronger, electorally and otherwise.

Indeed, when all parties have objectively turned themselves into peddlers of policies in the service of neoliberal capitalism and when most of them advocate some kind of collaboration with imperialism, making India a cheap labour platform for global capitalism and subjugating it to the global ambition of the US, there is a need for a party that distinguishes itself. There is no *objec-tive* basis for such distinction at a time when global capitalism, of which Indian capitalism is a part, is in an overall declining stage (as indicated by the decline in profitability and in investment in productive sectors), when neoliberal poli-cies are necessitated by capitalists to enhance profitability, and when the con-trol over businesses will not be tolerated by international finance capital along with its political backers primarily based in advanced countries. This creates a situation where lies, including religious/mythological lies, become the basis for creating a unique identity of right-wing parties who can say to common people: 'you have tried others, so try us now, we are different'; and 'if we cannot give you roti (bread), kapda (clothing) and makaan (shelter), we can give you some psychic-religious satisfaction'. Their appeal stems from a false sense of achievement, a sense of pride in ancient India that they artificially cultivate and worship. The subjective feeling of satisfaction is the main thing that the

---

22    The Congress party does include leaders with sympathy for Hindutva, and it does not con-sistently and forcefully confront right-wing Hindutva forces. One reason is that the party, more or less, shares the same neoliberal-capitalist agenda as the BJP does, an agenda that benefits from the division of common people based on religious and other such identi-ties. Another reason is that 'it might lead to the loss of the electoral support of the Hindus', as Panikkar says (in his Forward to *Rise of Fascism in India*, published by IPT, 2018). The extent of affinity between the two parties can be indicated by the fact that the Congress party includes within it politicians who were till the other day belonged to the BJP, and that many erstwhile Congress leaders are welcome, and do not do badly, in the BJP.

23    Note that earlier different sections of India's socialist left movement used to receive some support from the USSR and China, and that this is not the case anymore.

RWM, and the BJP at its political head, delivers. It is necessary for them to man-ufacture lies to tell the voter that 'we are different from that party' when in fact the right-wing party and the other bourgeois parties are equally pro-business, and indeed, if a comparison is to be made, the BJP is more pro-business and pro-corporate than the competing parties.

In India, as in other countries with a strong RWM, the lying is both a) the 'lying' of religious mythology and b) the lying that the capitalist system resorts to. In recent times, the technology of lies is cultivated with the help of online tools (WhatsApp and Facebook, etc.) and a servile cash-starved media depend-ent on government advertisements. There is an objective political need for lying. And if a party can come to power not because it provides concessions to people but because it peddles hatred against minorities, then this serves the business class too. When some material concessions, funded by common peo-ple's taxes, the main reason for this is to gain legitimacy for the political system which protects the capitalist class. But if the party in power can continue to be in power without having to give much concession, that is good for the capital-ist class: given that the more the masses consume to enjoy a better quality of life, the less money the business class gets, at a given point in time.[24] It is not that the BJP government does not provide any material concession. It does. For example, it gives a few thousand rupees to some people, and it gives a gas cylinder to some, and so on. The amount of concession is very much limited relative to people's needs. Wedded to a free-market policy when it comes to the business world and wedded to its own political interests, it does nothing to improve the employment and wages front, the main source of income for the vast majority. It does little to provide universal welfare support or state-funded collective consumption items (e.g., universal education and healthcare and universal provision of nutritious food). And whatever little material conces-sion is given, it is valorized through publicity to produce the false impression that a lot is done by the government.

---

24    It is not that the BJP government does not provide any material concession. It does. It
      provides small amounts of parcelized welfare in kind of cash to individuals (a gas cylinder
      here and a few thousand rupees there) to buy their votes, rather than universal bene-
      fits (e.g., a universal public food distribution system) and items of collective consump-
      tion (e.g., healthcare or education for all for free or at a heavily subsidized price, paid for
      through a tax on the richest layers of society). Then, by spending millions on publicity
      through the pliant media, it produces an impression that it provides more welfare than it
      actually does.

### 3.4    *Capitalism's Fascistic Agencies*

Capitalism does not only create the *structural* condition for fascistic tendencies by creating economic problems for the masses, who then falsely blame
their conditions on an enemy (e.g., religious minority). It also creates the *agencies* through which the fascistic project as a mass movement is carried out.
As in other countries, so in India, there is a section of the population with
an extremely backward level of consciousness that propagates Hindu supremacism. This process may have a degree of autonomy from the capitalist economic processes, but their reactionary ideas and politics are also partly a
response to the failure of the system to meet people's needs.[25] Economically
frustrated people with politically backward consciousness believe the lies
of post-truther politicians to be true and repeat these lies themselves. They
become the foot-soldiers of fascistic post-truth politicians. The capitalist system has created not only the logic of Hindutva type politics. It has also produced its willing foot-soldiers fed with the politics of hatred against minorities
and against progressives.

Firstly, competition for resources, employment, and government benefits
takes place on the terrain of cultural (religious) identity: if there is a shortage
of these things, it is blamed on a given religious group, and for this purpose, lies
have to be told. Secondly, when large sections of the population are deprived
of resources to meet their needs, when small amount of material assistance
comes from right-wing sources, this contributes to a degree of sympathy of
the masses towards the right-wing. When the right-wing government sends a
few hundred rupees directly to the bank accounts of people or gives a free or
subsidized item of consumption (e.g., cooking gas cylinder) or when the RSS
provides some help during times of need (e.g., flood relief) or provides subsidized elementary education thus filling a vacuum created by state failure,
the RWM obtains consent from the masses who fail to see the true colours of
the movement. Thirdly, the capitalist economic system has created millions of
un-employed and under-employed people, including lumpen elements. They
must engage in 'timepass' as they just have nothing much to do. As they do

---

25    The capitalist system will survive if religious bigotry against non-Hindus stops. What is
required is that the masses' consciousness be diverted from capitalism's failures, that they
give consent to it and that they remain divided ideologically and politically: these are the
ideological-political pre-condition for capitalism's reproduction. Anti-Muslim bigotry is
only one contingent mechanism. This means that capitalism's – big business owners' –
broader ideological and political needs happen to overlap with religious bigotry on the
part of some politicians' and their followers, and this situation is behind the right-wing
politics which resorts to truth-politics.

nothing, they have nothing to feel proud of in life. They lack a *sense* of control as they objectively have *no* control over their lives. So, one gains a false sense of achievement by heaping abuse on a Muslim or burning alive a Christian. One gains a false sense of achievement too by lynching someone for eating something one may not like or for falling in love in a way one may not endorse or demolishing a mosque or a statue of a socialist or a social reformer one hates,[26] or banning Muslim girls from school for wearing a head scarf, and so on. The process becomes therapeutic for economically frustrated mobs. Falsity or lies and action based on it can have some causal power. A chance to be recruited into communal politics and similar endeavours 'often gives them the much-needed purpose of life', and in the process, the aggressivity of posture that is so important for sheer survival in lumpen life can get easily transferred to communal/fascist kinds of organized violence' (Ahmad, 2013: 18–19). In fact, 'Bulk of the storm troopers for any fascism ... always come from among those victimized masses who have been spiritually destroyed and morally disoriented by the cruelties they suffer in their everyday life' (Ahmad, 2013: 3). This process is reinforced by a sense of religious belongingness, though it is 'a fictive sense of belonging to a real community' (ibid.). When there is so much suffering and, when poor Hindus identify themselves with rich Hindus on the basis of faith, it gives them an imaginary satisfaction, almost like a compensation for their objective suffering which the capitalist system does little about. The politics of religion is based on attachment to religious ideas and religious prejudice, and 'The deepest source of religious prejudice is poverty and ignorance' produced by a class society (Lenin, 1918).

One can explain the spread of RWM to the diaspora in the West (especially among the upper caste Hindu elements) in almost the same way. A large number of Indians leave India and permanently reside in economically developed countries with a better quality of life than India's.[27] A large proportion of the

---

26    Consider the demolition of the Babri masjid in 1992. Also consider the demolition of the Lenin statue in a town in the State of Tripura following the defeat of the Left in the 2018 provincial elections. A right-winger reasoned: 'For years, there has been resentment against this statue of Lenin. It was built by the municipality and funded by the taxpayers' money. Why should the taxpayer have to finance a statue of Lenin? What does this foreigner Lenin have to do with our people?' (BBC, 2018). But the right-wingers have no problem with the taxpayers' money being used to build statues of right-wing leaders as a part of the nation's built environment.

27    The total number of people giving up the citizenship of India in the past nine years is close to 1.25 million. 2022 saw more people renouncing the citizenship of India than in each of the past 11 years (Bhaumik, 2022). To the extent that many emigrants from India support Hindu nationalism, it is not clear how they reconcile their leaving India and their national-supremacist view about India.

diaspora in countries such as Canada, is reduced to almost-nothing, at least in the first several years of their lives, and in many cases, more or less, throughout their lives. Immigrants, many of whom were engineers and doctors, etc. at home, drive taxies or perform precarious manual/semi-skilled labour or engage in petty business and/or live on government benefits. They earn lower wages than native-borns.[28] They suffer from racial discrimination (explicit or not). Given all this suffering, identification with their own religion, with the nation (and Hindu-nation) back home, is therapeutic for these born-again Hindu Indians. Hindutva groups are actually supported by the extension of the Indian state in the form of its diplomatic missions: 'A new dimension has been added by the official patronage of Hindu groups by Indian diplomatic missions in foreign countries, which now show no compunction in privileging Hindus in NRI communities. [Religious leaders] of various kinds are hosted by the missions' (Bhatia, 2022).

It is interesting that while they sing songs in foreign countries about all things Indian being good, they will hardly be in that country (India) and identify themselves with the suffering of the common people. In fact, when millions of common people living in India fight for social and economic justice, the right-wing elements of the diaspora criticize them as being anti-India and anti-national. To criticize a government policy amounts to an illegal act, according to them.


4      A Critique of the Right-Wing Post-truth Politics and Thinking in India

### 4.1    The Right-Wing's Denigration of Dissent

Critique is fundamental to the culture of a civilized society. Indeed, ancient India has had a robust tradition of public debate and intellectual pluralism, as Amartya Sen (2005) has emphasized in his *Argumentative India*. This can be generally said about the India prior to the arrival of BJP on the political scene. Only a closed mind wants to say what powerful people want to hear. That mind is a servile mind. This is consistent with the obsession within the RWM with a strong leader who is surrounded by sycophants and unthinking foot soldiers.

---

28    In 2016, in Canada, wage gap between immigrants and those born in the country, and looking at the three of the most popular destinations for immigrants in the past decade (Toronto, Vancouver and Calgary), sits at 25, 17 and 23 per cent respectively (Magesan, 2017). Note that this applies to all immigrants and not just to South Asians.

The fundamental aim of post-truth politics in India, as elsewhere, is to defend the crisis-ridden capitalist economic system and, in the process, to pander to the politically backward layers of society, in the process. The defense of this economic system requires disabling criticism of the system, including the government which manages it. No wonder that any criticism of economic policies or governmental coercion against minorities or against critics is dubbed anti-national. Indeed, crushing political dissent against the big business and against right-wing politicians requires a broader culture of intolerance towards dissent.

When a progressive, especially, a socialist, is critical of any country/nation, he/she is basically being critical of the powerful people of that country – especially, i) the top 1–10% (the economic elite) who control the productive resources such as large land holdings and large enterprises, and ii) those who manage state's institutions and who seek to divide, mislead and misguide the common people by using religion, history, location, etc. with the purpose of ensuring that the common people can be ruled over by them in the interest of the economic elite. This elite, a small minority, is the real reason for the suffering of the real nation, i.e., common people (the wage-earners and petty producers or small-scale entrepreneurs). In this sense, the small minority is anti-national. The core of the RWM is its servility to capitalism (including especially its neoliberal form which also entails collaboration with imperialist capital). Therefore, its action (e.g. policies of the right-wing government) against the common people, the real nation, is anti-national too.[29] By calling its critics anti-national or anti-India, the RWM seeks to hide its own anti-national character.

It should be parenthetically added that being a nationalist is not necessarily a bad thing. If one is a nationalist against imperialist oppression, that nationalism is progressive, but ultra-nationalists are happy to subjugate India's foreign policy to America's geopolitical interests and to allow the unfettered operation of imperialist businesses in India. If one's nationalism defends the interests of the working masses, the real nation, that nationalism is progressive but ultra-nationalists in India conveniently ignore real facts about how most people live, and especially, in villages, small towns and urban slums. These spaces are the spaces, to use Marx's (1887: 451) words, 'misery, agony of toil, slavery, ignorance,

---

29    Ghosh (2016), an economist, rightly says that the goals of justice (social, economic and political), liberty (of thought, faith, etc.), equality, and fraternity (including dignity of individuals, and unity of the nation) define what Indians *as Indians* value, and that to be nationalists is to believe in these goals as Indians, that policies that go against these goals – including BJP's pro-business and anti-minorities policies – are anti-national.

brutality [and] mental degradation'. There is indeed very little to be proud of how the bottom 70% lives, or of the fact that India is one of the hungriest nations in the world.[30]

The right-wing idea that to criticize a government's *law* is to engage in *illegal* act and is anti-national, is genuinely anti-democratic, no matter how many votes the right-wing leaders get in (managed) elections. A (now-deceased) BJP politician, Arun Jaitley, indeed, warned BJP's critics by saying that 'weakening a sovereign elected government and strengthening the unelectable is only a sub-version of democracy' (quoted in Economic Times, 2019). The utterly undem-ocratic nature of any majoritarian tendency to crush dissent, as indicated in Jaitley's statement, is admirably explained by a former Supreme court judge, Justice Deepak Gupta (quoted in Choudhary, 2020):

> Rule of majority is an integral part of democracy but majoritarianism is the antithesis of democracy. ... [T]hose in power ... may be the elected government voted on the first past the post system by a large number of voters, but it cannot be said that they represent the entire will of the people.
>
> ... Even assuming they [an elected government] represent more than 50% of the electorate, can it be said that the remaining 49% of the pop-ulation has no voice in running the country? Can it be urged that the remaining 49% cannot speak for the next five years till next elections are held? Should these 49% be totally ignored if they oppose what is said by the Government? In my view, the answer has to be a big 'NO'.

Justice Gupta further clarified: 'Just because you hold a contrarian view does not mean that you are disrespectful to the country. You may be disrespectful to the government or the powers that be, but the government and the country are two different things' (ibid.).

If one accepts the idea that to criticize a government's *law* is to engage in an *illegal* act and is anti-national, then one has to also accept that Indians' strug-gle against British colonizers was an act of wrongdoing. When do big political changes happen if those seeking justice do not go beyond the bounds of given

---

30   According to a recent study, India fell six positions on the 2022 Global Hunger Index, ranking 107th out of the 121 countries included in the study. 'Based on data from 2019-2021, 16.3 percent of India's population was undernourished' (Al Jazeera, 2022). As expected, because these numbers did not agree with the right-wing government's inflated opinion about itself and the country, it criticized the Global hunger report for its "erroneous meas-ure of hunger", adding it "suffers from serious methodological issues".

laws? Indeed, in India, the 'forefathers' of those who now loudly call themselves nationalists had little to do with the fight against the British.[31] If one accepts the RWM's view, one has to also accept that the 2020–2021 farmers' protests against the three pro-big-business farm *laws* of the current government are *illegal*. It is interesting that under the pressure of the farmers' 15-month-long protest, the government was forced to take back the laws on November 20, 2021. If people had not participated in the protests on the ground that such participation is illegal and anti-government, how would the rollback of the laws happen?

Further, if the RWM is right that one should not criticize a government or its law, then most professors in social sciences and humanities, and progressive poets, novelists, artists as well as politically conscious natural scientists and philosophers of science in India, and in the world, would have no reason for existence. Without them, most people in the world would be just robot-like creatures, including the tech-coolies working in India for MNCs or in the diaspora in the West, without a conscience or an ability to think intelligently and critically about society. No wonder that India's right-wing government is against progressive intellectuals, as Hitler's was and as Trump's is.

The hyper-nationalistic character of India's RWM is evident in its approach to its foreign critics. In the RWM, the Indian government is to be trusted more than, say, Washington-based (or Western) news reports and studies. Why? The Indian government has been telling blatant and big lies. So, why should one automatically trust a piece of information just because it comes from the Indian government? Indeed, given that the current government has limited respect for facts and evidence,[32] there is all the more reason for being critical of its information.

Many ideas circulating in the (modern-day) West (including in the academia and the media) that are critical of the government are assumed by the RWM to be against India *because* they are from foreign countries and not from India. Here there is a typical right-wing attitude: whatever – facts or non-facts – suits its communal-nationalist agenda is right. If anyone in the West criticizes the atrocities against minorities in India, many in India say that such a criticism

---

31   In his appeal for release from jail in British India, Savarkar, a Hindu nationalist, said to the colonial government: 'If the Government in their manifold beneficence and mercy release me, I for one cannot but be the strongest advocate of ... loyalty to the English government' (quoted in Kulkarni, 2019).

32   India's opposition leader, Rahul Gandhi, who is usually very critical of the BJP's divisive politics, has said, BJP has been "institutionalising lies" (e.g., lies over COVID-19 deaths, the GDP figures, etc.).

is biased against India and against Hindus and that some 'vested interests' are conducting propaganda. The RWM suffers from a set of wrong conflations: the criticism of its (supreme) leader(s) = criticism of their party = criticism of the government = criticism of Hindus = criticism of contemporary and/or ancient India. Similarly, any criticism of the businesspeople supporting, and supported by, the BJP is seen as the criticism of India as such. In contrast, the ideas that emanate from ancient India or from current right-wingers are considered necessarily to be all good and correct. As well, when any idea that emanates from the West says things that the right-wing agrees with, that western information is fine. For example, many right-wing people endorse the view indicated in a survey by the US-based PEW that 'Indians value religious tolerance, though they also live religiously segregated lives' (Evans and Sahgal, 2021), without necessarily understanding the import of the survey findings as a whole.

To repeat: if an idea that happens to emanate from the West is against the RWM, then that idea is considered to be against the nation. But if a piece of information is from the West and supports the RWM, then it is good. Hitler, a Western leader, is a good model. Karl Marx, a western intellectual (or indeed Lenin, a Russian intellectual), or those from outside India writing critical reports on religious freedom in India, are not.

The RWM fails to see that: the geographical origin of an idea is not a definitive indicator of its truth status. If Newton's scientific ideas are correct, it is not because he was from Europe. If Marx was right about the fundamental dynamics of global capitalism, including about its progressive aspects relative to pre-capitalist societies (see Das, 2022b), it was not because he was from Europe. Those who believed that the earth was flat were wrong not because they were from Europe. If ancient Indians believed that turmeric and yoga had health-promoting effects, and if this has been scientifically proven to be true now, the ancient Indians were correct not because they were Indians (or Hindus) but because they had the intellectual power to observe nature and absorb ideas from other parts of the world to say useful things, even if proto-scientific. If some people (in India and in the Indian diaspora) believe the lies that ancient India made airplanes and practiced in vitro fertilization thousands of years ago, these people are wrong not necessarily because they are from India. Like everything, a place is a process. This is in the sense that it is a product of social processes, and it contributes to the ways in which they work (Pred, 1984). And it is a multi-scalar and a global process. What a place (e.g., a country or a subnational part of it) is capable of doing is partly because of its historical and contemporary connections to other places, from which it has received, and with which it has shared, good ideas, the ideas that are based on reason and evidence, or are, at least, are corroborable, and which are of some benefit to humanity. This is partly why the right-wing's ultra-nationalism – the idea that India – Hindu India – is superior to other nations – is mistaken. Feeling proud of a nation's achievements is legitimate, but national supremacism is not. And supremacism, when interpreted in religious terms (as in Hindu nationalism), is more reactionary.

Why is it not possible to admire good things about the history and heritage and the contemporary achievements of India (and indeed of any other nation), which are ultimately products of manual and mental labour of ordinary people, and yet be critical of those things that have happened, under 'Hindu rulers' or 'Muslim rulers' or British colonialists, that are against the interests of the common people and against the scientific temper, without antagonizing a given segment of society and/or neighbouring countries?[33] There *are* things to be proud of in India. Proto-scientific ideas and ideas about governance, etc. were developed in ancient India and in medieval India. In contemporary India, its public sector, led by people who were critical of both imperialism and domestic capitalist forces that drive inequality, has built dams, universities, factories, highways. It has produced countless numbers of natural and social scientists, poets, writers, engineers and doctors. In contemporary India, millions of people, including indigenous people, engage in intellectual and political fights against attacks on democratic rights, on secularism, on livelihood, etc. Armed with an alternative democratic and egalitarian vision, these people oppose inequality, exploitation, caste-oppression in Hindu society, attacks on secularism, corporate fraud, corporate take-over of nation's resources, India's capitulation to imperialism, and so on. But ultra-nationalists generally love to hate all these achievements or they under-emphasize them, even if these accomplishments are those of the real nation. They will not be proud of the fact that workers in the public sector have produced the wealth necessary for the nation and that they provide health, education and other services, as ultra-nationalists shrink the public sector, in the interests of their moneybags-sponsors. Nor will the ultra-nationalists be proud of the nations' political culture that envisions a democratic and egalitarian nation where people across religions and castes, etc. fight against the forces undermining that vision. Obsessed with their single-minded admiration for everything ancient (=Hindu), the RWM valorizes

---

33    Besides, if Washington/West is so bad, then should the Indian government(s) not delink
      themselves and their countries from Washington/West?! Indeed, those politicians who
      say Washington/West is anti-India are exactly the ones that are opening up India to
      exploitation and subjugation by Washington/West and making the country behave as a
      junior and subjugated partner in their global (anti-China) strategy.

India's scientific and other achievements *as* contributions of a Hindu society only, in the past or the present.

## 4.2     *Culturalism and Communalism in Right-Wing Post-truth Politics*

As already mentioned, in the discourse of the RWM, the main division in a society is between groups based on different cultural identity. In India, it is between Hindus and non-Hindus.[34] Therefore, if one criticizes and fights against the oppression/humiliation of non-Hindus by Hindu supremacists, one is automatically accused of undermining amity among religious groups and spreading hatred. But if one supports Hindu supremacists' thoughts/actions against religious minorities, one is considered a good citizen. And, if someone says that some elements of the minority religion are bad or that the majority religion is superior to the minority religion, then that person is considered to be telling the truth and creating harmony. So, the RWM suffers from another set of wrong conflations, supplementing the one mentioned earlier: the process of oppression (or justification for oppression of women and minorities) = creation of harmony. As well: the process of contestation of oppression/injustice = creation of unnecessary conflict = anti-nationalism.

Anyone who thinks that a given religion (certain religious ideas or practices) is under attack and that a political force is necessary to defend it should know better. Let people from different religions share their ideas and argue with one another. To the extent that adequacy of any religious idea can be settled through rational debate among people without any verbal and physical abuse, let there be a debate. If a given religion needs political defense, that smacks of an inferiority complex and fake victimhood on the part of its followers and/or their vanguard. It is interesting that many in India, even educated people, fail to distinguish between Hinduism (which is a religion in the sense of a collection of ideas about super-natural forces or gods, after-life, etc.) and Hindutva (the political utilization of people's identification with Hinduism with the aim of enforcing Hindu supremacism), although in terms of English grammar, the two terms sound similar.[35] To fail to make that distinction is almost like failing to distinguish between *metal* and *the metal used in predatory wars*.

---

34    In the US and Europe, it is between whites and non-whites and between the native-born people (especially, whites) and immigrants (especially, Muslims), and so on.

35    64% of Hindus in India (minus Jammu and Kashmir) say that being a Hindu is very important to being truly Indian, as per a recent PEW survey. Only a third of Hindu voters for whom neither being Hindu nor being able to speak Hindi is very important to national identity voted for the BJP in the 2019 parliamentary election. By comparison, 60% of Hindu voters who place great importance on Hinduism and Hindi as central to

A small detour is in order. All religions, including Hinduism, have ethical principles, some of which, if followed correctly and non-dogmatically and without falling for superstition, can enrich life to some extent, as long as adequate social conditions (e.g. decent employment; economic equality, etc.) exist for common people to meet their material needs. India's RWM appears to be loyal to Hinduism and seeks to mobilize people on the basis of that loyalty, but the RWM has very little concerns with the ethical principles of Hindu religion.[36] Consider one example. *Satyameva Jayate* (Translation: Truth Alone Triumphs) is the national motto of India. It is inscribed on India's national emblem. The national motto, as Kulkarni (2017) writes, is an abridgement of a line from an ancient philosophical text called *Mundaka Upanishad* that says: '*Satyameva jayate naanritam* (Translation: Truth alone triumphs, not falsehood)'. How odd it is that the BJP, a Hindu-nationalist party, appears to be wedded to Hinduism and its political defense, but discards the ethical principle of truthfulness embodied in Hinduism's texts.[37]

Contrary to the RWM, it is a lie, a deliberate deception, to say that the main divide in India is between Hindus and non-Hindus. The main divide, in all countries, including India, as mentioned before, is: between a) the majority of people who are suffering and are losing their rights, and b) a small minority which economically exploits, and politically subjugates, the majority. Those who seek to defend a given religion only defend their own selfish political interests and reactionary (anti-democratic) social consciousness,[38] and the interest of their business masters. By dividing common people along religious lines, some politicians peddling religion for votes, seek to weaken them. This benefits two groups: the big businesspeople, and the politicians, i.e., profit-seekers and vote-seekers, respectively. Where are these politicians when millions of people, Hindus and non-Hindus, are in poverty or near-poverty? What do they do to ensure that everyone, Hindus and non-Hindus, have a secure source of employment with a living wage and have access to shelter, education, healthcare, transit, etc.?

---

Indian identity voted for the BJP, so Hindus who are politicized on the basis of their religious identity have been made central to the right-wing agenda (Corichi and Evans, 2021).

36    The right-wingers 'in the name of God actually seek the destruction of all that is spiritual and peace loving not only in Hinduism but in other religions as well' (Gonsalves and Hashmi in IPT, 2018).

37    By making this argument, I am not saying that one has to be religious in order to be ethical. Nor am I saying that a given religion is not contradictory in the sense that while it may endorse good principles, it may also endorse ideas and actions that help reproduce an inegalitarian social order.

38    Politics is indeed not only a source of power but also money.

Matters of religion should be personal matters. The state should not be involved in these matters, except to stop religious sectarian conflicts. Every time, there is any policy that seeks to defend the rights of minorities, the right-wing shouts 'minority appeasement'. The right-wing sees only minority appeasement (i.e., any previous government action in support of minorities). But they do not see their own policy as the policy of majority appeasement (everything done to appease the majority) and minority anti-appeasement (actions aimed to destroy livelihood, lives, and dignity of minorities).[39] When the RWM accuses previous Indian governments of having appeased Muslims, they should look objectively at the economic conditions of Muslims: Muslims are disproportionately more poor than Hindus (and especially, upper caste Hindus) (see Tables 7.1–7.2).

The RWM is dangerous not only at home. It is also dangerous abroad (in the diaspora), even if it may have temporary therapeutic value (psychological compensation) here too.[40] Those people who believe that people of minority religions in a country are less than full citizens should think again, at least in their own interest! This especially applies to the immigrants from India living in developed western countries and also in Middle Eastern countries which are richer than India. In these countries, the religion of the majority is not the main religion of most immigrants. Hindus are a tiny minority.

India's RWM tells a big lie – a communal-Malthusian lie – that Muslim population growth is a threat to the numerical dominance of Hindus and contributes to society's problems. The RWM says this even if the Muslim fertility rate is very close to Hindu fertility rate (a difference of 0.5 – 0.6 child), even if the Muslim fertility rate in India is lower than the fertility rate for the un-educated people and the poorest, and even if the Muslim fertility rate in Kerala wihich, thanks to left government's policies, has the best record on human development, among major States is lower than the fertility rate for the whole population in less developed States. Now, consider the Middle East. According to *The Future of World Religions* report, some countries will see the doubling of the number of Hindus by 2050, thanks to the migration of Hindus. According to this report, Hinduism has become the fastest growing religion in Saudi Arabia (and in Pakistan too). In Saudi Arabia, Hindus currently make up about 1.1% of the population, and it will go up to 1.6% by 2050 (so it will rise by more than 40%). In Pakistan too, Hinduism has become the fastest growing religion since

---

39    Consider thousands of Muslims killed and Muslim businesses and houses destroyed in communal riots engineered by right-wingers, often with the support of their government.
40    The virulent presence of the ugly head of Hindu right-wing movement was recently came to the fore when it attacks Muslims in Leicester, England (Ellis-Peterson, 2022).

TABLE 7.1    Percentage of urban people in low-income category
(poverty) in India: different social groups

| | |
|---|---|
| Hindus upper caste | 8.3 |
| Hindu lower castes | 21.1 |
| Scheduled castes and tribes | 44.8 |
| Muslims | 38.6 |

TABLE 7.2    Percentage of rural people in low-income category (poverty)
in India: different social groups (somewhere here)

| | |
|---|---|
| Hindus upper caste | 9.3 |
| Hindu lower castes | 27.2 |
| Scheduled castes and tribes | 25.6 |
| Muslims | 26.9 |

SOURCE: GOI, 2006 (SACHAR COMMITTEE REPORT, P. 381)

1961. While the fertility rate of all religions in the world is about 2.5 children per woman, and only 2.1 in the Asia-Pacific region, Pakistan's Hindu fertility rate is 3.2; the Muslim fertility rate in India was 3.2 a decade or so ago. In Thailand, Hindu population will grow from 0.1% of the Thai population to 0.2% by 2050. While Europe's population will actually be contracting by about 6% over the next 40 years, the Hindu population will grow by 93%. It will grow especially in Ireland, Belgium, Italy and Greece (Venkataramakrishnan, 2015).

The fact that in the countries in Asia and in the wider world, people of different faiths are living together should be seen as a progressive tendency. However, if religious minorities are to be treated as second-class citizens in India, what would stop some right-wing people *in the West* (i.e., the counterparts of Hindu right-wingers *in India* or in the Indian diaspora), to argue that the Hindu minority in the diaspora should be treated as second-class citizens? What will happen if non-Hindus start being hostile to the Hindus in the countries where the minority Hindu population is increasing, the way the Hindutva Indians, the Indians with right-wing thinking, are being hostile towards non-Hindus in India? What will happen to the livelihood of millions of Hindus in the countries where the Hindus are a tiny minority? What if they face the anger of the non-Hindus who practice right-wing post-truth politics? The right-wing politics of religion, irrespective of which religious group practices it, is one of the biggest barriers to the development of solidarity among the working masses, within nations and globally, and to the exercise of democratic rights by common people.

## 5      Conclusion

There is a massive RWM that supports, and is supported by, a right-wing government in India, pointing to the strengthening of fascistic tendencies. It is characterized by a lack of commitment to objective truth and a consequent fetishization of a politically-motivated idealistic view about the world. Like the RWM in the US and elsewhere, the RWM in India engages in politics without facts (and reason). Its post-truth politics is the religious-cultural politics of majoritarianism. The anti-democratic religious majoritarianism has been expressed in the fact that the government presides over, and/or is complicit in a political environment where the following occurs nationally, or in different parts of the nation: 1) legally forbidding college students from wearing a hijab; 2) calls for a ban on Muslim traders selling goods near Hindu temples; 3) bulldozers demolishing Muslim homes and businesses; 4) destruction and desecration of non-Hindu places of worship; 5) Hindu mobs parading outside mosques and using abusive language; 5) Hindu religious leaders' open calls for genocide against Muslims; 6) punishment, by the government and the mobs, to those who call out hate-mongering; 7) criminalisation of inter-faith marriage; and 8) vigilante assaults on the freedom to propagate any religion (see Patel, 2022). It would be a mistake to see – as liberals and left-liberals do – the RWM as merely anti-democratic and anti-minorities, however. The anti-democratic religious majoritarianism must be seen as being expressed as follows: attack on the democratic rights of religious minorities as a part of 2) the attack on democratic rights as such, and the latter is linked to 3) the attack on the livelihood of common people and to 4) the single-minded worshipping at the altar of the god of big business. The right-wing is wrong as it is against the interest of the workers and peasants, the real nation. It is deeply anti-socialist. To fight it, what is needed is a lot more than liberalism.

The RWM resorts to post-truth politics in order to implement its pro-business, pro-market and authoritarian, anti-minorities, religious-supremacist vision, which is a fascistic vision. The emergence of fascistic tendencies points to a curious case of ideological and political inversion. This is one where the relation of class-antagonism between the common people (the real nation) and their *real* enemy (i.e., those who own/control large-scale enterprises) is transformed into an antagonistic relation between common people and their manufactured or fake enemies (e.g., minorities, democrats, and leftists/communists). There *is* a need to critique the RWM on its own terms. It is simply based on scientifically false and politically dangerous ideas.

The critique of right-wing politics in the sphere of culture and politics only is not enough. All cultural and political activities have underlying material conditions. The critique of the politics based on religious divides must be a critique of the conditions in the crisis-ridden capitalist society that not only create a need for religion on the part of people but also prompt people to fall for religion-based post-truth politics promoted by some politicians and groups. To paraphrase Marx, the demand to give up illusions about the politics based on religion (and attendant ultra-nationalism) must be the demand to give up a state of affairs which needs illusion, the mistaken belief that religion-based divisive politics can meet people's needs and that the minority religious groups are the main reasons for society's problems.

The critique of right-wing politics has to be more comprehensive. It must critique its political-economic foundation. There are indeed specific material reasons for the current popularity of post-truth politics in India. These will be recapitulated below.

1. The failure of a relatively backward and crisis-ridden capitalism, based on the hyper-exploitation of labour and brutal dispossession of petty producers, and the failure of post-colonial bourgeois-nationalist developmental-statism, have together produced a crisis of livelihood for common people. Such a crisis of livelihood leads to opposition from the masses, potential and real, thus creating the need for repression/authoritarianism (which is one aspect of fascistic tendency).

2. Repression needs justification on the basis of deception for which religious lies, and sometimes secular lies (another aspect of fascistic tendency), become a tool. Lies and deception also weaken the political consciousness and organization of the masses and divert their attention from real issues. 3. Political parties and movements outside of the RWM – those affiliated with Congress and non-Congress (e.g., left-democratic) parties – have failed to meet the needs of the masses, and such failure creates a vacuum which is filled by the BJP that engages in right-wing post-truth politics. 4. Capitalism in India, as a part of global capitalism, produces a reserve army of labour in a poor economy as well as layers of petty-producers through economic class differentiation and extra-economic dispossession. Millions of these people are available for lumpenization and criminality, which in turn appear to give them some sense of power. They are the foot soldiers of fascistic post-truth politics and thinking. Given the economic frustration and feeling of political-emotional powerlessness vis a vis the economic environment in which they live, identification with

a religion (and hyper-nationalism) along with the ability to humiliate minorities tend to produce narcistic form of hatred (= anti-*love,* or 'post-love') based on manufactured *lies.* These are elements of a fascistic environment.

# CHAPTER 8

# Conclusion

## 1    Brief Summary

There is a wide range of views on love, including those of Spinoza and Plato as well as more modern thinkers, including both leftists/Marxists and more mainstream thinkers. They offer some useful insights, but they are also problematic as I point out in my critique in Chapter 2.

By selectively building on the defensible ideas from that literature and more importantly, by utilizing the rich intellectual resources of the Marxist tradition, including Marx, Engels, Kollontai, Fromm, de Beauvoir, and others as well as the work outside of the Marxian tradition from neuroscience, psychology, and sociology, etc., I develop a Marxist approach to love (in Chapter 3-4). This approach locates love within historically specific social relations, and in particular, class relations. In terms of explaining the social nature of love, I did not begin with Kollontai, who is the Marxist who has written most about love. I begin with Marx and Marxist political economy and social theory inspired by him. But my conclusions firmly led me towards Kollontai. I also put Kollontai's ideas about the link between capitalism and love on a much firmer basis in Marxist political economy and Marxist social theory, including the theory consciousness than was the case in her own inspiring work. I also politicize love *under* capitalism in a stronger way than Kollontai and others do, in terms of the relation between love and class struggle.

Romantic love, like many other kinds of love, appears to be a relationship between two *individuals*, but upon closer analysis it is more than that. Love is a deeply *social* process. It is also more than a matter of a spontaneous neuro-biological impulse. Love involves conscious activity, both subjective and material. It is like a labour process. As a social process, love is shaped by social relations and not just by biology or purely individual level thinking and action. It is a social process at the level of human society. And, it is a social process at the level of class society, including capitalism: at this level, to say that love is a social process is to say that love has a class character: that is, it is shaped by class relations, which are the most important social relations.

Private property relations in all forms of class society shape relations of love. In capitalism, material conditions, which include capitalist private property, commodity relations, alienation, as well as certain forms of consciousness promoted by capitalism lead to certain conceptions and practices of love which do not serve the interests of the masses. Given the 'antagonistic character of capitalistic accumulation', where 'accumulation of wealth at one pole' coexists with 'accumulation of misery, agony of toil slavery, ignorance, brutality, mental degradation, at the opposite pole' (Marx, 1887: 451), and when there is so much alienation, competition, exploitation, inequality, etc., love in the widest sense of warm emotions, i.e. love as caring, compassion, solidarity, friendship, etc., is obviously difficult. The wings of love are clipped. The relations of oppression of women and minorities reproduced by capitalist class relations are also not conducive to a rich notion and practice of love. Love is social, so hatred (anti-love), and the politics of hatred, are also socially created. In fact, the conditions which undermine the basis for genuine love promote anti-love or hatred. How can someone brutally harmed by the police, lynched by a fascistic mob, struggling to put enough food on the table, having to perform (un-compensated) reproductive work for most of her waking time, and so on have a feeling of love or of joy as the essence of love (as Spinoza understood it).

And, with all its anti-people attributes, capitalism not only produces conditions for anti-love but also a very narrow view of romantic love, the romantic love that is isolated from love for the masses and for a political project of radical changes and that serves to distract attention of common people from the wider society, from the conditions that adversely affect their ability to truly experience love. The kind of love that capitalism allows is the kind of love that is generally reproductive of capitalism. Love *in* capitalism generally reproduces *love* with capitalism. Because love is social, it is political. It has to be so in a society with major class conflicts. Love in a political sense has a role to play in the fight against capitalism and in the process of the construction of socialism. Yet, one must avoid making extravagant claims about love's power, relative to the reality of capitalist production and exchange and the massive character of the project of changing that world.

Love must be rescued both from the principle of love of all humans as well as from the principle of love of two humans (as in romantic love in modern societies, isolated from wider concerns for society). In place of these principles, there is a need for a new principle of love that is dialectical. This principle promotes, or advocates, love of class brothers and sisters, within the context of love of the struggle against class enemies, in a manner that does not ignore passionate and erotic love between (two) individuals. Yet, this principle advances a socialist view of love that includes socialist anti-love, i.e., class hatred on the part of the exploited classes against the exploiting classes and their political/ideological backers; that class hatred is a part of the socialist class consciousness of the exploited classes, although the concept of class hatred does *not* advocate terroristic physical violence.

A critical examination of love from the standpoint of materialist dialectics allows us to address questions such as the following. What is the connection between love as a form of consciousness and class consciousness? Is there a difference between two fascistic bigots being in love vs two communists in love? Can a communist or even radical bourgeois-democrat have an enduring relation of love with a fascistic individual? Can a socialist have an enduring relation of love with one who has no respect for the right of workers and small scale producers to struggle for the improvement of their conditions or to defend their democratic rights? Is there a difference between two people in love who just care about each other and two people in love whose lives are devoted to the creation of a radically new society, i.e., socialist democracy? Is it a happenstance that partners of Marx, Engels, Lenin, Luxemburg, Trotsky, etc. were all politically progressive individuals? What kind of love might exist under communism, and how it might be different from love under capitalism?

It is not just that a commitment to a genuine sense of love, love as caring and solidarity, is missing. A commitment to truth is also increasingly absent. A post-truth phenomenon has arrived where lies and deception on a massive scale inform politics and everyday life as a normal state of affairs in capitalist societies. In post-truth capitalism, feelings are more accurate than facts, and lies are constantly told for the purpose of the political subordination of reality. The post-truth condition is deeply skeptical of objective truth and of experts/scientists. It is connected to (and gets nourishment from) the wider cultural environment shaped by the postmodernist idealist philosophy, and Far Right politics. The post-truth phenomenon is only partly because of Far Right politics, however, and that its ultimate cause lies in the capitalist system as a whole, i.e., in the crisis-ridden bourgeois political economy and bourgeois politics, including the contradictions of imperialism.

A specific example of post-truth politics is in India which is considered the largest democracy. In India, the right-wing movement has received a powerful impetus in 2014 with a right-wing political party, the BJP, capturing governmental power at the national level. As in America, so in India, blatant lies (or half-truths) and mistaken claims are deliberately produced and spread on a massive scale, for an ideological and political purpose. These are the lies and half-truths about ancient India, Hindu religion, and opponents of the right-wing movement. Such a strategy has important *intellectual* implications including right-wingers' view of society. For example, given its commitment to claims that have no objective basis, the right-wing movement sees society as divided into groups on the basis of subjective criteria (e.g., religion). Thus, it denies the basis for seeing a society as class-society on the basis of objectively existing criterion (e.g., exploitative social relations). The rightwing view also concomitantly denies the state as class-state. It sees the state as promoting *dharma* or morality. A direct *political* implication of post-truthism is the accumulation of lies by means of the suppression of dissent. When lies are exposed by progressives who are committed to the values of democracy, secularism and equality, right-wingers seek to negate such exposure by more lies. Indeed, in India's current political environment, the freedom of speech – the freedom to tell the truth and the freedom to criticize lies – is at great risk. The right-wing movement, including its post-truthism, does not hang in the air, however: it has a solid *economic* – or, political-economic – foundation.

The ways in which people think about, and experience, inter-personal love have practical implications. Similarly, the ways in which people think about truth/facts and act on such thinking have practical implications (from the standpoint of not only liberal-progressive critics of post-truth politics but also Lenin and Marx). Accepting narrow conceptions of love and jettisoning a commitment to truth – i.e. experiencing love in its bourgeois form, and holding views about the capitalist world that take the form of lying – help reproduce capitalism. Indeed, the dialectical approach employed in the book suggests that: ideas about how and why people experience love under capitalism as well as ideas about how and why people resort to political lying, have political implications: the fight for a broader view of love and the fight for a stronger commitment to truth are necessary parts of the fight for a world beyond the rule of capital, i.e. for socialist democracy.

## 2       Further Discussions

### 2.1     *Explanations*

My discussion on love is a response to the following ideas: that romantic love is driven by the biological pleasure-drive, that it is mainly a relation between two love-partners, that love is therefore a private matter, that love is class-neutral, and that love has little to do with politics. I examine love trans-historically, and historically. Trans-historically, love *is* based on a biological impulse, but its nature is shaped by social relations. Love is not the private matter it might seem to be at a first glance. Love is a deeply social process and therefore it is a political process too. Like everything else in society, love is connected to class relations: as class relations have changed, the concept and practice of love have changed. Love relations can contradict the interests of the ruling class or support these interests, so love relations are regulated by society. Love was shaped by the pre-capitalist relations of production and surplus appropriation which entailed extra-economic coercion/unfreedom. Love is shaped by capitalist class relations too.

Under capitalism, love is freer than it was earlier, but love is also shaped – constrained – by capitalist processes. Specifically important are the processes such as commodity fetishism, alienation, property relations and accumulation as well as the need for cheaper reproduction of labour power, all of which have had a deep impact on love relations. The different forms of consciousness that exist under capitalism impact love too: progressive forms of consciousness (democratic consciousness, trade union consciousness, class or socialist consciousness) have a different impact on love than capitalist values of competition and egoism, etc. do. Relations of oppression of women and minorities, reproduced by capitalism, also affect people's conception and experience love.

Love is more than an impulse, so people in love do think about qualities in each other. Love at first sight may produce the first romantic encounter but love does involve cognitive thinking and decision-making, especially for it to attain a degree of durability and intensity. Love is like labour process. The people in love are like Marx's architects: human beings erect the reality first in imagination before it is in existence. People fall in love based on certain common qualities, including physical attraction. But progressive forms of consciousness do *not* usually inform the choice of these qualities. Just as capitalism discourages and impedes progressive forms of consciousness and especially, class consciousness, similarly, capitalism is incompatible with a concept of love that is informed by progressive consciousness and that is in the interest of the masses.

Let us turn to lying now. The post-truth phenomenon, or simply, post-truth, is when business owners, political leaders and laypeople consciously lie for a political or ideological purpose. In the post-truth condition, how one feels about a matter matters more than what empirical evidence or reason says about it. Post-truth is on a spectrum which includes simple ignorance; falsehood; willful ignorance and lying. Post-truth not only privileges feelings over facts but also does it reject objectivity/truth. It privileges the common sense of common people. It is very critical of experts and scientists. '[S]cience denial is a precursor to post-truth' (McIntyre, 2018: 191). More generally, postmodernism is a precursor to post-truth which is turn associated with the right-wingers (Far Right). But ideas do not fly in the air. If large segments of people deny facts, science, reason and objectivity, the reason for this ultimately is in the objective material interests of the capitalist class and its ideological and political backers. It is ultimately capitalism – or the capitalist oligarchy – that is behind the mass-production of politically-motivated lies, or the phenomenon of post-truth, even if the relation between the two is mediated by a host of contingent factors.

Capitalism has certain contradictions (including the contradiction between political 'equality' and economic inequality and the contradiction between capital and labour). These contradictions need justification which in turn requires lying. Capitalism develops into imperialism, which also requires justification through lying. If capitalism inherently produces conditions where there is a threat to life and to the life-supporting environment, and if these conditions can be and must be *at least* regulated by the state, such regulation will hurt the capitalist class. This means that regulation must be resisted. To do this, the relevant scientifically-established facts that support the need for regulation must be denied on the basis lying. When all political parties, more or less, resort to austerity to serve the capitalist class, and when they fail to meet the needs of the masses, a condition is thus created for some political party to emerge that engages in lies, including about the fake enemies (minorities, immigrants, and foreign countries, etc.), to claim its superior electoral value relative to other parties. But such a party serves the exploited classes no better than any previous ruling political party. To naturalize the problems created by capitalism, to cover the contradictions of capitalism, to counter any resistance to capitalism and its state, and thus to present the problems created by the capitalist system as those created by God or nature or by the actions/thinking of 'unwanted' minorities or by experts, etc., lies must be manufactured and spread. As Arenchibia and Velazquez (2021), two scholars from History and Marxism Department at Cuba's University of Informatics Sciences, say:

> Post-truth is a phenomenon with an absence of rigor and integrity, ideologically biased by supporters of deception, who respond to business models associated with manipulation, in a political context, in which truth is defined by the predominant power relations of the international financial oligarchy ...
>
> The phenomenon of the "post-truth era" is a reflection of the crisis of ideology and politics of contemporary capitalism, which desperately resorts to sources of power to manipulate the mind, as the new territory of the conquest of capital.
>
> p. 125

Just because there is a structural need for lies on the part of the capitalist system or on the part of the capitalist class, a need that is created by the contradictions of capitalism and imperialism and the capitalist state, does not adequately explain how lies are produced and disseminated. Capitalists (and politicians) have specific strategies in which they produce lies. Production of lies requires a network of liars and an enterprise of lying. Lies have become a capitalist commodity produced for profit. Capitalism also produces opportunities – via capitalist media – whereby the lies can be spread and magnified. The media that spreads lies is a capitalist commodity.

While capitalism needs lies and produces the means of lying, and while Far Right politicians tell lies, why do *common people* accept the lies? There are specific reasons for this too. Lying has become an opium in their lives over which they have limited control. When people's suffering is increasing while they have little control over the conditions that cause this as they live in a system where the control over society's productive resources is in the hands of a tiny minority class of the super-wealthy people which engages in production and exchange for private profit at the expense of the masses, lying serves as an opium of the masses. This lying is both religious and secular.

With some justification, one can use Marx's (1843a) views on religion to think about political lying in post-truth capitalism, especially on the part of the ordinary people acting as foot soldiers of post-truth politicians serving the big business. Common people's political lying[1] is a symptom of their 'real suffering'. And it is 'a protest against real suffering', a protest against all those institutions that claim to serve common people and to defend truth but do exactly the opposite. Political lying, to paraphrase Marx's point about religion, 'is the sigh of the oppressed creature, the heart of a heartless world, and the soul of soulless conditions. It is the opium of the people'. Lying gives the appearance of some control over their conditions. A sort of imaginary happiness is produced by lies, including lies about their deities and about their religion, about their nation and its past that they know little about, about their race or nationality, etc., the lies that make them feel they are superior to others. So, to call for the elimination of lying as the *illusory* possession of control over their lives is the demand for their *real* control. To call on them to give up their illusions about their condition is to call on them to give up a condition that requires illusions and lying. The socialist criticism of post-truth lying is, therefore, in embryo, the criticism of that vale of contradictions between what is true and what is claimed to be true and between the promise of a crisis-ridden capitalism and what it actually delivers.

---

1   Political lying exists in the sense of not being faithful to facts, including to the facts that justify political action to serve the planet and humanity. Political lying includes holding illusory views about the world for an ideological and political reason. It includes common people's willing acceptance of routine and massive lies by the business world and politicians.

As in the US and many other countries, so in India, there is a massive RWM that supports, and is supported by, a right-wing government. It is characterized by lack of commitment to objective truth and a consequent fetishization of an idealistic view about the world. Concomitantly, its politics is one that requires no reasoning and evidence. Its post-truth politics is the cultural politics of majoritarianism. Like the RWM in the US and elsewhere, the RWM in India engages in politics-without-facts. Or, it ignores inconvenient facts.

The RWM resorts to post-truth politics in order to implement its pro-business, pro-market and authoritarian, anti-minorities, religious-supremacist vision. This is a fascistic vision. The emergence of fascistic tendencies points to a curious case of ideological and political inversion. This is one where the relation of class-antagonism between the common people (i.e., the real nation) and their real enemy (i.e., those who own/control large-scale enterprises) is transformed into an imaginary antagonistic relation between them and their manufactured enemies (e.g., minorities, democrats, and leftists/communists). There *is* therefore a need to critique the RWM on its own terms. It is based on scientifically false and politically dangerous ideas. But it is not enough to critique it at the level of ideas. The critique has to be more comprehensive. It must critique its political-economic foundation. There are indeed specific material reasons for the current popularity of post-truth politics in India.

Firstly, the failure of a relatively backward and crisis-ridden capitalism, including hyper-exploitation and brutal dispossession processes that it is based on, and the failure of bourgeois-nationalist developmental-statism, have produced a crisis of livelihood for common people. Such a crisis of livelihood leads to opposition from the masses, potential and real, thus creating the need for repression. Repression needs justification on the basis of deception for which religious and sometimes secular lies become a tool. Lies and deception also weaken the political consciousness and organization of the masses and divert their attention from real issues. Secondly, political parties and movements outside of the RWM – those affiliated with Congress and non-Congress (e.g., 'left-democratic') parties – have not succeeded significantly to meet the needs of the masses, and such failure creates a vacuum which is filled by the BJP that engages in right-wing post-truth politics. Thirdly, capitalism in India, as a part of global capitalism, produces a reserve army of labour in a poor economy as well as layers of petty-producers through class differentiation and dispossession, and millions of these economically frustrated and precariously living people are available for acts such as lumpenization, vigilantism, and criminality in service of Far Right politicians, the acts that in turn appear to give these millions some limited sense of power (power to, and power over). They are the foot soldiers of fascistic post-truth politics and thinking.

According to Karl Marx (1844b), while one should be critical of everything, 'The weapon of criticism cannot ... replace criticism by weapons, material force must be overthrown by material force'. The RWM seems to have turned this revolutionary idea of Marx on its head: it tries to counter the weapon of criticism from its liberal and left critics by using the 'criticism by weapons' i.e., by using its 'material force' (i.e., physical abuse, or online/offline threat of physical abuse). And, if Marx (1843b) says there is a need for 'ruthless criticism' against the unequal system, the right-wing's motto is to ruthlessly deny to its critics the right to criticize. Its ruthless denial of the right to dissent is internally connected to another trait of the RWM: its tendency to tell blatant lies repeatedly (i.e., to engage in post-truth politics with a Hindu-supremacist content). The world of post-truth politics, more or less, coincides with the world of Far Right or fascistic politics, a politics that is not only pro-market and pro-capitalist but also anti-minorities and authoritarian.

Much of what I have said about RWM thinking applies to countries beyond India, i.e., where-ever the ugly and poisonous snake of the RWM has been raising its head. There is no scientific basis for the politics of hatred (anti-love) based on religion or race or any other cultural identity. Such politics is reactionary. It will take humanity nowhere with its immense existential problems of poverty, ecological damage, inequality, etc.

Love and lying are connected in many ways. Class relations, and capitalism in particular, shape both love relations and the reasons for lying. They are connected in other ways. Lying is not conducive to loving, and this is true not only inter-personally but also at the societal level. To understand this, let us begin with lying. Lies are lies because they do not reflect the real state of affairs. Lies 'are designed to prevent us from being in touch with what is really going on' while being in touch with the real state of affairs ... is in our interest. The liar 'tries to impose *his* will on us' and 'aims at inducing *us* to accept *his* fabrication as an accurate account of how the world truly is' (Frankfurt, 2006: 77; italics added). If, and in so far as the liar succeeds in lying to us, its consequence for us is as follows: 'we acquire a view of the world that has its source in *his* imagination' rather than *our own*, and 'rather than being directly and reliably grounded in the relevant facts', we are forced to live in 'an imaginary world' (Frankfurt, 2006: 77–78). This consequence is anti-democratic. Our sovereignty is violated against our own wish.

This anti-democratic consequence has a psychological effect too. The culture of lying injures us psychologically. 'When we encounter people who lie to us, or who in some other way manifest a disregard for truth, it tends to anger and upset us' (Frankfurt, 2006: 73–74). We get angry and upset because 'they have certainly injured us' (ibid.). Lies injure us because they 'contrive to interfere with, and to impair, our natural effort to apprehend the real state of affairs' (ibid.: 76–77). Not just that. When we believe in the lies and feel injured on discovering that we have been lied to, we begin to doubt our own ability to know the world, our own ability to be rational, i.e., our own rationality itself. We feel that we cannot rely on our own 'feelings of trust', that we have been betrayed in our effort to 'identify people in whom [we] can have confidence', that we have missed 'the truth rather than ... attain it', and that we are 'out of touch with reality' (Frankfurt, 2006: 86).[2] When we believe someone we should not, we feel that 'we cannot realistically be confident of our own ability to distinguish truth from reality' (ibid.: 83). Since the post-truth condition is an extreme variant of lying, what is true about the relation between lying's anti-democratic consequences applies to the post-truth condition.

Love requires that the people in love know each other correctly, i.e., as they really are. One will know another through the latter's truthful self-disclosure. This requires mutual trust which is an aspect of love. Eagleton (2016: 56) says this about the relation between knowledge (truth) and love:

> A selfless concern for what lies beyond the boisterous ego is traditionally known as love. Love and knowledge [truth] are in this sense allied, an affinity most obvious when it comes to knowledge of other persons. We can know others only through their voluntary self-disclosure, which in turn involves trust, which is itself a species of love.

Lying makes love, including at the interpersonal level, difficult.

Indeed, 'With our close friends' whom we love, and unlike with others who we hardly know, we take it for granted that 'our friends are generally honest with us' and '[w]e tend to trust whatever they say, and we do so, mainly, not on the basis of a calculation establishing that they are currently telling us the truth, but because we feel comfortable and safe with them', that is, we feel at home with them (Frankfurt, 2006: 81–82). 'With friends, the expectation of access and intimacy has become natural [and] is grounded not in a calculated judgement but in our feelings [of love]' (Frankfurt, 2006: 82).

When two people are in love, they 'commit themselves mutually to fulfill various expectations and requirements that are defined by morality or by local custom. Each gives an assurance to the other that he or she can confidently be trusted to be true, at least so far as concerns the fulfillment of those particular

2  One can then understand Immanuel Kant's point that 'without truth social intercourse and conversation become valueless' and that 'a lie ... harms mankind generally' (quoted in Frankfurt, 2006: 70).

requirements and expectation' (Frankfurt, 2006: 68–69). To repeat a point from a philosopher made earlier, when one says at the wedding 'I pledge you my troth' [I promise you my truth], it means that 'I will be faithful to you' (Dudiak, 2022: 13–14). It is not only in the contexts of marriage, seen as a longer-term relation of love, that trust is important. 'Social and communal relationships generally ... can be efficient and harmonious only if people have a reasonable degree of confidence that others are on the whole reliable. If people are generally dishonest and untrustworthy, the very possibility of peaceful and productive social life would be threatened', so 'lying decisively undermines the cohesion of human society' (Frankfurt, 2006: 69).

However, things are different with liars. The liar 'hides his own thoughts, pretending to believe what he does not believe' (ibid.: 80). By doing so, 'the liar refuses to permit himself ... to be known' and thus 'denies them access to an elementary mode of human intimacy that is normally taken more or less for granted: the intimacy that consists in knowing what is on, or what is in, another person's mind' (Frankfurt, 2006: 80; 90). Intimacy is an aspect of love in its broad sense. The liar's refusal to be known 'is an insult to his victims. It naturally injures their pride'. Love cannot be a cause of injury in any form. Lying on the other hand can injure: lying and love (or friendship) cannot go together. The relationship between a liar and the person lied to is not only undemocratic. It also cannot generally be a relation of love.

Our wishes and feelings matter. These are important aspects of our life. But there are 'certain aspects of our experience' that fail to submit to our wishes or how we feel about them, and that means that they are not part of us, of our identity (Frankfurt, 2006: 99). Our understanding of who we are depends on 'our appreciation of a reality that is definitely independent of ourselves', and 'over which we cannot hope to exercise direct or immediate control' (ibid.: 100-101). Postmodernism/post-truth-ism denies that there are parts of our life's experience which is objectively outside of us. What is objectively outside of us is not just the stock market and the rule that if I don't go to work for a few days I will starve. Objectively outside of us are also real people with real need. They have a need for food and housing, and they have a need for love and recognition, and they have need for their democratic rights to be respected. If a set of ideas/practices has a tendency to ignore aspects of the reality that are outside of us, that are not a part of us and that are objective, such a thinking/practice cannot be conducive to love. As Iris Murdoch (1959: 51) says in 'The Sublime and the Good': 'Love is the extremely difficult realisation that something other than oneself is real. Love ... is the discovery of reality'. Murdoch further says: 'Love is the perception of individuals ... [W]e all have an indefinitely extended capacity to imagine the being of others [who are] different from ourselves ... Love is the imaginative recognition of, that is respect for, this otherness. ' (p. 51–52). Capitalist economy and capitalist politics make it extremely difficult to practice that love. If the reality is not objective, if there aren't people with objective needs, if one's friends and enemies are merely socially constructed (for example, Muslims and immigrants are seen as enemies), then it is *not* difficult to see how it is that: Far Right's politics of post-truth is also a politics of hatred (anti-love, or 'post-love'). This is seen when opponents of Donald Trump repeat 'love trumps hate' at protests and on placards. Indeed, indicative of this politics of anti-love is the fact that the Far Right is obsessed with not only fascistic mob violence against minorities, democrats and communists, but also with police/prisons. 'Prisons embody a failure of love in institutional form: they deprive individuals of the tenderness of social contact', while decarceration would be 'an attempt to bring love to the fore' (Harris, 2017).

The hatred that Far Right politics encourages/engages in can be described by using some of the ideas of Spinoza (1954) mentioned earlier in the book. The hatred of Far Right politicians and their foot-soldiers is characterized by 'an attempt to bring evil upon' their victims, i.e. those they hate (p 158). Far Right politics practices contempt which is 'hatred in so far as it affects a man so that he thinks too little of the [people] he hates' (p. 179). Far Right politicians practice envy which 'is hatred in so far as it affects a man so that he is sad at the good fortune of another person and is glad when any evil happens to him' (p. 179). Far Right politics is full of anger where 'Anger is the desire by which we are impelled, through hatred, to injure those whom we hate' (p. 183). Far Right politics engages in vengeance where 'Vengeance is the desire which, springing from mutual hatred, urges us to injure those who, from a similar emotion, have injured us' (p. 183). Although Spinoza treats hatred at an interpersonal level, it is important to stress that the hatred that characterizes Far Right's politics has a true basis in political economy.

### 2.2    Political Implications

There are two different ways in which class relations and capitalism, including capitalist contradictions, can be thought about. One is objectivist. Another is materialist (or dialectical-materialist), which is a class-based approach:

> The objectivist speaks of the necessity of a given historical process; the materialist gives an exact picture of the given social-economic formation and of the antagonistic relations to which it gives rise. When demonstrating the necessity for a given series of facts, the objectivist always runs the risk of becoming an apologist for these facts: the materialist discloses the class contradictions and in so doing defines his standpoint. The

objectivist speaks of "insurmountable historical tendencies"; the materialist speaks of the class which "directs" the given economic system, giving rise to such and such forms of counteraction by other classes. Thus, on the one hand, the materialist is more consistent than the objectivist, and gives profounder and fuller effect to his objectivism. He does not limit himself to speaking of the necessity of a process, but ascertains exactly what social-economic formation gives the process its content, *exactly what class* determines this necessity. In the present case, for example, the materialist would not content himself with stating the "insurmountable historical tendencies," but would point to the existence of certain classes, which determine the content of the given system and preclude the possibility of any solution except by the action of the producers themselves. On the other hand, materialism includes partisanship, so to speak, and enjoins the direct and open adoption of the standpoint of a definite social group in any assessment of events.

LENIN, 1894

Using the materialist approach, I have discussed capitalism and its contradictions, in relation to love and lying, as objectively existing processes and relations but not in an objectiv*ist* manner. My approach to capitalism also encompasses the fact that a) the objective nature and contradictions of capitalism create a need for, and prompt the ruling class and its state to take steps towards, actions to cover up capitalism's true nature and to distract people's attention from this, and b) exploited classes' action is necessary to overthrow capitalism because overthrowing capitalism is possible and necessary (Das, 2020b). An objectivist approach to capitalism has no problem with brilliantly pointing to the contradictions of capitalism but at the same time saying that capitalism is too big to fail. This is what David Harvey, does, for example:

capital in general is too big to fail. ... [W]e cannot allow it to fail. We have to actually spend some time propping it up, trying to reorganize it, and maybe shift it around very slowly and over time to a different configuration....[A] revolutionary overthrow of this capitalist economic system is not anything that's conceivable at the present time. It will not happen, and it cannot happen, and we have to make sure that it does not happen. But at the same time, the other side of the coin is capital is too big, too monstrous, too huge to survive, that it cannot survive in its current form. So on the one hand, we can't do without it; on the other hand, it is on a suicidal path. So this is, if you like, what I think the central dilemma is.

HARVEY, 2019

A materialist (or a materialist-dialectical) approach, the kind of approach that Lenin advocates, cannot reach the sort of defeatist conclusion that Harvey and others reach, especially at this stage of humanity's social evolution when global capitalism is in its terminal decline.

There are indeed specific political implications of my analysis of the bourgeois views of love and bourgeoise-reactionary approach to truth/facts, for the revolutionary struggles of the masses. Let me begin with love.

Because love is a social process, it is a class-process in a class society. So, the usefulness of love of humanity as a concept is limited in a class society. It is a utopian concept. Ideologists of pre-capitalist societies, through ancient and religious scriptures, as well as ideologists of modern society, advise people to love humanity, to love everyone. Love of humanity *is* a good concept. But it cannot be practiced in a *class-divided* society. If it is the case that a person who loves a thing necessarily tries to preserve it and meet its interests (Spinoza, 1954: 139), what would be the meaning of a person's love for landlords and peasants or love for capitalists and workers or love for imperialist powers and oppressed nations? Should the exploited peasants practicing universal love or love of humanity preserve the interests of their exploiting landlords? Should workers practicing universal love preserve the interests of their capitalists? Certainly not. Love of/for humanity, universal love, only makes sense under two conditions. One is when there are no class divisions (and divisions based on social oppression) in society. Another condition is when humanity (or humankind, or human race, or human beings) as a category is seen as the exploited and oppressed masses. This is indeed how Engels (1845) uses humankind or human race.[3] For the similar reason, love for a nation or the state – as opposed to love for the masses, as a class or as a bloc of exploited classes -- is a reactionary and anti-democratic view.[4] When a nation/country is class

---

3   Dedicating his first book, *Condition of the Working Class in England*, to England's workers, Engels says: 'I found you to be more than mere *Englishmen,* members of a single, isolated nation, I found you to be ... members of the great and universal family of [humankind], who know their interest and that of all the human race to be the same. And as such, as members of this Family of "One and Indivisible" [humankind], as Human Beings in the most emphatical meaning of the word, as such I ... hail your progress in every direction and wish you speedy success. Go on then [fighting for your rights], as you have done hitherto. Much remains to be undergone; be firm, be undaunted – your success is certain, and no step you will have to take in your onward march will be lost to our common cause, the cause of Humanity!' (Engels, 1845).
4   Real love is 'not really tied to any country's institutions or even national identity'; it instead 'transmutes into amor humanitas, a love of humanity, exceeding any and all nations' (Marasco, 2010: 649), where humanity is seen in terms of the exploited classes and oppressed masses.

divided, and when the state's fundamental role is to serve the interests of the ruling class, the notion and practice of love for the nation and love for the state help reproduce the class order. That kind of love must be rejected.

The concept of love of humanity is something that Mao lambasts in his *Talks at the Yenan Forum on Literature and Art*: 'Love as an idea is a product of objective practice. Fundamentally, we do not start from ideas but from objective practice' (quoted in Labayne, 2020). 'As for the so-called love of humanity, there has been no such all-inclusive love since humanity was divided into classes. All the ruling classes of the past were fond of advocating it, and so were so-called sages and wise men, but nobody has ever really practiced it, because it is impossible [to practice it] in class society.' (ibid.). Eagleton writes that 'a utopian thinker might exhort us to rise above these conflicts in the name of love and fellowship', but 'Marx himself takes a very different line. He does indeed believe in love and fellowship, but he does not think they will be achieved by some phoney harmony' (Eagleton, 2011: 78).

Marxism recognizes that it is class struggle and *class hatred* of the exploited classes as a part of their class consciousness that is the motor of change in a context where there are massive conflicts between productive forces and productive relations and between nation-states. Marxism avoids fetishizing the power of love, especially, for macro political-social change. So a Marxist cannot agree with the author of A *Politics of love*, Williamson (2019: 10) making an exaggeration about love when she says: 'It was love that abolished slavery, it was love that gave women suffrage, it was love that established civil rights'. Likewise,, Lerner (2022) mistakenly makes an exaggerated claim that a civilization infused with love could put an end to its major problems such as global poverty and homelessness. Spinoza's idea is that 'hatred is increased by reciprocal hatred, and, on the other hand, can be extinguished by love' and that 'he who lives according to the guidance of reason will strive to repay the hatred of another, with love, that is to say, with generosity' (Spinoza, 1954: 223). This may have *some* relevance at an inter-personal level in some contexts, but not when it comes to the politics of hatred practiced by Far Right in post-truth politics.

Not surprisingly, Engels is against the extravagant 'deification of love' of the type Negri, etc. engage in. Engels (1886) is critical of Feuerbach who argued for 'the liberation of mankind by means of "love" in place of the emancipation of the proletariat through the economic transformation of production' on the basis of class struggle. Engels is also critical of the idea of Feuerbach's that: 'love is everywhere and at all times' working as 'the wonder-working god' who helps people 'to surmount all difficulties of practical life and at that in a society which is split into classes with diametrically opposite interests'. Engels is rightly critical of the Feuerbachian advice: 'Love one another – fall into each other's arms regardless of distinctions of sex or estate – a universal orgy of reconciliation!' (ibid.). Contrary to 'the Feuerbachian theory of morals' which 'is designed to suit all periods, all peoples and all conditions, and precisely for that reason it is never and nowhere applicable', is the actual reality behind the moral claims. This reality is where 'every class, even every profession, has its own morality, and even this it violates whenever it can do so with impunity'. A part of the reality is also the fact that 'love, which is to unite all, [actually] manifests itself in wars, altercations, lawsuits, domestic broils, divorces, and every possible exploitation of one by another' (ibid.).

Whether it is from Fromm or Negri, love of humanity and its utility in politics *is* mistaken.

> What they fail to consider is the possibility that amor patriae cannot be universalized without relinquishing its political claim. In other words, they do not show how love might assume a real political force that pertains to humanity as a whole, which would require an admission that the world is not such a loving place.
>
> MARASCO, 2010: 649

In modern society for most of the people in romantic love, their love life revolves around that relationship, in abstraction from the sufferings of the masses. Their love for one another is not connected to their love for others, the ordinary suffering people. But there is a reason for this as we have seen. Such views/practices of love reflect the objective conditions including alienation. To paraphrase Marx (1843a), to call on people to love humanity, to reject the concept of romantic love as practiced in a class society, and to give up their illusions about love, is to really call on them to *give up a condition that requires them to conceive love in that manner.* The criticism of the restricted form of love in modern society is, therefore, *in embryo, the criticism of that vale of tears* of which their private love life is the *halo* and an escape route and a source of the solution to their problems. Moralizing about love and advising people to be selfless and loving under heartless conditions is not the task of communists. Marx and Engels (1845: 58) say:

> Communists do not oppose egoism to selflessness or selflessness to egoism, nor do they express this contradiction theoretically either in its sentimental or in its highflown ideological form; they rather demonstrate its material source, with which it disappears of itself. The Communists do not preach morality at all [at an individual level]. They do not put to people the moral demand: love one another, do not be egoists, etc.; on

the contrary, they are very well aware that egoism, just as much selfless-ness, is in definite circumstances a necessary form of the self-assertion of individuals. Hence, the Communists by no means want to do away with the "private individual" for the sake of the "general", selfless [lov-ing] man.

Therefore, strictly speaking, Fromm's (1956: 26) following statement is not accurate or it is that his conception of love as implied below cannot quite be practiced in a class society:

> If I truly love one person I love all persons, I love the world, I love life. If I can say to some-body else, "I love you," I must be able to say, "I love in you everybody, I love through you the world, I love in you also myself."

Indeed, 'satisfaction in individual love cannot be attained without the capacity to love one's neighbor' (ibid.). For this to be true, however, class relations must be abolished. A Marxist cannot say 'I love you all', to landlords, capitalists and bourgeois politicians as well as to workers and peasants. A worker or a peasant cannot say to a landlord or capitalist or bourgeois politician who may be their neighbours 'I love you all'.

Love is important not only in socialist theory but also in socialist politics. A socialist politics of love requires an understanding of how class relations including especially, of capitalism, make love difficult. A socialist politics of love is therefore bound to a commitment to the radical reforms of the con-ditions where possible and to the socialist project of the revolutionary aboli-tion of class relations and injustices against women and minorities. A socialist politics of love must be expressed in political activities of socialist mobiliza-tion too. Indeed, 'the true revolutionary is guided by great feelings of love. It is impossible to think of a genuine revolutionary lacking this quality .... [They] must idealize this love of the [common] people, of the most sacred causes' (Guevara, 1967: 7). This is different from ordinary love, for socialists 'cannot descend, with small doses of daily affection, to the level where ordinary people put their love into practice' (ibid.). Also, the fight for genuine love based on care and solidarity, must be a part of the demand for the fight for socialism. In the class society love is not free (as in pre-capitalist societies), or when slightly free, love is narrowly confined to two individuals as a private matter as in cap-italism. The latter conception of love must be replaced by a conception of love where love is a social matter and serves the lives and political struggles of the masses.

If the concept and practice of love have changed to serve the interests of the ruling classes, then the concepts and the practice of love should change too in order to serve the interest of the new rising class, the working class. Capitalism is based on political separation (or dis-unity) within the working class, for without that separation, and consequent disorganization, the separation of the working class from private property and from production and surplus value (i.e., its alienation) cannot be reproduced. This alienation which is behind not only the suffering of the people but also the mutilated form of love that people commonly experience. But socialism is based on the opposite, i.e., both non-separation between people and nature, and non-separation (i.e., unity) among working people, and love can play a small sole here. Indeed, 'The working class derives its ideal from the labour co-operation and inner solidarity that binds the men and women of the proletariat together; the form and content of this ideal naturally differs from the conception of love that existed in other cultural epochs', that is, in pre-socialist class societies (Kollontai, 1923). Love in socialism will be such that two people in love, whether of the same sex or different sexes, will also 'be capable of responding to the distress and needs of other members of the class' (ibid.). The proletarian 'advocacy of love-comradeship' and of socialized conception of love, does not imply that in the militant atmosphere of its struggle for the dictatorship of the proletariat the working class [will] mercilessly [try] to remove all traces of tender emotion from relations between the sexes', or from relations between two sexually related people of the same sex or different sexes, nor does it imply that it will 'destroy "winged Eros"' i.e. love based on desire'. The proletarian 'advocacy of love-comradeship', in fact, will 'clear the way for the recognition of the value of love as a psychological and social force' (ibid.), whether, once again, it is the love between people of the same sex or different sexes. The idea of socialist love, as a part of socialist concept of life as a totality, recognizes the power of love. As Kollontai (1911) says, 'Love is in itself a great creative force: it develops and enriches the psyche of the person who experiences love and of the person to whom love is given'. Yet, socialists recognize that romantic 'love [is] not the main goal of our life' and that 'work and the longing for love can be harmoniously combined *so that work remains as the main goal of existence*' (Kollontai, 1926; italics added). But work (or labour) remains the main goal of life where, just like love, it has also been transformed so much so that 'labour has become not only a means of life but life's prime want' (Marx, 1875), i.e., as a source of pleasure, just like romantic love is.

Socialist politics of love also encompasses relationships of compassion and care *among* socialists themselves in their everyday life, the relationships that can take romantic/erotic form under certain conditions.[5] Fighting against racism, fascism, capitalist exploitation, imperialism, war and avoidable ecological damage, etc. and the consciousness associated with these fights, can bring two people together in a relationship of love that is social-political as well as romantic and reinforce whatever else (e.g. physical attraction, etc.) makes them closer. In the socialist conception, inter-personal love or romantic love between two people must be a part of, or must be linked to, revolutionary love.

The future is in the spaces of the present. There were glimpses of capitalism in the feudal society. Similarly, within the limits imposed by the logic of capitalism and its culture, there are glimpses of socialism in the capitalist society, which indeed creates some of the necessary conditions for socialism. Socialists living in capitalism try to have a conception of what I would call 'as if socialism' and they live according to that conception, i.e. as socialistically free and socialistically solidarizing individuals. In such an 'as if socialism', men and women live their lives according to the values of the future socialist society, to the extent possible. The concept and the reality of 'as if socialism' reflect what Lenin calls the sparks of socialist consciousness, within capitalism. Socialists try to live as citizens of 'as if socialism' when, bathed with their love for the cause of justice and for the people suffering from injustice under capitalism and armed with the vision of a future socialist society, they join a demonstration in a cold weather against injustice, when it is in one's own material interest to stay near the fireplace at home. Socialists think, write and talk as Marxists even if not being a Marxist is in one's own immediate interest, as indicated by the fact that numerous people give up on Marxism because doing Marxism may not be good for one's career.

At an individual level too, a socialist tries to live as a citizen of 'as if socialism'. This is when a socialist gives another person pure unconditional love and does things primarily in this person's interest, even if not doing so might be in the interest of the socialist individual; this is a glimpse of love in its socialistic form. Indeed, selflessly doing something *for others* becomes an *individual* need, because the individual is inherently a social thing in the socialist conception. In the spaces of 'as if socialism' (i.e. spaces of sparks of socialism within capitalist society), socialistic love as a part of socialist culture can be expressed and experienced, however limited that expression/experience may be. There are surely objectively existing limits to how developed the glimpses of socialism – including socialistic love – can be within capitalism, and it would be utopian

---

5  'A radical politics of love recentres the significance of solidarity and mutual care within activist movements, reminding individuals of the need for self-care and self-love' (Harris, 2017).

to think otherwise. But constraints do not entirely determine what individuals and collectives of individuals do and can do to make history.[6]

Human beings have hitherto fallen in love in the world in various ways. The point, however, is to change that world. And the act of changing the world must include the act of changing the ways in which we think about, and fall in, love. The fact is that: genuine love – at inter-personal level and in the wider society – requires socialism.

Just as the socialist critique of mutilated form of love presented in the book, the critique of the culture of lying too has political implications. To live well, not only is love (as caring, warmth, solidarity, etc.) necessary. Truth is also necessary. 'Truth is objective'; 'it is good to believe what is true', 'truth is a worthy goal of enquiry', 'truth is worth caring about for its own sake', says Lynch, a professor at Cornell (Lynch, 2005: 4). 'Science's quest for knowledge about reality presupposes the importance of truth, both as an end in itself and as a means of resolving problems. How could truth become passé?' (Higgins 2016). 'Truth still matters, as it always has' (McIntyre, 2018: 172). The concept of truth will never die because 'to believe anything at all is itself to take a stand on its truth' (Blackburn, 2018: 11). Without truth, without the views about how the world works that are more or less true (although subject to revision when new evidence comes), we cannot intervene in the world. Truth is necessary for practice which in turn shapes our pursuit of truth (Das, 2022g)

There is therefore a 'need to reject the idea', often coming from the post-truth political world 'that truth doesn't exist anymore' (Levitin, 2017: ix). Or as Lockie (2016) says, 'Misinformation must ... be countered ... with solidarity'. This solidarity must be among the members of the exploited classes, among their ideological and political representatives, and between them. Truthers' of the world must unite. Truthers must oppose post-truthers, in all the spaces of life, whether in the newsroom, classroom, public fora, parliament, restaurants, parks, social media, trade unions, or on the street.

There is indeed a need to defend science and scientific temper. The struggle against Far Right forces which are forces of bourgeois reaction and which use political lying like no other group must include a struggle against post-truth, i.e., a struggle in defense of truth. As Higgins (2016) notes: 'Scientists

––––––––––––

6   If capitalist economic and political rules, customs and ideas entirely determined our action and thought, then there would be no Marxism either in theory or action. Because of the objective constraints, revolutionary activists and scholars, while trying to create ideological and political conditions for revolution, act and think in *specific ways*, in order not to attract undue attention of those – the state, family and owners of private property, etc. – who would police socialist thought and action.

and philosophers should be shocked by the idea of post-truth, and they should speak up when scientific findings are ignored by those in power or treated as mere matters of faith' (Higgins, 2016).[7]

The philosopher, McIntyre, says: 'one must always fight back against lies'. A lie is told because the person telling it thinks there is a chance that someone will believe it' (McIntyre, 2018: 155). Those who care about truth must call out an act of political lying out what it is. A lie must be called by a proper name: a lie. The point of challenging a lie may not be to convince the liar, who is likely too far gone in his or her dark purpose to be rehabilitated, McIntyre says. But because every lie has an audience, there may still be time to correct them. 'If we do not confront a liar', then it is possible that 'those who have not yet moved from ignorance to "wilful ignorance" [will] just slip further down the rabbit hole toward full-blown denialism, where they may not even listen to facts or reason anymore' (ibid.: 155). Or as Lockie (2016) says:

> Facts may be the first casualty of post-truth politics but – to the extent post-truth propagandists enjoy electoral success – material consequences for people and ecosystems follow closely behind. It makes absolute sense, in this context, that many of our colleagues, in both the social and natural sciences, see increased involvement in grassroots activism.

Truthers must reject the idea of false equivalence, i.e., giving equal emphasis to truth and to falsehood which is sold as alternative facts. Truth is not a matter of, or a product of, arithmetic or algebraic average. To say that truth is necessarily the midpoint between two ideas, one of which is false, is dangerous. Is global warming happening? The answer does not lie between 'yes, it is happening' and 'no, it is not happening'. The only answer is the former.

There is already *some* reason for optimism, howsoever limited. This optimism is on theoretical and empirical grounds. Theoretically speaking: 'human beings are not normally drawn to falsehoods and thus tend to progress towards good sense' (Davis, 2018: XIII). Indeed, it is true that 'we as a species have managed to advance away from superstitious nonsense towards a more scientific era', that our 'mistakes tend to be rectified in the long term' (ibid.) and that 'good sense normally prevails in the end' (p. 302; 299). This is because we are rational and because we do need truth in our everyday life. Or, as a

---

7  As Higgins (2016) further says: 'Scientists must keep reminding society of the importance of the social mission of science – to provide the best information possible as the basis for public policy. And they should publicly affirm the intellectual virtues that they so effectively model: critical thinking, sustained inquiry and revision of beliefs on the basis of evidence'.

contemporary philosopher has said: as human beings, we are known for 'our *natural* effort to apprehend the real state of affairs' (Frankfurt, 2006: 76–77), and lying interferes goes against this tendency. As a species, we are deeply – even if not entirely – natural. This is in at least three senses. Our needs – need for food, shelter, transit, medicine, etc. — are biologically driven: our physical body needs these things. Then, the things that we need, directly indirectly, come from nature and its interaction with labour. Besides, our ability to perform manual and mental labour, including the labour needed to produce the things to meet our needs, is partly a force of nature.[8] The naturalness of human life in all these senses is objective – it exists independently of how we think at a given point in time – and cannot permit lying. Being truthful is simply essential for life, as we have seen. But there is another aspect of the objectivity of human life: in meeting our needs, we are involved in the social relations of production and exchange (e.g., labour market; stock market, state-society relations; etc.) that are objective, even if socially constructed. So, the pursuit of objectivity, of truth, is one of our essential 'natural' traits. And being anti-truth or post-truth is against our interests.

There are also empirical or concrete reasons for some optimism. In the US, the media stopped telling both sides of the story about vaccines and autism once there was a measles outbreak in 14 States in 2015. Similarly, in 2014, the BBC decided to stop giving equal airtime to climate change deniers. Such principled defiance must be widely demanded by citizens who must exercise their right to know facts/truths. There are also various factcheck initiatives in numerous countries – e.g., Snopes, Fact-Check.org, Altnews, Politifact, BBC Reality check– that seek to expose post-truth lies. As well, and more importantly, people are resisting post-truth every time they fight against capitalists not paying an adequate wage or against unnecessary predatory imperialist wars (proxy or direct) by states, or against the political mismanagement of the pandemic, etc., all of which are explained away on the basis of lies. Every time people fight against the conditions behind their suffering, the conditions that

---

8   'So far therefore as labour is a creator of use value, ...it is a necessary condition, independent of all forms of society, for the existence of the human race; it is an eternal nature-imposed necessity, without which there can be no material exchanges between man and Nature, and therefore no life' (Marx, 1887: 31). The labour that human beings engage in is the labour that is 'a process in which ...man of his own accord starts, regulates, and controls the material reactions between himself and Nature. He opposes himself to Nature *as one of her own forces*, setting in motion arms and legs, head and hands, the natural forces of his body, in order to appropriate Nature's productions in a form adapted to his own wants' (ibid.: 127; italics added).

require massive political lying (religious and/or secular lying) to hide them or to distract attention from them, people resist post-truth.

The fight against post-truth must include a fight not only for state-funded education but also for an education where the institutions will a) 'pass along an accurate and balanced history to our children', b) 'communicate to them the importance of reason ... and of using evidence to arrive at conclusions' as well as c) teach the importance 'of trying to overcome bias' against socially oppressed groups such as women, religious or racial minorities and homosexuals and so on (Cheney, 1995: 20). So, there must be a fight for an education at all levels, including schools, colleges and universities, so students learn about the importance of reason and evidence and about the need for a critical attitude towards the structures of social relations that cause inequalities and other problems, which are prompting the need for political lying. There must be a fight against on-going rightwing attacks on university curriculum on inequality and oppression based on gender, racial, caste and religious differences.

If my analysis of the reason for post-truth is correct, then it follows that there is a limit to the extent to which liberals can fight post-truth. Society cannot be significantly and durably defended against post-truthers by people or organizations that accept the basic premises of capitalism, or that accept the deliberately produced mistaken claims about imperialist wars or accept the idea that capitalist austerity benefits common people or indeed that socialism is against human nature and the dignity of human nature, and so on. Both the Right and the center support capitalism which is fundamentally behind the post-truth culture we are in. So, one cannot fight the lies of a Trump about his election or about China, etc. without fighting the lies of a Biden about the Ukraine war, etc. Indeed, as a senior American journalist says: 'I have found little difference between the two parties on this basic fact: They will both stretch the truth if they believe it will give them a political advantage' (Kessler, 2020: XIV).[9] If capitalism is behind the massive political lying – i.e. post-truth – that we are experiencing, this conclusion points to the fact that only socialism can gradually create conditions for a truthful public sphere, where the structural need for ideological-political lying ceases to exist.

The defense of truth ultimately requires a truthful defense of communism. 'Communists must be ready at all times to stand up for the truth, because truth is in the interests of the people' (Mao, 1945). Lenin's (1922) thinking is crucial to

---

9  At the same time, lies about the regimes which have falsely called themselves socialist must also be exposed.

the communist fight against the post-truthers we encounter today.[10] It is a part of communist ideological class struggle. This is in two senses.

Firstly, what Lenin had said about the need to fight against the autocracy in capitalist Russia applies to the current conjuncture, including what are called major liberal democracies (e.g. India, the United States of America, Italy, Sweden, Poland, Brazil, etc.) where fascistic tendencies, armed with a post-truth attitude, are growing and crushing the democratic rights of people, including, especially, of the minorities. Indeed, 'The post-truth approach is the approach of the autocrat: by a campaign of attrition, trust in institutions such as the state, the judiciary and the media [is] undermined, until public discourse is simply a clash of competing narratives' (Ball, 2017: 278). This is a clash, or 'a contest which can then be won by the side willing to make the boldest plays towards emotion and mass-appeal – often …. through the demonization of minority groups' (ibid.). To return to Lenin and to paraphrase him, the right-wing thinking and right-wing autocratic politics in capitalist countries, which includes 'the persecution of the religious sects' and 'the barrack methods in the treatment of the students and liberal intellectuals' and many other 'manifestations of tyranny', must be the basis for the 'political agitation and for drawing the masses into the political struggle' against the capitalist economic and political system (Lenin, 1902: 35). Once again, the defense of truth – and the fight against post-truth – must be a part of a socialist struggle against class society.

Secondly: Lenin advocates collaboration between scientists and Marxists/communists, in their common fight against superstition/irrationalism, the power of which has increased in the current post-truth world, and which is generating hatred against a significant proportion of the population. In doing so, Lenin makes a general point that speaks to his non-sectarian strategic thinking: 'One of the biggest and most dangerous mistakes made by Communists … is the idea that a revolution can be made by revolutionaries alone'.[11] Assistance of non-communists is necessary, he says rightly. Lenin, for whom the defense of science is a crucial Marxist task, continues:

---

10    To paraphrase Zizek (2011: 128), it is important to be a friend of truth and a scientific worldview as well as a friend of specific leaders and scholar-activists such as Lenin who help us to explore truth.
11    'On the contrary', Lenin adds, 'to be successful, all serious revolutionary work requires that the idea that revolutionaries are capable of playing the part only of the vanguard of the truly virile and advanced class must be understood and translated into action' (ibid.).

> This [principle] also applies to the defence of materialism and Marxism ... [There are] materialists [i.e. scientists] from the non-communist camp, and it is our absolute duty to enlist all adherents of consistent and militant materialism in the joint work of combating philosophical reaction and the philosophical prejudices of so-called educated society' [which includes] the professors of philosophy in modern society [who] are in the majority of cases nothing but "graduated flunkeys of clericalism".
>
> LENIN, 1922

Lenin could have been talking about postmodernists of our times such as a Latour or a Lyotard or a Foucault, etc. Lenin explicitly emphasizes the need for collaboration of Marxists with non-communist scientists, i.e., 'with those modern natural scientists who incline towards materialism and are not afraid to defend and preach it as against the modish philosophical wanderings into idealism and scepticism which are prevalent in so-called educated society' (ibid.). Here Lenin could have been talking about natural scientists such as Alan Sokal. Given his firm belief that interpretations/explanations of the world are ultimately connected to – they reflect and reinforce – class interests, Lenin (1922) stresses the need for 'a militant materialist [approach] ... in the sense of unflinchingly exposing and indicting all modern "graduated flunkeys of clericalism", irrespective of whether they act as representatives of official science or as free lances calling themselves "democratic Left or ideologically socialist" publicists'. Lenin advises that one must be cognizant of 'the connection between the class interests and the class position of the bourgeoisie and its support of all forms of religion on the one hand, and the ideological content of the fashionable philosophical trends [such as idealism] on the other' (ibid.). And, as we have seen, the modern-day idealism in the form of postmodernism is deeply linked to the post-truth attitude to society and politics.

Post-truth politics in the world's largest democracy, India, takes the form of god politics, the politics in the name of gods one worships. God politics can never be good politics.[12] That is: the politics conducted in the name of gods, or religious politics, which has no basis in facts or reason, and which is therefore inherently post-truth, can never be good for common people (the bottom 70% or so). God politics also effectively undermines the many beautiful ethical or

---

12  'Love of God cannot be turned into hatred' (Spinoza, 1954: 265), so if one really loves God or gods, their politics can never be the politics of hatred, assuming that the traits that religious believers apply to God are those that properly apply to the human species-essence of which God is an imaginary representation, as Feuerbach argued.

spiritual principles that preach peace, love and happiness embodied in world's major religions, including Hinduism itself.

The politics of people, people's politics, would have to be actually 'anti-god' and anti-post-truth. In fact, if gods existed, they would never allow sectarian violence in their names. One god would never want a place of worship of another god to be destroyed. Gods would never demand that land and wealth be devoted to the construction of their abodes (places of worship) while millions are without land, food and housing. Gods could never discriminate against people based on their faith. If they did, they could never be gods. God politics must be subjected to serious materialist critique, but one that also critiques the suppression of religious freedom and oppression of religious minorities. Such a critique must be against the oppression of the non-Hindu minorities by Hindus and against the oppression of the Hindu minority by non-Hindus.

Right-wing post-truth politics in India (as elsewhere) is absolutely wrong on all counts. It must be soundly discarded by all democratic and secular-minded people. The right-wing politics is bad because it is pro-big-business and authoritarian. And it is bad because it seeks to disunite the ordinary men and women in their fight against big capital and against authoritarianism and against state's pro-corporate policies. There is a need to fight for the defense of democratic rights of *all* irrespective of their religious and other forms of cultural identity. The battle for democracy must be won, because, as a Supreme court judge of India has said, 'A democracy welded to the ideal of reason and deliberation ensures that minority opinions are not strangulated and ... that every outcome is not a result merely of numbers but of a shared consensus' (quoted in *The Wire* 2020). Given that 'the Indian New Right ... [is] the political accompaniment of neoliberal capitalist development' (Desai, 2013), a fight against right-wingers' post-truth thinking and politics must be a part of the fight against their pro-market, pro-big-business policy. There is indeed a need for all the workers and small-scale producers to be united against the forces that exploit them, that subjugate them and that weaken and divide them, including on the basis of post-truth politics. For durable and significant success, the fight against right-wing thinking and post-truth politics *ultimately* depends on these classes who must be organized independently of all bourgeois forces in politics. Such a struggle must be a class struggle, i.e., a struggle against the attacks on democracy and against anti-secular politics of religious hatred, as a part of the fight for socialism, an egalitarian and participatory-democratic world beyond the rule of big capital.

For a world of genuine love, the world needs love of socialism. Similarly, for a truthful world, the world needs the truth of socialism. Indeed, 'The regime of the proletarian dictatorship', i.e. political and cultural hegemony of the proletariat, that must happen in a society that has just overthrown capitalism, 'is irreconcilably hostile both to the objectively false mythology of the Middle Ages and to the conscious falsity of capitalist democracy (Trotsky, 1973: 249). In fact, 'The revolutionary regime is vitally interested in laying bare social relations, not in covering them up. This means that it is interested in political truthfulness, in saying what is' (ibid.). Socialism will 'create the possibility and necessity of a higher degree of truthfulness than has hitherto been attained in relations between rulers and ruled' (ibid.). 'Relations in either socialist or communist society, i.e., in socialist society's highest development, will be thoroughly transparent and will not require such auxiliary methods as deception, lies, falsification, forgery, treachery and perfidy'. (ibid.: 247). The latter are characteristic traits of a class society, and especially, of capitalism. The contradictions of capitalism that require political lying will cease to exist, as will the capitalist media and thinktanks to propagate lies, so the objective reasons for political lying will cease to exist.

However, this massive cultural change towards truthfulness will not happen immediately following the revolutionary overthrow of capitalism. Socialism will not immediately get rid of the culture of 'many lies of both serf-owning and bourgeois origin' (ibid.: 247). This is because of two reasons: political and economic-cultural. Socialism, strictly speaking, is transitional between capitalism and communism (which is classless society). The socialist stage, a lower stage of communism, would be much better than an economically advanced capitalist society, but it *will* also mark some of the features of capitalism. Socialist society is not yet a class-less society proper. It is 'the regime of revolutionary dictatorship', and because it is 'a transitional regime', it is 'therefore a contradictory one' (p. 249). There is always a threat of overthrown classes coming back to power. 'The existence of powerful [class] enemies' will make it necessary for the proletariat state and the common people 'to resort to military cunning, and cunning is inseparable from falsehood' (ibid.). Yet, such falsehood will be different from post-truth capitalism or bourgeois lying as such. This is because of the requirement of the socialist revolution and of the socialist society that 'the cunning used in the struggle against foes not be employed for the deluding of one's own people, that is, of the working masses and their party' (ibid.).[13]

The second reason why lying will not immediately vanish in socialism is economic-cultural: i.e., 'poverty ..., the insufficient supply of goods, ... [the inherited] economic and cultural backwardness' and 'the entire heritage of

---

13    This idea was 'like a red thread through all of Lenin's work' (ibid.).

the past' (p. 248). The extent to which and the pace at which political lying as a part of culture can be gotten rid of depends on economic development and on the democratization of social and political relations, i.e., broader political culture. Indeed, in a transitional society following the overthrow of capitalism, and especially, under conditions of the previous epoch of capitalist under-development, 'the lack of the necessary good things of life [will set] ... its mark heavily on our life and on our morals, and will continue to do so for a number of years' (p. 249). Such a situation will cause 'contradictions big and small' as well as 'struggle connected with these contradictions, and – connected with this struggle – cunning, lies, deceit' (ibid.). Only a sufficient level of economic development, with the necessary technological improvements in 'both pro-duction and trade', can 'improve "morals"' and obviate the need for massive ideological-political lying that is characteristic of capitalism, especially, in its current declining stage. Indeed, 'The interaction of improved technology and morals will advance us along the road to a social order of civilized cooperators, that is, to socialist culture' (ibid.) that would be far superior to, and overcome the contradictions of, capitalist society and culture.

# Bibliography

Abraham, P., & Mathew, R. (2021). *The Post-Truth Era: Literature and Media*. New Delhi: Author Press.

Acevedo, B., Aron, A., Fisher, H., & Brown, L. (2012). Neural correlates of long-term intense romantic love. *Social Cognitive and Affective Neuroscience*, 7(2), 145–159.

Adler, E., & Drieschova, A. (2021). The epistemological challenge of truth subversion to the liberal international order. *International Organization*, 75(2), 359–386.

Agha, Z. (2022). How credible is the 'Muslim outreach' of the RSS? National herald. https://www.nationalheraldindia.com/india/how-credible-is-the-muslim-outreach-of-the-rss-what-is-mohan-bhagwat-up-to. (Accessed October 2022).

Ahmad, A. (2013). Communalisms: Changing forms and fortunes. *The Marxist, xxix*(2).

Albright, M. (2018). *Fascism: A warning*. New York: Harper.

Ali, A. (2019). *Why Does the BJP Get Away with Lies?* The Wire. https://thewire.in/politics/bjp-kashmir-terrorist-threat-lie-article-370. (Accessed April 2021).

Al Jazeera. (2022). India slips in Global Hunger Index, ranks 107 out of 121 nations. https://www.aljazeera.com/news/2022/10/15/india-hunger (Accessed November 2022).

Althusser, L. (1968). Philosophy as a Revolutionary Weapon. Marxists.org. https://www.marxists.org/reference/archive/althusser/1968/philosophy-as-weapon.htm (Accessed April 2022).

Althusser, L. (2001). *Lenin and Philosophy and Other Essays*. New York: Monthly Review Press.

Arenchibia, M., & Velazquez, M. (2021). A critical look at post-truth Thinking. *History Research*, 9(2), 118–126.

Arnett, J. (2011). Sex love and sensuous activity in the work of historical materialism. *Mediations* 25(2), 79–102.

Badhwar, N. (2003). Love. In LaFollette H. (ed.), The Oxford Handbook of Practical Ethics. New York: Oxford University Press, pp. 42–69.

Badiou, A. (2012). *In Praise of Love*. Paris: New Press.

Bakunin, M. (1870). *The Red Association*. Marxists.org.https://www.marxists.org/reference/archive/bakunin/works/writings/ch05.htm. (Accessed April 2022).

Ball, J. (2017). *Post-truth: How Bullshit Conquered the World*. London: Biteback Publishing.

Banaji, J. (2006). (Ed.) *Fascism: Essays on Europe and India*. New Delhi: Three Essays Collective.

Baron, I. (2018). *How to Have Politics in a Post-Truth Era*. Manchester: Manchester University Press.

Baroud, R. (2022). Chomsky on the Root Causes of the Russia Ukraine War. *Kashmir Reader*. https://kashmirreader.com/2022/07/03/chomsky-on-the-root-causes-of -the-russia-ukraine-war/.

Barrett, E. and Ellis-Petersen, H. (2023). Adani crisis: Indian group has value cut in half after stock market rout. The Guardian. February 3. (Accessed February 2023).

Barry, D. (2017). In a Swirl of 'Untruths' and 'Falsehoods'. Calling a Lie a Lie. New York Times. https://www.nytimes.com/2017/01/25/business/media/donald-trump-lie -media.html?searchResultPosition=1. (Accessed April 2021).

BBC (2018). India crowd pulls down Tripura Lenin statue after Communist defeat. https://www.bbc.com/news/world-asia-india-43297477 (Accessed March 2019).

Biener, V. (2018). *Dangerous Minds: Nietzsche, Heidegger, and the Return of the Far Right*. Philadelphia: University of Pennsylvania Press.

Bhadrakumar, M. (2019). Modi's post-truth politics. The Week. https://www.theweek.in /columns/mk-bhadrakumar/2019/04/12/modis-post-truth-politics.html. (Accessed April 2020).

Bhatia, S. (2022). Communal Virus Injected into Diaspora, and the Culture is Growing. The Wire. https://livewire.thewire.in/rights/communal-virus-injected-into-diasp ora-and-the-culture-is-growing/. (Accessed October 2022).

Black, G. (2022). Critical resources, imperialism and the war against Russia. https: //www.wsws.org/en/articles/2022/05/28/mine-m28.html (Accessed June 2022).

Blackburn, S. (2018). *On truth*. New York: Oxford University Press.

Blee, K., & Creasap, K. (2010). Conservative and right-wing movements. *Annual Review of Sociology, 36*(1), 269–286.

Boghossian, P. (2006). *Fear of Knowledge*. Oxford: Clarendon Press.

Brooks, A. (2019). *Love and Intimacy in Contemporary Society*. London: Routledge.

Cacioppo, S. (2022). *Wired for Love: A Neuroscientist's Journey Through Romance, Loss and the Essence of Human Connection*. New York: Flatiron Books.

Cadwalladr, C. (2017). Interview: Daniel Dennett: 'I begrudge every hour I have to spend worrying about politics'. *The Guardian*. https://www.theguardian.com/scien ce/2017/feb/12/daniel-dennett-politics-bacteria-bach-back-dawkins-trump-inter view. (Accessed April 2022).

Callinicos, A. 1991. *Against postmodernism*. Cambridge (UK): Polity Press.

Castro, G. (2014). The Neuroscience of Love, *Emotion, Brain, & Behavior Laboratory*. https://sites.tufts.edu/emotiononthebrain/2014/12/08/the-neuroscience-of-love/. (Accessed December 2021).

Chappell, D. and Di Martino, V. (2006). *Violence at work*. Geneva: International labour office. https://www.ilo.org/wcmsp5/groups/public/@dgreports/@dcomm/@publ /documents/publication/wcms_publ_9221108406_en.pdf (Accessed April 2021).

Cheney, L. (1995). *Telling the Truth*. New York: Simon & Schuster.

Choi, J. (2022). Both political parties unpopular with Americans in new poll. The Hill. https://thehill.com/blogs/blog-briefing-room/news/591215-both-political-part ies-unpopular-with-americans-in-new-poll. (Accessed April 2022).

Chomsky, N. (1989). Manufacturing Consent: The Political Economy of the Mass Media (a lecture delivered at University of Wisconsin-Madison). https://chomsky.info /19890315/ (Accessed April 2022).

Choudhary, A. (2020). Majoritarianism is the antithesis of democracy. *The Times of India.* https://timesofindia.indiatimes.com/india/governments-not-always-right -wrong-to-term-people-with-dissent-view-as-anti-national-sc-judge-deepak-gupta /articleshow/74288153.cms. (Accessed March 2021).

Cidam, C. (2013). A politics of love? Antonio Negri on revolution and democracy. *Contemporary Political Theory* 12(1), 26–45.

Conger, K. and Hirsch, L. 2022. Elon Musk Completes $44 Billion Deal to Own Twitter. *The New York Times.* https://www.nytimes.com/2022/10/27/technology/elon-musk -twitter-deal-complete.html (Accessed December 2022).

Coughlan, S. (2017). What does post-truth mean for a philosopher? *BBC.* https://www .bbc.com/news/education-38557838. (Accessed May 2021).

Corichi, M., & Evans, J. (2021). *For most of India's Hindus, religious and national identi- ties are closely linked.* Pew Research Center. https://www.pewresearch.org/fact-tank /2021/07/20/for-most-of-indias-hindus-religious-and-national-identities-are-clos ely-linked/. (Accessed October 2021).

Costa, K. and Hanover, N. (2013). Seattle schools propose race-centric "ethnomathe- matics" curriculum. wsws.org. https://www.wsws.org/en/articles/2019/12/06/ethn -do6.html (Accessed June 2021).

Cozzarelli, T. (2018). *Love and socialism. Left Voice.* https://www.leftvoice.org/love-and -socialism/.(Accessed August 2021).

D'Ancona, M. (2017). *Post-Truth: The New War on Truth and How to Fight.* London: Ebury Press.

Damon, A. (2022). The historical background to the US-NATO war against Russia in Ukraine. wsws.org. https://www.wsws.org/en/articles/2022/12/10/mdkj-d10.html (Accessed December 2022).

Das, G. (2003). *Democracy and capitalism in India: What is unique about India's experi- ence with democracy and capitalism? The Globalist.* www.theglobalist.com/democr acy-and-capitalism-in-india/. (Accessed May 2020).

Das, R. (2014). *A Contribution to the Critique of Contemporary Capitalism: Theoretical and International Perspectives. New York:* Nova Science Publisher.

Das, R. (2017a). *The Marxist Class Theory for a Skeptical World.* Leiden/Boston: Brill.

Das, R. (2017b). 'David Harvey's Theory of Accumulation by Dispossession: A Marxist Critique.' *World Review of Political Economy,* 8(4): 590–616.

Das, R. (2018). A Marxist perspective on sustainability: Brief reflections on ecological sustainability and social inequality. Links. http://links.org.au/marxism-ecologi cal-sustainability-social-inequality. (Accessed April 2022).

Das, R. (2019a). Indian Election 2019: A Marxist Interpretation. *International Socialism: A Quarterly Review of Socialist Theory, 164.*

Das, R. (2019b). Contradictions of India's right-wing government, and growing disenchantment. *Journal of Contemporary Asia 49*(2), 313–328.

Das, R. (2020a). Identity Politics: A Marxist View, *Class, Race and Corporate Power*: Vol. 8: Iss. 1, Article 5. pp. 1–33.

Das, R. (2020b). 2020. On the Urgent Need to Re-Engage Classical Marxism. *Critical Sociology*, Vol. 46(7–8) 965–985.

Das, R. (2021a). *Critical Reflections on Economy and Politics in India. Volume 2.* Chicago: Haymarket.

Das, R. (2021b). *Critical Reflections on Economy and Politics in India. Volume 1.* Chicago: Haymarket.

Das, R. (2022a) Politics of love, and love of politics: Towards a Marxist theory of love. *Class, Race and Corporate Power*, Vol. 10: 2 (forthcoming).

Das, R. (2022b). On the Communist Manifesto: Ideas for the Newly Radicalizing Public. *World Review of Political Economy, 13*(2), 209–244.

Das, R. (2022c). *Marikx's Capital, Capitalism, and Limits to the State: Theoretical Considerations.* London: Taylor and Francis.

Das, R. (2022d). Social Oppression, Class Relation, and Capitalist Accumulation, D. Fasenfest (ed). *Marx matters.* Leiden: Brill.

Das, R. (2022e). Marxism and revisionism in the world today. *Capital & Class.* https: //doi.org/10.1177/03098168221139287 (Accessed December 2022).

Das, R. (2022f). *Capital*, Capitalism and Health. *Critical Sociology* (forthcoming in print):https://journals.sagepub.com/doi/full/10.1177/08969205221083503.(Accessed December 2022).

Das, R. (2022g). Theory and class struggle: A dialectical approach. Links: *Links: International Journal of Socialist Renewal.* http://links.org.au/theory-and-class-strug gle-dialectical-approach. (Accessed December 2022).

Das, R. (2023a). Why is identity politics not conducive to achieving sustained social justice?. Dialec*tical* Anthropo*logy* 47, 19–31.

Das, R. (2023b). The Post-truth condition in capitalist society: A critical enquiry, *International Critical Thought*, Vol 13: 1 (forthcoming).

Das, R. (2023c) Post-truth politics in India's right-wing ecosystem, *International Critical Thought*, Vol 13: 2 (forthcoming).

Das, R. and Chen, A. (2019). Towards a Theoretical Framework for Understanding Capitalist Violence against Child Labor. *World Review of Political Economy.* 10(2): 191–219.

Das, R., Gough, J. and Eisenschitz, A. (2023). *Which Local Politics: Social Capital or Class Struggle?* Leiden: Brill (forthcoming).

Davidson, R. (2012). *The Emotional Life of the Brain.* New York: Avery.

Davidson, R. (2019). *A Neuroscientist on Love and Learning.*https://onbeing.org/progr ams/richard-davidson-a-neuroscientist-on-love-and-learning-feb2019/. (Accessed January 2022).

Davidson, R., & McEwen, B. (2012). Social influences on neuroplasticity: stress and interventions to promote well-being. *Nature Neuroscience, 15*(5), 689–695.

Davis, E. (2018). *Post-truth: Peak Bullshit and What We Can Do about It.* London: Abacus.

de Beauvoir, S. (2011). (1949). *The Second Sex.* New York: Vintage Books.

Desai, R. (2013). *India's New Right.* Frontline. https://frontline.thehindu.com/cover -story/article30198807.ece. (Accessed February 2021).

Desai, R. (2016.) Hindutva and fascism. *Economic and Political Weekly*, LI(53), 20–24.

DiMaggio, A. (2015). Class Sub-Conscious: Hegemony, False Consciousness, and the Development of Political and Economic Policy Attitudes, *Critical Sociology*, 41: 3, 493–516.

Du Bois, W. (1935). *Black Reconstruction in America.* New York: Hartcourt.

Du, J. (2022). *Post-truth: Facts and Faithfulness.* Eugene, Oregon: WIPF & Stock.

Dukes, R. (2019). *Thoughts on: Post-truth Politics and Magical Thinking.* London: Mouse that spins.

Eagleton, T. (1996). *Illusions of Postmodernism*, Oxford: Blackwell.

Eagleton, T. (2011). *Why Marx Was Right.* New Haven: Yale University Press.

Eagleton, T. (2016). *Materialism.* New Haven: Yale university press.

Ebert, T. (1999). Alexandra Kollontai and Red Love. Marxists.org. https://www.marxi sts.org/history/etol/newspape/atc/1724.html (Accessed December 2021).

Economic Times (2019). Compulsive Contrarians are manufacturing logic to run prop-aganda against Modi govt: Arun Jaitley. *Economic Times*. https://economictimes.ind iatimes.com/news/politics-and-nation/compulsive-contrarians-are-manufactur ing-logic-to-run-propaganda-against-modi-govt-arun-jaitley/articleshow/67568 156.cms?from=mdr. (Accessed January 2021).

Ellis-Peterson, H. (2022). What is Hindu nationalism and how does it relate to trou-ble in Leicester? *The Guardian.* https://www.theguardian.com/world/2022/sep/20 /what-is-hindu-nationalism-and-who-are-the-rss. (Accessed October 2022).

Ellis-Petersen, H. (2023). India invokes emergency laws to ban BBC Modi documen-tary *The Guardian.* https://www.theguardian.com/world/2023/jan/23/india-emerge ncy-laws to-ban-bbc-narendra-modi-documentary (Accessed January 2023).

Engels, F. (1845). *Condition of the Working Class in England.* Marxists.org. https://www .marxists.org/archive/marx/works/download/pdf/condition-working-class-engl and.pdf (Accessed January 2020).

Engels, F. (1883). Karl Marx's Funeral. Marxists.org. https://www.marxists.org/arch ive/marx/works/1883/death/dersoz1.htm (Accessed January 2020).

Engels, F. (1884). *Origin of the Family, Private Property, and the State.* Marxists.org. https://www.marxists.org/archive/marx/works/download/pdf/origin_family.pdf. (Accessed January 2020).

Engels, F. (1886). *Ludwig Feuerbach and the End of Classical German Philosophy.* Marxists.org.https://www.marxists.org/archive/marx/works/download/pdf/Ludwig _Feuerbach.pdf. (Accessed January 2020).

Engels, F. (1891). Letter to Conrad Schmidt. Marxists.org. https://www.marxists.org /archive/marx/works/1891/letters/91_11_01.htm (Accessed February 2020).

Esch, T., & Stefano, G. (2005). The Neurobiology of Love. *Neuro Endocrinol Lett, 26* (3): 175–192.

Evans, J., & Sahgal, N. (2021). Key findings about religion in India. Pew Research Center. https://www.pewresearch.org/fact-tank/2021/06/29/key-findings-about-religion-in -india/. (Accessed July 2021).

Evans, M. (2002). *Love: An Unromantic Discussion.* Cambridge: Polity Press.

Fisher H. (1998). Lust, attraction, and attachment in mammalian reproduction. *Human Nature.* 9(1): 23–52.

Fisher, H. (2004). *Why We Love: The Nature and Chemistry of Romantic Love.* New York: Henry Holt.

Frankfurt, H. (2004). *The Reasons of Love.* Princeton: Princeton University Press.

Frankfurt, H. (2006). *On Truth.* New York: Alfred A. Knopf.

Fromm, E. (1956). *The Art of Loving.* New York: Harper & Row.

Fujii, W. 2021. (2021) 'My Order, My Rules': China and the American Rules-Based Order in Historical Perspective, *E-International Relations.* https://www.e-ir.info/2021/12/28 /my-order-my-rules-china-and-the-american-rules-based-order-in-historical-pers pective/ (Accessed April 2022).

Gabriel, M. (2011). *Love and Capital.* New York: Back Bay Books.

Gettleman, J., & Kumar, H. (2019). India's Leader Is Accused of Hiding Unemployment Data Before Vote. *New York Times.* https://www.nytimes.com/2019/01/31/world/asia /india-unemployment-rate.html. (Accessed May 2021).

Ghosh, J. (2016). On anti-national economics. In R. Azad, J. Nair, M. Singh and M. Roy. (Eds.), *What the Nation reAlly Needs to Know.* Noida: Harper Collins.

Giles, J. (1994). A Theory of Love and Sexual Desire. *Journal for the Theory of Social Behaviour,* 24(4), 339–357.

Gilman-Opalsky, R. (2020). *The Communism of Love.* Chico (California): A. K. Press.

Gilman-Opalsky, R. (2021a). *The communism of love.* Public Seminar.https://publicsemi nar.org/essays/the-communism-of-love/. (Accessed December 2021).

Gilman-Opalsky, R. (2021b). *The communist secret of love.* Ill Will. https://illwill.com /the-communist-secret-of-love. (Accessed December 2021).

Gimenez, M. (2019). *Marx, Women, and Capitalist Social Reproduction.* Chicago: Haymarket.

GOI (Government of India) (2006). *Sachar commission report.* Government of India. https://www.minorityaffairs.gov.in/sites/default/files/sachar_comm.pdf (Accessed February 2021).

Goldstein, R. (2001). *Political Repression in Modern America.* Champaign: University of Illinois Press.

Goleman, D. (ed). (2003). *Destructive emotions.* New York: Bantam Books.

Goleman, D., & Davidson, R. J. (2017). *Altered traits: Science reveals how meditation changes your mind, brain, and body.* New York, NY: Avery.

Golwalkar, M. (1960). Bunch of Thoughts. The Hindu Centre. https://www.thehinducen tre.com/multimedia/archive/02486/Bunch_of_Thoughts_2486072a.pdf. (Accessed January 2021).

Gregoratto, F. (2017). Love is a losing game: power and exploitation in romantic relationships. *Journal of Political Power, 10*(3), 326–341.

Guevara, C. (1967). Man and Socialism in Cuba. Marxists.org. https://www.marxists.org /archive/guevara/1965/03/man-socialism-alt.htm (Accessed October 2022).

Hardt, M., & Negri, A. (2009). *Commonwealth.* Cambridge, Massachusetts: Harvard University Press.

Harris, M. (2017). Join the party of love. https://aeon.co/essays/it-is-time-for-love-to -become-a-radical-force-in-politics (Accessed October 2022).

Harsin, J. (2018). *Post-truth and Critical communication studies.* Oxford Research Encyclopedia of Communication. https://oxfordre.com/communication/view/10 .1093/acrefore/9780190228613.001.0001/acrefore-9780190228613-e-757. (Accessed January 2021).

Harvey, D. (2004). The 'new' imperialism: accumulation by dispossession. *Socialist register.* Vol. 40, pp. 63–87.

Harvey, D. (2005). *A brief history of Neoliberalism.* Oxford: Oxford University press.

Harvey, D. (2014). *Seventeen Contradictions and the End of Capitalism.* Oxford: Oxford University Press.

Harvey, D. (2019). Anti-Capitalist Chronicles: Global Unrest. https://www.democrac yatwork.info/acc_global_unrest?fbclid=IwAR10GRcltaL_oI2N1ixYuAS-cT-HhjF7 cErSXBswcWPAvkNmPVaDndYU1xQ. (Accessed March 2021).

Heilbroner, R. (1999). *The Worldly Philosophers.* New York: Simon & Schuster.

Henig, R. (2006). Looking for the lie. *The New York Times.* https://www.nytimes.com /2006/02/05/magazine/looking-for-the-lie.html (Accessed March 2021).

Herman, E. and Chomsky, N. 2002. *Manufacturing Consent: The Political Economy of the Mass Media.* New York: Pantheon Books.

Higgins, K. (2016). Post-truth: a guide for the perplexed. *Nature 540*(9), https://doi.org /10.1038/540009a. (Accessed August 2021).

Hill, C. (1971). *Lenin and the Russian Revolution*. London: Penguin Books.

Ikenberry, G. (2018). The end of liberal international order?, *International Affairs*, Volume 94, Issue 1, 7–23, https://doi.org/10.1093/ia/iix241 (Accessed April 2021).

Illing, S. (2017). *"Post-truth is pre-fascism": A Holocaust historian on the Trump era*. Vox.https://www.vox.com/conversations/2017/3/9/14838088/donald-trump-fasc ism-europe-history-totalitarianism-post-truth. (Accessed June 2021).

Illouz, E. (1997). *Consuming the Romantic Utopia: Love and the Cultural Contradictions of Capitalism*. Berkeley: University of California Press.

Illouz, E. (2010). *Love in the Time of Capital.* Guernica https://www.guernicamag.com /illouz_6_1_10/. (Accessed December 2021).

Illouz, E. (2021). *The End of Love: A Sociology of Negative Relations.* Cambridge: Polity Press.

IPT (Independent People's Tribunal) (2018). *The rise of Fascism in India*. New Delhi: Human Rights Law Network.

Jafri, A., & Apoorvanand (2021). *How the RSS network's incessant generation of lies has actively damaged our brains*. The Wire. https://thewire.in/politics/rss-bjp-hindu tva-communal-misinformation. (Accessed January 2022).

Jha, A. (2021). India's top 10% reach highest wealth level. *Hindustan Times.* https: //www.hindustantimes.com/india-news/indias-top-10-reach-highest-wealth-level -101638898391710.html (Accessed January 2022).

Joshi, R. (2021). *The contours of India's post-truth State.* The Wire. https://thewire.in /politics/the-contours-of-indias-post-truth-state. (Accessed January 2022).

Kakutani, M. (2018). The death of truth: how we gave up on facts and ended up with Trump, *The Guardian.* https://www.theguardian.com/books/2018/jul/14/the-death -of-truth-how-we-gave-up-on-facts-and-ended-up-with-trump (Accessed May 2021).

Kakutani, M. (2019). *The death of truth.* New York: Penguin Random House.

Kalpokas, I. (2018). Post-truth: The condition of our times. In I. Kalpokas (Ed.), *A Political Theory of Post-Truth.* London: Palgrave.

Kessler, G. (2020). *Donald Trump and the Assault on Truth.* New York: Scribner.

King, S. (2021). *Imperialism and the development myth. How rich countries dominate in the twenty-first century.* Manchester: University press.

Kofman, A. (2018). *Bruno Latour, the post-truth philosopher, mounts a defense of science.* New York Times. https://www.nytimes.com/2018/10/25/magazine/bruno-lat our-post-truth-philosopher-science.html. (Accessed April 2021).

Kollontai, A. (1911). *Love and the new morality.* Marxists.org.https://www.marxists.org /archive/kollonta/1911/new-morality.htm. (Accessed December 2021).

Kollontai, A. (1921). *Theses on Communist Morality in the Sphere of Marital Relations.* Marxists.org. https://www.marxists.org/archive/kollonta/1921/theses-morality.htm. (Accessed December 2021).

Kollontai, A. (1923). Make way for Winged Eros: A Letter to Working Youth. Marxists. org.https://www.marxists.org/archive/kollonta/1923/winged-eros.htm. (Accessed December 2021).

Kollontai, A. (1926). *The Autobiography of a Sexually Emancipated Communist Woman.* Marxists.org. https://www.marxists.org/archive/kollonta/1926/autobiography.htm. (Accessed December 2021).

Kováts, E. (2015). Preface. In E. Kováts (Ed.), *Love and Politics.* Budapest: Friedrich-Ebert-tiftung.https://library.fes.de/pdf-files/bueros/budapest/12134.pdf. (Accessed December 2021).

Kreitner, R. (2016). Post-Truth and Its Consequences: What a 25-Year-Old Essay Tells Us About the Current Moment. The Nation. https://www.thenation.com/article/arch ive/post-truth-and-its-consequences-what-a-25-year-old-essay-tells-us-about-the -current-moment/. (Accessed March 2021).

Kulkarni, P. (2019). *How Did Savarkar, a Staunch Supporter of British Colonialism, Come to Be Known as 'Veer'?* The Wire. https://thewire.in/history/veer-savarkar-the-sta unchest-advocate-of-loyalty-to-the-english-government. (Accessed February 2021).

Kulkarni, S. (2017). *Nailing Modi's Lies On Pak And Gujarat Election.* NDTV.com.https: //www.ndtv.com/opinion/nailing-modis-lies-on-pak-and-gujarat-election-1786649. (Accessed April 2021).

Langeslag, S., & van Strien, J. (2016). *Regulation of Romantic Love Feelings: Preconceptions, Strategies, and Feasibility.* Plos One. https://doi.org/10.1371/journal.pone.0161087. (Accessed January 2022).

Labayne, I. (2020). *A possible Communist redefinition of love.* Monthly Review Online. https://mronline.org/2020/02/06/a-possible-communist-redefinition-of-love/. (Accessed December 2021).

Latour, B. (2004). Why has critique run out of steam? From matters of fact to matters of concern. *Critical Enquiry, 30,* 225–248.

Latour, B. (2018). *Down to Earth.* New York: Wiley.

Lazzarato, M. (1996). Immaterial labor. In P. Virno; M. Hardt (eds.). Radical Thought in Italy : A Potential Politics. Minneapolis: University of Minnesota Press. pp. 142–157.

Lenin, V. (1894). The Economic Content of Narodism and the Criticism of it in Mr. Struve's Book(The Reflection of Marxism in Bourgeois Literature). https://www .marxists.org/archive/lenin/works/1894/narodniks/ch02.htm. (Accessed January 2022).

Lenin, V. (1902). *What is to be done?* Marxists.org.https://www.marxists.org/arch ive/lenin/works/download/what-itd.pdf. (Accessed January 2022).

Lenin, V. (1908a). *Materialism and Empirio-criticism: Critical Comments on a Reactionary Philosophy.* Marxists.org. https://www.marxists.org/archive/lenin/works/cw/pdf /lenin-cw-vol-14.pdf (Accessed January 2022).

Lenin, V. (1908b). Marxism and Revisionism. Marxists.org. https://www.marxists.org/archive/lenin/works/1908/apr/03.htm (Accessed January 2022).

Lenin, V. (1917a). A From *Can the Bolsheviks Retain State Power?* Marxists.org. https://www.marxists.org/archive/lenin/works/subject/women/abstract/17_09.htm (Accessed January 2022).

Lenin, V. (1917b). The state and revolution. Marxists.org. https://www.marxists.org/ebooks/lenin/state-and-revolution.pdf (Accessed January 2022).

Lenin, V. (1917c). The Tasks of the Proletariat in Our Revolution. Marxists.org. https://www.marxists.org/archive/lenin/works/1917/tasks/ch04.htm (Accessed March 2022).

Lenin, V. (1918). Speech at the First All-Russia Congress of Working Women. Marxists.org. https://www.marxists.org/archive/lenin/works/1918/nov/19.htm (Accessed March 2022).

Lenin, V. (1922). *On the Significance of Militant Materialism.* Marxists.org.https://www.marxists.org/archive/lenin/works/1922/mar/12.htm. (Accessed February 2022).

Lenin, V. (1964). *Collected Works vol 26.* Moscow: Progress Publishers.

Lenin, V. (1977). *Imperialism: The Highest Stage of Capitalism* in Vl. Lenin. Selected Works. Vol 1. Moscow: Progress Publishers.

Lerner, M. (2022). *Revolutionary Love: A Political Manifesto to Heal and Transform the World.* Oakland: University of California press.

Levitin, D. (2017). Weaponized Lies: How to Think Critically in the Posy-truth Era. New York: Penguin Books.

Lipold, P. (2014). "Striking Deaths" at their Roots: Assaying the Social Determinants of Extreme Labor-Management Violence in US Labor History—1877–1947. *Social Science History*, 38(3–4).

Lockie, S. (2016). Post-truth politics and the social sciences. *Environmental Sociology*, 3(1), 1–5.

Lotz, C. (2015). Against Essentialist Conceptions of Love: Toward a Social-Material Theory. In D. Enns and A. Calcagno (Eds.), *Thinking About Love: Essays in Contemporary Continental Philosophy.* (Pp. 1310148). University Park: Penn State University Press.

Loye, D. (2000). *Darwin's Lost Theory of Love: A Healing Vision for the 21st Century.* New York: Writers Press club.

Lutz A, Brefczynski-Lewis J, Johnstone T, Davidson R. (2008) Regulation of the neural circuitry of emotion by compassion meditation: effects of meditative expertise. PLoS One. 3(3):e1897. https://pubmed.ncbi.nlm.nih.gov/18365029/ (Accessed January 2022).

Lynch, C. (2017). *Trump's war on environment and science are rooted in his post-truth politics and maybe in postmodern philosophy. Salon.* https://www.salon.com/2017/04/01/trumps-war-on-environment-and-science-are-rooted-in-his-post-truth-politics-and-maybe-in-postmodern-philosophy/. (Accessed April 2021).

Lynch, M. (2005). *True to Life: Why Truth Matters*. Cambridge, Mass.: MIT Press.

Macfarlane, A. (1987). Love and Capitalism in *The Culture of Capitalism*. Oxford: Oxford University Press. http://www.alanmacfarlane.com/TEXTS/LOVE_l ong.pdf. (Accessed January 2022).

Mackey, J and Sisodia, R. (2013). Conscious Capitalism: Liberating the Heroic Spirit of Business. Boston: Harvard Business Press.

Magesan, A. (2017). *New figures show just how big Canada's immigrant wage gap*. Macleans. https://www.macleans.ca/news/canada/new-figures-show-just-how-big -canadas-immigrant-wage-gap-is/. (Accessed January 2021).

Manjoo, F. (2008). *True Enough: Learning to Live in a Post-fact Society*. Hoboken, New Jersey: John Wiley.

Mao, T. (1945). *On Coalition Government*. Marxists.org. https://www.marxists.org/referen ce/archive/mao/selected-works/volume-3/mswv3_25.htm. (Accessed January 2022).

Marasco, R. (2010). 'I would rather wait for you than believe that you are not coming at all': Revolutionary love in a post-revolutionary time. *Philosophy & Social Criticism*, *36*(6), 643–662.

Marcuse, H. (1955). Epilogue: Critique of Neo-Freudian Revisionism. Marxists.org .https://www.marxists.org/reference/archive/marcuse/works/eros-civilisation /epilogue.htm. (Accessed May 2022).

Marx, K. (1843a). *A Contribution to the Critique of Hegel's Philosophy of Right*. Marxists. org. https://www.marxists.org/archive/marx/works/1843/critique-hpr/intro.htm. (Accessed January 2022).

Marx, K. (1843b). *Marx to Ruge*. Marxists.org. https://www.marxists.org/archive/marx /works/1843/letters/43_09.htm. (Accessed January 2022).

Marx, K. (1844a). *Economic and Philosophical Manuscripts*. Moscow: Progress Publishers.

Marx, K. (1844b). The introduction to Contribution to the Critique of Hegel's Philosophy of Right. *Marxists.org*. https://www.marxists.org/archive/marx/works/1844/df-jah rbucher/law-abs.htm. (Accessed January 2022).

Marx, K. (1845). *Theses On Feuerbach*. Marxists.org. https://www.marxists.org/arch ive/marx/works/1845/theses/theses.htm. (Accessed January 2022).

Marx, K. (1857). *Grundrisse*. Marxists.org.https://www.marxists.org/archive/marx /works/1857/grundrisse/ch01.htm. (Accessed January 2022).

Marx, K. (1859). *A Contribution to the Critique of Political Economy*. Marxists.org.https: //www.marxists.org/archive/marx/works/1859/critique-pol-economy/preface.htm. (Accessed January 2022).

Marx, K. (1875). *The critique of the Gotha programme*. Marxists.org.https://www.marxi sts.org/archive/marx/works/1875/gotha/ch01.htm. (Accessed January 2022).

Marx, K. (1887). *Capital volume 1*. Marxists.org.https://www.marxists.org/archive/marx /works/download/pdf/Capital-Volume-I.pdf. (Accessed January 2022).

Marx, K. & Engels, F. (1845). *German Ideology*. Marxists.org. https://www.marxists.org /archive/marx/works/1845/german-ideology/preface.htm. (Accessed January 2022).

Marx, K., & Engels, F. (1848). *Manifesto of the Communist Party*. Marxists.org. https: //www.marxists.org/archive/marx/works/download/pdf/Manifesto.pdf. (Accessed January 2022).

Mažeikis, G. (2015). Approaches to romantic love in early Marxist tradition. In E. Kováts (Ed.), *Love and Politics*. Budapest: Friedrich-Ebert-Stiftung.

McIntyre, L. (2015). *The attack on truth*. https://www.math.mcgill.ca/rags/JAC/124/Atta ck_On_Truth-CoHE.html. (Accessed January 2021).

McIntyre, L. (2018). *Post-truth*. Cambridge (MA): MIT Press.

Misra, U. (2022). Explained: How electoral bonds work, and why they face criticism. Indian Express. https://indianexpress.com/article/explained/explained-how-electo ral-bonds-work-why-criticism-7856583/.(Accessed May 2022).

Monbiot, G. (2016). Neoliberalism is creating loneliness. That's what's wrenching society apart. *The Guardian*. https://www.theguardian.com/commentisfree/2016/oct/12 /neoliberalism-creating-loneliness-wrenching-society-apart (Accessed May 2021).

Moore, J, ed. (2016). *Anthropocene or Capitalocene? Nature, history, and the crisis of capitalism*. Oakland, CA: PM Press.

Moore, J. (2017). The Capitalocene, Part 1: on the nature and origins of our ecological crisis, *The Journal of Peasant Studies*, 44: 3, 594–630.

Morley, D. and Alizadeh, H. 2022. Marxism versus postmodernism. https://www.marx ist.com/marxism-versus-postmodernism.htm (Accessed February 2022).

Morrison, C., Johnston, L., & Longhurst, R. (2012). Critical geographies of love as spatial, relational and political. *Progress in Human Geography*, 37(4): 505–521.

Murdoch, I. (1959). The Sublime and the Good, *Chicago Review*, 13: 3, 44–55.

Murray, A. (2018). *Saving Truth. Finding Meaning & Clarity in a Post-truth World*. Grand Rapids: Zonderban.

Murti, A. (2020). *India plummets from B to D Grade on international scale of academic freedom. The Swaddle*. https://theswaddle.com/india-plummets-from-b-to-d-grade -on-international-scale-of-academic-freedom/. (Accessed May 2021).

Nanda, M. (2002). *Breaking the Spell of Dharma and Other Essays*: New Delhi: Three Essays Collective.

Naranjit, D. (2020). *The Post-truth Society*. Washington D.C.: Just World Publications.

Nichols, T. (2014). *The death of expertise*. The Federalist. https://thefederalist.com/2014 /01/17/the-death-of-expertise/. (Accessed May 2021).

Nichols, T. (2019). *The Death of Expertise*. New York: Oxford University Press.

Norman, M. (2016). *Whoever wins the US presidential election, we've entered a post-truth world – there's no going back now*. Independent. *https://www.independent.co.uk/*. (Accessed January 2021).

North, D. (2015). *The Frankfurt School, Postmodernism and the Politics of the Pseudo-left.* Oak Park: Mehring Books.

Oreskes, N. (2023). Eight Billion People in the World Is a Crisis, Not an Achievement. *Scientific American.* https://www.scientificamerican.com/article/eight-billion-peo ple-in-the-world-is-not-a-crisis-not-an-achievement/ (Accessed March 2023).

Oreskes, N. and Conway, E. (2011). *Merchants of Doubt.* New York: Bloomsbury.

Orwell, G. (1939). *Review of Russell's Power: A New Social Analysis.* Lehman. https://www .lehman.edu/faculty/rcarey/BRSQ/o6may.orwell.htm. (Accessed January 2021).

Oxford Dictionaries (2016). *Word of the year.* Oxford Languages. https://languages.oup .com/word-of-the-year/2016/. (Accessed January 2021).

Pagan, N. (2019). Jung Chang's Wild Swans: Love as a political concept. *Southeast Asian Review of English 56*(2), 102–115.

Parmar, I. (2018). The US-led liberal order: imperialism by another name?, *International Affairs* 94: 1, 151–172.

Patel, A. (2022). India's aspiration for a greater role on the global stage is incongruous with its present behaviour, *National Herald*, https://www.nationalheraldindia.com /opinion/indias-aspiration-for-a-greater-role-on-global-stage-is-incongruous-with -its-present-behaviour. (Accessed December 2022).

Pathak, S., Frayer, L., & Silver, M. (2021). *India's pandemic death toll estimated at about 4 million: 10 times the official count.* NPR. https://www.npr.org/sections/goatsands oda/2021/07/20/1018438334/indias-pandemic-death-toll-estimated-at-about-4-mill ion-10-times-the-official-co. (Accessed October 2021).

Patnaik, P. (2010). *The State under Neo-liberalism.* MR Online. https://mronline.org /2010/08/10/the-state-under-neo-liberalism/. (Accessed January 2021).

Pennock, R. (2010). The Postmodern Sin of Intelligent Design Creationism. *Science & Education, 19*(6–8), 757–778.

People's Democracy. (2023). Adani's fraudulent empire exposed. *Monthly Review Online.* https://mronline.org/2023/02/06/adanis-fraudulent-empire-exposed/ (Accessed February 2023).

Peters, M., McLaren, M and Jandrić, P. (2022). A viral theory of post-truth, *Educational Philosophy and Theory,* 54: 6, 698–706.

PEW. (2022). Public Trust in Government: 1958–2022. https://www.pewresearch.org /politics/2022/06/06/public-trust-in-government-1958-2022/ (Accessed July 2022).

Phillips, T. (2020). *Truth: a Brief History of Total Bullshit.* New York: Hanover Square Press.

Plato (1956). *Symposium.* London: Penguin Classics.

Popova, M. (2016). *Lying in politics.* The Marginalian. https://www.themarginalian.org /2016/06/15/lying-in-politics-hannah-arendt/. (Accessed February 2021).

Pred, A. (1984) Place as Historically Contingent Process: Structuration and the Time Geography of Becoming Places, *Annals of the Association of American Geographers* 74: 2, 279–97.

Rabin, N. (2006). *Stephen Colbert.* AV Club. https://www.avclub.com/stephen-colb ert-1798208958. (Accessed January 2021).

Rabin-Havt, A. (2016). *Lies, Incorporated: The World of Post-truth Politics.* New York: Anchor Books.

Rao, M. (2011). Love jihad and demographic fears. *Indian Journal of Gender Studies, 18*(3), 25–430.

Rao, S. (2021). India Gained Nothing From Modi's Toxic Affair With Trump. https: //www.haaretz.com/world-news/2021-01-27/ty-article-opinion/.premium/india -modi-trump-legacy/0000017f-e191-d568-ad7f-f3fb06700000 (Accessed May 2021).

Rao, V. (1960). *Introduction to a bunch of thoughts.* The Hindu Centre. https://www.the hinducentre.com/multimedia/archive/02486/Bunch_of_Thoughts_2486072a.pdf. (Accessed May 2020).

Roberts, M. (2016). *The Long Depression.* Chicago: Haymarket.

Roberts, M. (2022). Russia under Putin. https://thenextrecession.wordpress.com/2022 /08/15/russia-under-putin/ (Accessed August 2022).

Robinson, W. (2022a). Global capitalism has become dependent on war-making to sustain itself *Truthout.* https://truthout.org/articles/global-capitalism-has-bec ome-dependent-on-war-making-to-sustain-itself/ (Accessed January 2023).

Robinson, W. (2022b). *Can global capitalism endure?* Atlanta: Clarity press.

Rodrik, D. (2012). *The Globalization Paradox. Democracy and the Future of the World Economy.* New York: W.W. Norton & Company.

Roelofs, J. (2018). Alexandra Kollontai: Socialist Feminism in Theory and Practice. *International critical thought 8*(1), 166–175.

Roy, A. (2023). Modi's model is at last revealed for what it is: violent Hindu nationalism underwritten by big business. *The Guardian.* https://www.theguardian.com/com-mentisfree/2023/feb/18/narendra-modi-hindu-nationalism-india-gautam-adani (Accessed February 2023).

Roy, I. (2021). *India: From the World's Largest. The India Forum: A Journal-magazine of contemporary Issues.* https://www.theindiaforum.in/article/india-world-s-largest -democracy-ethnocracy. (Accessed January 2022).

Roy, I. (2022). India: The Hollowing Out of the World's Largest Democracy. *Political Insight, 13*(2), 26–31.

Sahu, S. (2022). How to defend India and swaraj. *Newsclick.* https://www.newsclick.in /how-defend-india-and-swaraj. (Accessed October 2022).

Sarkar, S. (2006). The fascism of the Sangh Parivar. In J. Banaji (Ed.), *Fascism: Essays on Europe and India.* New Delhi: Three Essays Collective.

Sathyamurthy, T. (1994). *State & Nation in the Context of Social Change.* Delhi: Oxford University Press.

Sen, A. (2005). *The Argumentative India.* London: Penguin Books.

Shandro, A. (2007). Lenin and Hegemony: The Soviets, the Working Class, and the Party in the Revolution of 1905 In S. Budgen, S. Kouvelakis and S. Žižek (eds) *Lenin Reloaded: Toward a Politics of Truth*, Durham: Duke University press.

Sloss, D. (2022). 'Introduction: Preserving a Rules-based International Order', in David L. Sloss (ed.), *Is the International Legal Order Unraveling?* (New York, 2022; online edn, Oxford Academic, 20 Oct. 2022), https://doi.org/10.1093/oso/9780197652 800.003.0001. (Accessed October 2022).

Smith, R. (2003). *From Blackjacks To Briefcases — A History of Commercialized Strikebreaking and Unionbusting in the United States*. Athens, Ohio: Ohio University press.

Smith, T. 1993. Postmodernism: Theory and Politics. Marxists.org. https://www.marxists.org/history/etol/newspape/atc/4881.html (Accessed February 2022).

Spinoza, B. (1954). *Ethics and on the improvement of the improvement of the understanding*, New York: Hafner Publishing company.

Snyder, T. (2017). *On Tyranny*. New York: Crown.

Snyder, T. (2021). *The American Abyss. The New York Times*. https://www.nytimes.com /2021/01/09/magazine/trump-coup.html. (Accessed January 2021).

Soble, A. (1990). *The Structure of Love*. New Haven: Yale University Press.

Sokal, A. (2008). *Beyond the Hoax: Science, Philosophy and Culture*. Oxford: Oxford University Press.

Sokal, A. and Bricmont, J. (1998). *Fashionable nonsense: Postmodern intellectuals' abuse of science*. New York: Picador.

Solomon, R. (1988). *About Love: Reinventing Romance for Our Times*. New York: Simon & Schuster.

Stanley, J. (2018). *How fascism works*. Vox. https://www.vox.com/2018/9/19/17847 110/how-fascism-works-donald-trump-jason-stanley. (Accessed February 2021).

Sternberg, R. (1986). A triangular theory of love. *Psychological Review, 93*(2), 119–135.

Stiglitz, J. (2018). *Globalization and Its Discontents Revisited: Anti-Globalization in the Era of Trump*. New York: Norton & Co.

Suskind, R. (2004). Faith, Certainty and the Presidency of George W. Bush. New York Times. https://www.nytimes.com/2004/10/17/magazine/faith-certainty-and-the -presidency-of-george-w-bush.html. (Accessed January 2021).

Tomasi, J. (2014). Democratic Capitalism: A Reply to Critics, *Critical Review*, 26: 3–4, 439–471.

The Hindu (2017). Hard work is more powerful than Harvard: Modi. *The Hindu*. https: //www.thehindu.com/elections/uttar-pradesh-2017/hard-work-more-power ful-than-harvard-narendra-modi/article61809632.ece (Accessed January 2021).

The White House (2023). Statement from President Joe Biden on Travel to Kyiv, Ukraine. https://www.whitehouse.gov/briefing-room/statements-releases/2023 /02/20/statement-from-president-joe-biden-on-travel-to-kyiv-ukraine/ (Accessed Februrary 2023).

The Wire (2020). *Labelling dissent anti-national strikes at heart of democracy*. The Wire. https://thewire.in/rights/justice-chandrachud-dissent-anti-national-democ racy-caa. (Accessed May 2021).

Trotsky, L. (1973). *Problems of Everyday Life*. New York: Pathfinder Press.

Trotsky, L. (2007). *My Life*. New York: Devon Press.

Twain, A. (2022). Let's remember Madeleine Albright for who she really was. *Aljazeera* https://www.aljazeera.com/opinions/2022/3/25/lets-remember-madeleine-albri ght-as-who-she-really-was (Accessed April 2022).

US Congress. (2023). Denouncing the horrors of socialism. https://www.congress.gov /bill/118th-congress/house-concurrent-resolution/9/text (Accessed February 2023).

Vanaik, A. (1990). *The Painful Transition: Bourgeois Democracy in India*. London: Verso.

Vanaik, A. (2017). *The Rise of Hindu Authoritarianism*. London: Verso.

Varma, S. (2020). *BJP's Jan-jagran: the calculus of lies. Newsclick*.https://www.newscl ick.in/CAA-NRC-NPR-BJP-Narendra-Modi-Government-Lies. (Accessed April 2021).

Velleman, J. D. (1999). Love as a Moral Emotion. *Ethics*, 109: 338–374.

Venkataramakrishnan, R. (2015). *A little-known fact: Hinduism is the fastest-growing reli-gion in both Pakistan and Saudi Arabia*. Scroll.in. https://scroll.in/article/733474/a -little-known-fact-hinduism-is-the-fastest-growing-religion-in-both-pakistan-and -saudi-arabia. (Accessed May 2021).

Vij, S. (2020). Why the Modi government gets away with lies, and how the opposi-tion could change that. *The Print*. https://theprint.in/opinion/why-modi-governm ent-gets-away-with-lies/422211/ (Accessed April 2021).

Viner, K. (2016). *How technology disrupted truth*. The Guardian. https://www.theg uardian.com/media/2016/jul/12/how-technology-disrupted-the-truth. (Accessed June 2021).

Vogel, L. (2013). *Marxism and the Oppression of Women*. Leiden: Brill.

Walsh, D. (2020). The campaign to smear novelist Charles Dickens as a racist. Wsws.org. https://www.wsws.org/en/articles/2020/07/10/cdck-j10.html (Accessed April 2022).

Warner, J. (2011). Fact-free science. *New York Times*. https://www.nytimes.com/2011/02 /27/magazine/27FOB-WWLN-t.html (Accessed January 2021).

Weng, H. Y., Schuyler, B. S., & Davidson, R. J. (2017). The impact of compassion training on the brain and prosocial behavior. In E. Seppala, E. Simon-Thomas, S. L. Brown, M. C. Worline, D. Cameron & J. Doty (Eds.), Handbook of compassion science (133–46). Oxford, UK: Oxford University Press.

White, R. (2001). *Love's Philosophy*. Lanham (MD): Rowman & Littlefield.

Wilber, K. (2017). *Trump and a Post-truth World*. Boulder: Shambhala.

Williamson, M. (2019). *A Politics of Love*. New York: Harper One.

Wong G, Sun R, Adler J, Yeung KW, Yu S and Gao J (2022) Loving-kindness medita-tion (LKM) modulates brain-heart connection: An EEG case study. Front. Hum. Neurosci. 16: 891377. doi: 10.3389/fnhum.2022.891377.

Wood, E. (1981). The Separation of the Economic and the Political in Capitalism. *New Left Review*, 1/127, pp. 66–95.

Wu, H. (2017). *'Anti-national': Is free speech being stifled at Indian universities?* CNN. https://www.cnn.com/2017/03/20/asia/india-universities-nationalism-abvp/index .html. (Accessed June 2021).

Zeki, S. (2007). The neurobiology of love. *FEBS Letters*, *581*(14), 2575–2579.

# Index